IRELAND'S FATE
The Boyne and After

IRELAND'S FATE
The Boyne and After

Robert Shepherd

AURUM PRESS

First published 1990 by Aurum Press Limited,
33 Museum Street, London WC1A 1LD
Copyright © 1990 by Robert Shepherd

The author and publishers are grateful to
Faber and Faber Limited for permission to reproduce
lines from *The Battle of Aughrim* by Richard Murphy.

The author and publishers are grateful to the following for
permission to reproduce illustrations: Bank of Ireland,
Dublin for Plate XVIII; Belfast City Hall for Plate XXII
right (James Prinsep Beadle); Mansell Collection, London
for Plates IV left (W. Holl) and right, XV; National Army
Museum, London, courtesy of the Director, for Plates IX
(Smith, after Kneller), X (Jan Wyck), XIV (Schoonebeeck),
XVI (C. O. Murray, after Swains), XIX (W. Walker and
W. Angus, after P. Sandbey); National Gallery of Ireland
for Plates VII (attributed to John Riley), XIII right (Sir
Godfrey Kneller), XXI (Francis Wheatley); National
Library of Ireland for Plates VIII, XI (Theodor Maas), XII
(Romeyn de Hooghe), XVII, XX left (after West), XXII
left; National Maritime Museum, London for Plate V
(Willem van de Velde the Younger); National Portrait
Gallery, London for Plates I (Sir Godfrey Kneller), II left
(William Wissing), and right (after Wissing), III (after Sir
Peter Lely), VI (French school), XIII left (AH. J.
Closterman); Popperfoto, London for Plate XXIII; Ulster
Museum, Belfast for Plate XX right.

British Library Cataloguing in Publication Data
Shepherd, Robert
  Ireland's Fate: the Boyne and after.
  1. Ireland. Battle of the Boyne
  I. Title
  941.506
ISBN 1 85410 101 3

Typeset by Wyvern Typesetting Ltd, Bristol
Printed in Great Britain by Butler and Tanner Ltd, Frome

CONTENTS

CONTENTS

PART FOUR
IRELAND BESIEGED

PART FIVE
LEGACIES AND LEGENDS

THE EUROPE OF WILLIAM III AND LOUIS XIV

SWEDEN

North Sea

DENMARK

IRELAND
Galway
Belfast
Dublin
Limerick
Cork
Waterford
Kinsale

Edinburgh

Preston
Chester Derby

ENGLAND
Newbury

BRANDENBURG
Bremen
Berlin

DUTCH REPUBLIC
Amsterdam

Milford Haven
Bristol
Plymouth
Exeter
Torbay
Portsmouth
Beachy Head
Brest

London
Faversham
Dover
St. Omer
Brussels
Dieppe Mons
Le Havre

Maastricht
Cologne
Bonn
Namur
Lux.
Trier

THE
EMPIRE

English Channel

Seine
Paris

St. Malo

Loire

FRANCHE-COMTÉ

FRANCE

Bay of Biscay

Garonne

Rhône

SAVOY

Orange

Santander

Madrid

SPAIN

Philippsburg
Strasbourg
BAVARIA
AUSTRIA
Danube
Vienna

Rhine

Oder

Elbe

Rome

Mediterranean
Sea

0   300 miles

IRELAND IN THE 1690s

NORTH CHANNEL

MULL OF KINTYRE

LOUGH SWILLY

LOUGH FOYLE

Coleraine

Derry

Carrickfergus

Bangor

Donegal

Omagh

ULSTER

Lisburn

Belfast

Belleek

Charlemont

Hillsborough

LOUGH ERNE

Armagh

Loughbrickland

Sligo

Enniskillen

Newtonbutler

Killala

MONAGHAN

Newry

MOYRA PASS

Boyle

Dundalk

CAVAN

CONNAUGHT

Ardee

LOUTH

ROSCOMMON

Lanesborough

Drogheda

Boyne

Skerries

Suck

Shannon

Mullingar

Dublin

LAMBAY ISLAND

Athlone

LEINSTER

Galway

Aughrim

Bray

Jamestown

Kilcullen

Castledermot

Carlow

Arklow

CLARE

Nenagh

Kilkenny

Limerick

Ballyneety

Cashel

Tipperary

Kilmallock

Carrick

Wexford

MUNSTER

Waterford

Duncannon

Mallow

Blackwater

KERRY

Cork

Lee

Bandon

Kinsale

BANTRY BAY

DUNMANUS POINT

CAPE CLEAR

• FASTNET ROCK

–·–·– Provincial boundaries

0   50 miles

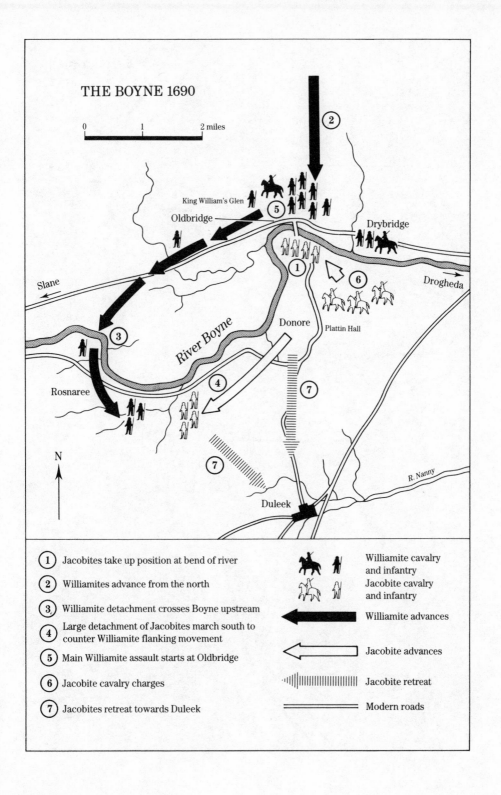

THE BOYNE 1690

0   1   2 miles

King William's Glen
Oldbridge
Slane
Drybridge
Drogheda
River Boyne
Donore
Plattin Hall
Rosnaree
Duleek
R. Nanny

N

1 Jacobites take up position at bend of river
2 Williamites advance from the north
3 Williamite detachment crosses Boyne upstream
4 Large detachment of Jacobites march south to counter Williamite flanking movement
5 Main Williamite assault starts at Oldbridge
6 Jacobite cavalry charges
7 Jacobites retreat towards Duleek

Williamite cavalry and infantry
Jacobite cavalry and infantry
Williamite advances
Jacobite advances
Jacobite retreat
Modern roads

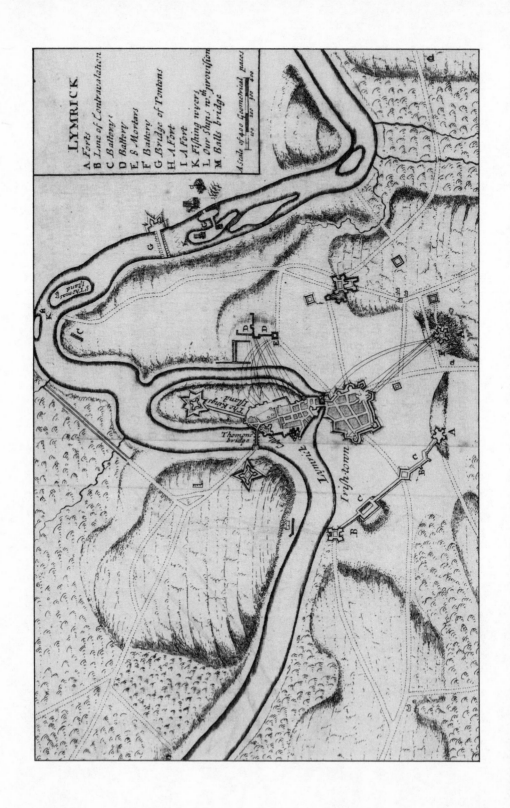

LYMRICK

A. *Forts*
B. *Line of Contravalation*
C. *Battery*
D. *Battery*
E. 8. *Mortars*
F. *Battery*
G. *Bridge of Pontons*
H. *A Fort*
I. *A Fort*
K. *Fishing wyers*
L. *Our Ships wᵗʰ provision*
M. *Balls bridge*

A Scale of 400 Geometrical paces

AUTHOR'S NOTE

All dates before 1752 in the narrative are expressed in Old Style; that is, according to the Julian calendar in use in Britain and Ireland. Dates according to the Gregorian calendar (New Style) in use on the Continent of Europe were ten days later from 1600 to 1699, and eleven days later thereafter. Dates before 25 March in any year have been expressed in accordance with modern usage, with each new year starting on 1 January.

I have tried wherever possible to retain the original language for the direct quotations from eye-witnesses and contemporary documents. This accounts for eccentricities of spelling and grammar. In some cases, however, the usage proved too arcane, or the spelling too difficult, to be easily understood. In such instances, I have modernized the language, without, I hope, losing too much of its original flavour or sense. In other cases, earlier editors have already brought the language into more modern usage.

PREFACE

Three centuries ago, Ireland was enveloped in a major European war. It was also a civil and family war, which would decide the destiny of the crowns of the three kingdoms of England, Scotland and Ireland; and a political and religious war, which would determine who ruled Ireland. Resonances of the conflict have echoed down the centuries.

The aim of the main part of the narrative is to explain what happened in Ireland between 1689 and 1691, and why it happened. I have made extensive use of eye-witness accounts, drawn from diaries, documents, letters and memoirs, which reveal people's experiences and feelings at the time. In the final part of the book, where I trace the principal legacies and legends of the war as they have affected Irish people, the approach is necessarily thematic and does not claim to represent a comprehensive history of Ireland over the past three centuries.

In the summer of 1690 two European armies, each led by a king of England, Scotland and Ireland, fought on the banks of the River Boyne, 30 miles north of Dublin. Such was the political and psychological impact of the battle that it subsequently became, and still remains, a potent symbol of the loyalist tradition in Ireland. The Treaty of Limerick of 1691, which finally concluded the Irish war, resulted in the 'flight of the Wild Geese', as thousands of Irish soldiers followed Patrick Sarsfield into exile, creating one of the most romantic legends in history. It was not the Treaty, but the flouting of its terms by the English and Irish Parliaments which ushered in the era of penal laws and what has been termed the 'Protestant Ascendancy'.

The war of 1689–91 in Ireland was accorded only a passing reference in most of the ceremonies and exhibitions held in Britain to commemorate the tercentenary of the 'Glorious Revolution'. The impression created, with the notable exception of the National Army Museum, was that events across the Irish Sea, and for that matter in Scotland, were mere postscripts, or sideshows, to what had occurred in England. No doubt a wish to avoid adding fuel to the flames of discord in Northern Ireland was part of the reason, but the result was to perpetuate the myth of a 'bloodless revolution'. This is contradicted by

Ireland's experience, which entailed, in James II's phrase, 'so much blood and treasure'.

The impetus for this book dates from my time as political adviser to the Rt Hon. Lord Prior, formerly Northern Ireland Secretary, and my work in current affairs television, which increased my interest in the historical background. In recent years, an array of new research has appeared on Irish history. I am indebted to the many historians who have undertaken detailed studies, most especially the late J. G. Simms.

I should like to thank Gillian Shepherd for her invaluable help with the research, and Michael Alcock and Michael Shaw for their advice and enthusiasm. I am grateful to all those with whom I have talked about the issues discussed in this book, members of the Military History Society of Ireland, and the staffs of the British Library, the London Library, the National Army Museum, the National Gallery of Ireland, the National Library of Ireland, the Royal Irish Academy, Trinity College, Dublin, the Ulster Museum, Derry City Council, the Apprentice Boys of Derry, the Grand Orange Lodge of Ireland, the Bord Fáilte and the Northern Ireland Tourist Board. I am particularly grateful to Joe Gallagher for all his help and generous hospitality. Before completing the book, I was fortunate to visit Lahinch, County Clare, for the 1989 Merriman Summer School on 'Derry, Aughrim, Enniskillen and the Boyne: Orange and Green 1689–1989'.

Robert Shepherd
London, 1989

PART ONE

EUROPE IN CRISIS

CHAPTER ONE

'UNPARALLELED ASTONISHMENT'

I

At Dublin Castle on Tuesday 18 December 1688, Richard Talbot, the Earl of Tyrconnel, James II's Catholic Lord Deputy of Ireland, wrote to the Earl of Antrim, the premier Catholic peer in Ulster. 'Three pacquets came in this morning but brought very little newes,' explained Tyrconnel, 'the King is at Windsor in the head of his Army, which lyes all along the Thames, the Prince of Orange is about Newbury, the Queen and the Prince are at Whitehall.'

Ireland was in turmoil after the invasion of England by William of Orange, the Protestant nephew and son-in-law of King James. 'The transactions of England strike unparalleled astonishment into the hearts of all the Irish,' wrote Dennis Scott in Dublin to his kinsman across the Irish Sea, Sir Edward Scott, Deputy Governor of Portsmouth. But the Irish had to rely on news that could take anything between five days and two weeks to arrive from London, depending on tide and wind. The political crisis only added to the delays. On the morning that Tyrconnel reported the King 'at Windsor in the head of his Army', James II was in reality being escorted from Whitehall Palace by Catholic soldiers of the Dutch Guards and taken by barge to the Kent coast, destined for France and exile.

Tyrconnel's Catholic Administration in Dublin, appointed in early 1687 by the Catholic James II, was in jeopardy. The Lord Deputy's immediate concern was the revolt by Protestants in Derry, where the apprentice boys had shut the city gates in Antrim's face. Tyrconnel was determined to reassert his authority, as he wrote to Antrim:

Finding the people of Londonderry continue obstinate in their rebellion and that there appears no likelyhood of reducing them by fair means I desire your lordship to give orders presently, to all companies of your regiment, to be in readiness to march at an hour's warning, it being my resolution in case I doe not hear by Friday's post, that the Citty of Derry has submitted, to order them, with severall other regiments of horse, foot and dragoons, to march against it, and will soon follow them myself.

Throughout Ireland, rumour and panic had taken hold. Talk of a Catholic uprising, allegedly planned for Sunday 9 December, was unsubstantiated but stirred Protestant folk-memories of the Catholic uprising of 1641,[1] prompting defiance in Derry and triggering an exodus of Protestants across the Irish Sea.

Many refugees landed at Chester and began their journeys to English relations or friends. Not everyone welcomed their arrival. 'For no sooner were we seated in our coach,' wrote John Stevens, an English Catholic excise officer heading for London, 'but our fugitive Irish [began] lamenting the imaginary calamities of their Protestant brethren in Ireland . . .' They were not the ideal travelling companions for Stevens, who had resolved to follow James II through thick and thin. Stevens would later travel to Ireland and become an important eye-witness of events.

As reports of James's predicament filtered through to Dublin during late December, Catholics in Ireland grew increasingly apprehensive. According to a Protestant Dubliner 'About this time news came from England of the King's being taken and abused, and Princess Ann's leaving him, which put a damp on the Roman Catholics here, and made some of the most active provide for themselves, by disposing of their goods into places of safety.'

Mutual suspicion was never far beneath the surface in seventeenth-century Ireland. English and Scottish colonization had been superimposed on the Gaelic Irish and their ever-changing alliances. Between the 1580s and 1640s an influx of 100,000 'new English' immigrants had made Ireland one of England's most important colonies. Yet the authorities in London rarely accorded the problems of governing Ireland anything more than the most cursory attention, until a crisis suddenly alarmed them. Instead, they thought primarily in terms of security, viewing Ireland as a potential base for enemy attacks on the Atlantic trade routes or for invasion through England's 'back-door'. This perceived, strategic imperative was reinforced by English suspicions of the true allegiance of both the Irish Catholic majority and Protestant dissenter minority. 'The bulk of common people in Ireland are either Papist or Dissenters,' commented William King, the Church of Ireland Bishop of Derry, who regarded them as 'equally enemies to the Established Church'.

Only a minority of Ireland's inhabitants belonged to the state Church, the Church of Ireland, the equivalent of the Church of England. Although it was by no means exceptional for the established church of a state, whether Protestant or Catholic, to be accorded a special status, the state religion was generally practised by a majority, and discrimination was exercised against the minority. Ireland was a mirror image. Until Tyrconnel's Catholic Administration, the vast majority of Irish people had been barred from participating in politics, or public or military service. Catholics comprised approximately 70 per cent of Ireland's estimated total population of 2.2 million in 1687. The majority of Protestants also suffered discrimination. These included about one-third of Protestants who were Presbyterians, mainly of

Scottish origin or descent living in Ulster, and the best part of a further third who belonged to smaller denominations, such as Quakers like William Penn, a convert whose father owned estates in County Cork.[2] The remainder of Ireland's Protestants, a minority within a minority, who belonged to the established state Church, the Church of Ireland, thus enjoyed a remarkably privileged status. They owned over three-quarters of the land, and, except during Tyrconnel's administration, monopolized the army, the law, the government, and politics.

Ireland was also distinctive because its small, ruling elite was a colonist class. The so-called 'new English' were generally set apart by their Protestant religion from the long-established 'old English' families, such as the Butlers, the Fitzgeralds, the Luttrells, the Nugents, the Plunketts and the Talbots, of whom Tyrconnel was a member. The 'old English' had settled in Ireland from Norman times, initially within the 'Pale', and after the Reformation had generally held to their Catholicism. But their religion and independence were at odds with the centralizing power of the Tudor and Stuart state. They were driven from political power, along with the last of the Gaelic chieftains, by Elizabeth I and James I. During the first quarter of the seventeenth century, 'new English' and Scottish settlers were vigorously encouraged by James I (VI of Scotland). The plantation of Ulster is the most dramatic and widely remembered initiative of this period, but immigrants were settling in all counties of Ireland.[3]

The different identities in Ireland – Gaelic Irish, 'old English', 'new English' and the Scots – were not exclusive or discrete entities. They mixed, intermarried and influenced one another. The famous Jacobite commander, Patrick Sarsfield, for example, was descended from the 'old English' on his father's side and Gaelic Irish on his mother's. Some of the 'new English' condescendingly regarded the 'old English' as having 'gone native', indistinguishable to all intents and purposes from the Gaelic Irish, the 'Os and the Macs'. These prejudices were perpetuated in the work of the nineteenth-century English historian, Lord Macaulay, who described the Talbots as 'an old Irish family which had been long settled in Leinster, which had there sunk into degeneracy, which had adopted the manners of the Celts, which had, like the Celts, adhered to the old religion, and which had taken part with the Celts in the rebellion of 1641'. On the other hand, it was alleged that Tyrconnel, 'sometimes in his rants, talked with Norman haughtiness of the Celtic barbarians'.

The economic and cultural distinctions between Ireland's identities were real enough. In Jonathan Swift's mordant comment on the impact of Oliver Cromwell's land settlement, 'the Catholics of Ireland lost their estates for fighting in defence of the king, while those who cut off the father's head and forced the son to fly for his life got the very estates which the Catholics lost'. Despite their shared deprivation, 'old English' Catholics demanded the return

of estates taken from them in the Cromwellian settlement, whereas the Gaelic
Irish pressed for the restitution of land expropriated over a longer period,
partly by the 'old English'. And while the Catholicism of Gaelic Ulster traditionally looked to Spain for support, 'old English' Catholicism looked to England and France.

The 'old English' were particularly disappointed that Charles II, restored to
the throne in 1660, did so little to reverse the Cromwellian settlement. He had
promised to return their estates while preserving the interests of Cromwellian
beneficiaries, a compromise born of his initial dependence on the army in
Ireland but bearing no relation to what was feasible. As the Duke of Ormonde,
Charles's long-serving Lord Lieutenant in Ireland, commented, 'there must
be new discoveries made of a new Ireland, for the old will not serve to satisfy
these engagements'.

The reforms of Charles II's reign were extremely modest. The Act of
Settlement in 1662 and the Act of Explanation in 1665 were passed by an Irish
Parliament still dominated by Protestants. In August 1666, Charles dissolved
the Irish Parliament. No further meetings were held for the remaining
nineteen years of his reign. Predictably, the Restoration land settlement
brought very limited recovery of Catholic lands. Catholics had owned an
estimated 59 per cent of the land before the Cromwellian confiscations. Even
after the Restoration settlement, they owned only 22 per cent, their predicament prompting Robert Southwell to write of 'the old proprietors who
evermore haunt and live about their lands whereof they were dispossessed, and
cannot forbear to hope and reckon a day of repossession'.

Yet the whole outlook was dramatically transformed in the latter half of
the 1680s. James II, who acceded to the throne in 1685, was a convert to
Catholicism. He naturally possessed no doubts about Catholic loyalty, and had
included Irishmen, among them Tyrconnel, in his circle since his days in exile
thirty years earlier. Like his predecessors on the English throne, however,
James viewed Ireland first and foremost in terms of its strategic importance to
England.

It was James's religious affinity for his Irish subjects which Tyrconnel set
about exploiting with such panache. The 'old English' families were given a
tantalizing glimmer of hope. It seemed that their dream of recovering their
estates and being freed from religious discrimination might just come true.
But Protestants, Church of Ireland and Presbyterian alike, came to suspect
that their worst nightmare of a Catholic state in Ireland might well be
realized.

II

One of the few character sketches which survive of Richard Talbot, Earl of
Tyrconnel, was written by Thomas Sheridan, his secretary and First Commis-
sioner of Revenue in Ireland:

He was a tall proper handsome man, but publicly known to be most insolent in prosperity and most abject in adversity, a cunning dissembling courtier, of mean judgement and small understanding, uncertain and unsteady in his resolutions, turning with every wind to bring about his ambitious ends and purposes, on which he was so intent that to compass them he would stick at nothing and so false that a most impudent notorious lie was called at Whitehall and St James's one of Dick Talbot's ordinary truths.

A less than flattering portrait, but then Sheridan had never wanted to serve Tyrconnel and was eventually dismissed amid allegations of corruption. The second Earl of Clarendon, Tyrconnel's great rival, saw him as 'a man of monstrous vanity as well as pride and furious passion', and observed 'how wonderfully false he is in almost everything he does'. A more balanced judgement comes from the Duke of Berwick, James II's illegitimate son, who summed up Tyrconnel as 'a man of very good sense, very obliging, but immoderately vain and full of cunning'.

The evidence reveals Tyrconnel as a skilled political operator, adept at court intrigue, necessarily duplicitous, but also a passionate advocate and a courageous soldier. His qualities were applied to a single purpose: championing the cause of Ireland's dispossessed 'old English' Catholic aristocracy. It was a combination guaranteed to generate fierce rivalries and create bitter enemies.

Tyrconnel had long pinned his hopes of restoring the power and fortunes of his fellow Irish Catholic aristocrats on James, Duke of York, Charles II's Catholic brother. But it seemed that the time available in which to effect radical change would be limited. By 1685, James was already fifty-one years old, was no longer in the best of health and had no male heir. His second wife, Mary of Modena, had given birth to five children, but none had survived more than a few years. On James's death the throne would pass to Mary, his eldest daughter from his first marriage to Anne Hyde, who was born before his conversion to Catholicism and was brought up a Protestant. Tyrconnel was fifty-four years old and a man in a hurry. But his perspective was long-term. His efforts would count for naught unless the Catholic revival in Ireland outlived James.

At Charles II's court, Richard Talbot, as Tyrconnel then was, had been one of the leading members of the Irish faction, and was involved in the court intrigue against the Duke of Ormonde, the King's long-serving Lord Lieutenant in Dublin. Ormonde was a Butler, one of an 'old English' family in Ireland like the Talbots, but was not a Catholic. In October 1684, Ormonde was finally recalled. Shortly afterwards, Charles accepted the principle of commissioning Catholics in the Irish army, which had previously been the preserve of Protestants. Moreover, all Irish commissions were to be issued by the Secretary of State in London, not the Lord Lieutenant in Dublin.

On the death of Charles in February 1685, the new King, James II, immediately sought to reassure the Privy Council that 'he would endevour to maintaine the Government both in Church & state as by Law established, its Principles being so firme for Monarchy, & members of it shewing themselves so good and loyal subjects'. Yet doubts were soon being voiced about James's intentions in Ireland, prompted in part by Talbot's advancement. 'The zealous Protestants say loudly that this Prince [James II] has departed from what he said to the Council,' wrote the French Ambassador in London, Barrillon, to Louis XIV on 20 April. As the diarist, John Evelyn, noted, James had 'formally promised to do nothing against the Protestant religion, although he has since given a regiment in Ireland to Colonel Talbot, which is, they say, to advance Popery and to begin to destroy the Protestant religion'.

In his King's Speech to the new Parliament,[4] James repeated the reassurances he had given the Privy Council, and then 'acquainted them with that morning['s] news of Argyll's being landed in the West highlands of Scotland from Holland, and the Treasonous declaration he had published'. The Duke of Argyll was a Protestant, and his uprising prompted fears of trouble from the Ulster Scots. James ordered that 'disaffected' subjects in northern Ireland should be disarmed, entrusting Talbot with the task. In June, James elevated his long-standing associate to the peerage of Ireland as Baron of Talbotstown, Viscount Baltinglas and Earl of Tyrconnel.

Less than a month after Argyll's landing, a second Protestant Duke, Monmouth, a son of Charles II, invaded the English west country, which in Evelyn's words 'wonderfully alarmed the whole kingdome, fearing the joyning of disaffected people'.[5] In Ireland, Tyrconnel exploited the climate created by Protestant-led rebellions and sought to label all Protestants as 'disaffected'. James had extended his order for disarming Protestants to cover the English in Ireland as well as the Scots. The arms of the Irish militia, an entirely Protestant force, were also called in. Tyrconnel continued to disarm Protestants after the immediate emergency had died down and pressed ahead with recruiting Catholic soldiers. By the end of 1685, an estimated 850 Catholics had joined the army.

Within months of Tyrconnel's arrival in Ireland, however, his plans were dealt a severe blow. Remaining in Dublin throughout the summer, he was unable to exert any influence over the fierce power-struggle being waged at the English court. In August 1685, James appointed Clarendon Lord Lieutenant. Clarendon was a brother of the late Anne Hyde, James's first wife, and was thus the King's brother-in-law. He was an experienced administrator and politician, and with his brother, the Earl of Rochester, whom James appointed to the Treasury, was regarded in England as a stabilizing influence in the Government.

Tyrconnel was furious at the appointment of Clarendon, who regarded the Irish as a 'conquered people'. Any prospect of advancement for 'old English' Catholics in Ireland seemed to have been scuppered. Having helped bring down one Lord Lieutenant, the Duke of Ormonde, Tyrconnel set about undermining another. He immediately wrote a letter to James, designed to exploit the King's natural affinity for his Catholic subjects and elicit James's sympathy for their plight in Ireland. Tyrconnel left James in no doubt that Clarendon's appointment was a further, serious setback for them. 'All those methods', claimed Tyrconnel, 'by which your authority as well as the true worship of God began to take root in this kingdom seem utterly disappointed by lodging your authority in a person from whom they have so little reason to expect any favour'. At the same time, Tyrconnel implied that Irish Protestants were inherently disloyal and were preventing James from being as powerful as he might be in Ireland.

Clarendon did not arrive in Dublin until 9 January 1686, the day on which Tyrconnel reappeared at court in London and began his campaign to discredit the new Lord Lieutenant. At the end of January, Tyrconnel was accorded the honorary position of Marshal of Ireland, and in March was appointed lieutenant-general. At the same time, his fellow Catholic Irish soldiers, Justin MacCarthy and Richard Hamilton, were appointed respectively major-general and brigadier. James also agreed to sanction the appointment of Catholics to public office. With Tyrconnel securing overall command of the Irish army Clarendon's authority was grievously weakened.

Tyrconnel's return 'to Ireland with greate powers & commissions' in June 1686 gave 'as much cause of talk', in Evelyn's account, as James's appointment of Catholic Privy Councillors and judges. Tyrconnel vigorously stepped up the recruitment of Catholics to the Irish army. Over 4000 Catholic soldiers were recruited in the six months to the end of September. By the autumn of 1686, on these calculations, about two-thirds of the 7500 ordinary soldiers were Catholic, as were two in five of the 400-plus commissioned officers and one in three of around 750 NCOs. Within less than eighteen months, Tyrconnel had wrought a radical transformation in what had been an entirely Protestant army. But there was a price to pay. The inexperience of the new Catholic officers rendered the Irish army a less efficient military machine.

Discrimination against Catholics was eased in the legal system and public service. Tyrconnel persuaded James to appoint one Catholic judge to each of the four Irish law courts. James also approved the appointment of Catholics to the Irish Privy Council, to the commissions of the peace and to posts in central and local government. Tyrconnel and his fellow Catholics, the Earl of Limerick, Justin MacCarthy and Richard Hamilton, were appointed Irish Privy Councillors.

Yet the greatest challenge still awaited Tyrconnel. The loss of land under Cromwell's rule was the source of strongest resentment among the 'old English' Catholic aristocracy. The recovery of their estates was the cause dearest to Tyrconnel's heart. 'These Acts of Settlement and this New Interest are damned things,' he reportedly commented to Clarendon. Reversing the Cromwellian and Restoration land settlement, however, would provoke bitter opposition, stir Protestant unrest in Ireland, and give rise to deep anxiety in England.

If Tyrconnel was to achieve his objective, he would need to secure Clarendon's removal from Dublin Castle and persuade James to summon the Irish Parliament. In August 1686, Tyrconnel returned to the English court and started plotting his next move. Clarendon was plainly irritated by Tyrconnel's campaign against him. A month later, Evelyn replied sympathetically to a letter from the beleaguered Lord Lieutenant in Dublin. Caricaturing Tyrconnel as 'the huffing great man', the diarist observed 'How the noyse he makes will operate I know little of; what it does with you (and would do everywhere else) is sufficiently evident.'

III

Tyrconnel was a match for anyone at court. After months of intrigue during the autumn of 1686, James eventually agreed that Clarendon should be recalled from Ireland and Tyrconnel appointed in his place. 'Lord Tyrconnel gon to succeede my Lord Lieutenant in Ireland,' commented Evelyn, 'to the astonishment of all sober men, & to the evident ruine of the Protestants in that Kingdome.'

Tyrconnel's appointment provoked strong opposition. Although the powerful Catholic convert the Earl of Sunderland and many of the other English Catholics at court had wanted Clarendon ousted, they were against installing Tyrconnel at Dublin Castle. They feared that this would so alarm English Protestants as to ruin all prospect of a compliant Parliament at Westminster. As a concession to Tyrconnel's opponents, James accorded him only the inferior title of Lord Deputy, not Lord Lieutenant.

Echoes of the deep controversy over Tyrconnel's appointment live on to this day. The tune 'Lilliburlero', which is played before the World News in the BBC Radio World Service, owes its title to the mock Irish refrain of a savage satire, composed when Tyrconnel embarked for Dublin in February 1687.[6] The verses were penned by Thomas Wharton, a staunch critic of the Government, and were set to a catchy tune, attributed to the English composer Henry Purcell, although it first seems to have appeared in London in 1661 with the lyric, 'There was an old man of Waltham Cross'.[7]

Wharton's attack on an Irish Catholic being appointed Lord Deputy was written in an insulting, mock Irish brogue, and opened with an offensive reference to 'Teague', the slang name for an Irishman:

> Ho, brother Teague, dost hear de decree,
>   Lilli Burlero, bullen a-la;
> Dat we shall have a new debittie,
>   Lillie burlero, bullen a-la;
>   Lero lero, lero lero, lilli burlero, bullen a-la;
>   Lero lero, lero lero, lilli burlero, bullen a-la.

Ho, by my shoul, it is a Talbot,
And he will cut de Englishman's troat.[8]

Yet it would be a further eighteen months before 'Lilliburlero' was transformed into the 'smash hit' of its day.

Not only was Tyrconnel denied the title of Lord Lieutenant by James, but the King also appointed Fitton as Lord Chancellor and Sheridan as the Lord Deputy's secretary, neither of whom Tyrconnel wanted with him in Dublin Castle. Moreover, according to Sheridan, James expected both of them to report on Tyrconnel. James also repeatedly insisted that no one should be appointed or dismissed in Ireland purely on religious grounds, although by this stage Catholics comprised most of the army and held many Government and municipal posts. His fears that Tyrconnel's Irish reforms would stir up trouble in England led him to forbid further efforts to disarm the Scots in Ulster and to order that no disputes over the land settlement should come before the courts.

James had initially said that he had no plans to repeal the Restoration land settlement in Ireland, wanting only to compensate Catholics who had a deserving case. Crucially, however, Tyrconnel dissuaded James from adopting a proposal of Sunderland's for a proclamation to confirm existing titles to land. This would have killed stone dead any hope of recovering Catholic estates. Moreover, Tyrconnel restored land reform to the political agenda by persuading James that the Irish Parliament should meet.

In August 1687, James summoned Tyrconnel to England, where they met at Shrewsbury before travelling on to Chester. It was a crucial meeting. Initially arranged to discuss signs that Government revenues in Ireland were likely to slump, fears which proved premature, Tyrconnel brilliantly turned the talks to his advantage. From this point on, his position in Ireland was secure. James agreed to let him prepare legislation to modify the land settlement. The draft bills would require Protestant landowners to return about half their land to the former Catholic owners. Tyrconnel's proposals were strongly opposed by the Privy Council in London, but his letters suggest that James approved his plans, a view confirmed in a letter from Barrillon to Louis XIV a couple of months later. The French Ambassador reported Sunderland as saying that James was 'resolved to reverse the Act of Settlement', and added that 'this was as yet kept very secret; but it would soon be gone about, and that measures are taken to accomplish it'.

It was also rumoured that Irish independence was on Tyrconnel's agenda, although the evidence remains sketchy. Immediately before the meeting at Chester, a contact claiming to represent Tyrconnel approached a senior French official in London. The contact told Bonrepaus, who served in Seignelay's Ministry of Marine, that after James's death Tyrconnel would 'take measures not to come under the rule of the Prince of Orange and to put himself under the protection of the King [Louis XIV]'. Bonrepaus promised not to reveal the plan to Barrillon, since it was feared that the Ambassador would tell Sunderland, whom Tyrconnel did not trust. 'I am fully convinced', Bonrepaus concluded,

> that the intention of the King of England is to bring about the loss of this kingdom [Ireland] to his successor and to fortify it so that his Catholic subjects may find there an assured asylum. His plan is to put matters on this footing in the course of five years. But my Lord Tyrconnel presses him unceasingly that this may be done in less time; and in fact his Britannic Majesty has within the past eight days sent thither a vessel laden with powder, arms and mortars, at the entreaty of the person who spoke to me.

Louis XIV gave this piece of intelligence high priority, but deferred acting upon it until Bonrepaus confirmed the credentials of his source and opened direct correspondence with Tyrconnel. Bonrepaus failed and nothing more was heard of the alleged plan.

Within a month the outlook was transformed by the news that Mary of Modena was expecting a child. James's Protestant daughter might not succeed after all, and Ireland might not come 'under the rule of the Prince of Orange'. The founding of a Catholic dynasty would provide the King's Catholic subjects with the strongest protection imaginable. James's perspective remained that of an English king determined to retain control of Ireland.

In Ireland itself, Tyrconnel was doing his utmost to restore and entrench the position of the 'old English' Catholic nobility. He ensured that any Jacobite Irish Parliament would be a very different animal to its predecessor, which had last met more than twenty years earlier. Following the precedent set by Charles II in the latter years of his reign, Tyrconnel used the Crown's authority to rewrite town charters. Protestant domination of borough corporations the length and breadth of Ireland was replaced by two-thirds Catholic majorities. This in turn would lead to the election of a predominantly Catholic Irish House of Commons. James, however, stoutly held to his position that the Irish Parliament should meet only after the English Parliament. He wanted nothing to happen in Ireland which might antagonize English Protestants and jeopardize his plans for repealing the laws discriminating against Catholics and dissenters in England.

Tyrconnel guaranteed a majority for the recovery of Catholic estates in Ireland, whenever the Irish Parliament might be summoned. James's support for his Lord Deputy at Chester seemed to indicate that the King was ready to accept the consequences, provided that religious toleration had first been established in England. The upsurge of optimism among Ireland's 'old English' nobility was reflected in the poetry of their champion, Dáibhídh Ó Bruadair. In 'A Hundred Thanks to God', which he composed around 1687–8, he wrote (translated from the Irish):

Pray for King James, the bright shining star of bliss,
Who hath shed on both sides of the ocean a brilliant light,
Pray also that God may vouchsafe him a son and heir,
Who shall be for our country a shelter and sanctuary.

After your rightful king pray undistractedly
That Tyrconnell may live to defeat the barbarians;
It is he hath cleared Erin from sorrowful mists and clouds.
Drink ye his health all around then with fervent zeal.

No one could have foreseen the extraordinary circumstances in which James's Irish Parliament would eventually assemble in Dublin. Events in Europe and England were about to take a dramatic hand in Ireland's destiny.

CHAPTER TWO

'INTRIGUES AND PREPARATIONS'

I

As Bishop Burnet observed, the death in the early summer of 1688 of Maximilian-Henry of Wittelsbach, the elderly Archbishop Elector of Cologne, 'came in very luckily to give a good colour to intrigues and preparations'. The choice of a new archbishop became the catalyst for a great Continental power-struggle, which would soon envelop Britain and Ireland.

The canons of Cologne, whose duty it was to elect a new archbishop, were lobbied by envoys from the powerful French and German supporters of the two contestants. Louis XIV's candidate was William Egon von Fürstenberg, the Bishop of Strasbourg and a former adviser to the old Archbishop, while Leopold I, the Austrian Emperor, and his German allies were supporting Prince Joseph Clement of Bavaria. At their chapter on 9 July, most votes were cast for Fürstenberg, but he failed to win the necessary two-thirds majority. The contest would have to be settled by Pope Innocent XI. Louis and the Pope were on extremely bad terms as a result of the French King's persistent refusal to acknowledge the superior authority of the papacy. In September, the see of Cologne was conferred on Joseph Clement.

The Pope's decision triggered a military démarche by Louis. 'Appearances of wonderful stirs in this part of Europe', recorded Evelyn on 22 September 1688, as 70,000 French troops invaded the Rhineland, on a front stretching from Liège in the north to Philippsburg, 100 miles south of Cologne, where they laid siege to the great riverside fortress. Louis did not intend that his assault should provoke a major conflict, but he miscalculated. Within a matter of months, Ireland would become a theatre of war in the European power-struggle, with lasting effect over the generations.

The English had long been fearful of European intervention in Ireland. The island's history had been shaped by Continental influences. The Celts, Vikings and Normans were all European invaders. The Dark Ages were characterized by cultural links between Ireland and the Continent. The great religious tides of Reformation and Counter-Reformation shaped Irish, as much as European, society. Under English rule, penal laws against the Catholic clergy served to strengthen their ties with Continental Catholic Churches. Trade routes stretched across the seas from Irish ports to Europe. In the autumn of 1588, the remnants of the Spanish Armada were scattered along Ireland's storm-tossed northern and western coasts. In 1601, Spanish troops had landed at Kinsale in support of the Gaelic earls. During the war with Spain in the 1620s, the English were again afraid that Ireland would be used as a base for invasion.

Since the 1580s, when the chieftains of Munster and their followers took refuge in Spain after their defeat by Elizabeth I, generations of Irishmen had fought in Continental wars, though not on their own soil. The coming of European war to Irish soil in the late 1680s, was all the more remarkable in an age of protracted sieges and setpiece battles. The chain of events by which Ireland entered the European equation can be traced back twenty years earlier, to the late 1660s. A great shift in the balance of power was under way. As the Spanish Empire entered a decline, which was to prove irreversible, France was emerging as the first great, modern state.

The cockpit of Franco-Spanish rivalry was the Spanish Netherlands, largely coterminous with present-day Belgium. After assuming power in 1661, Louis XIV was concerned to secure the weak points on his northern and eastern borders, the so-called 'gates' to France. But French aggression in the late 1660s antagonized their erstwhile Dutch allies. The Dutch no longer had cause to fear their former Spanish masters and instead saw the Spanish Netherlands as a buffer-state against a resurgent France. Reaction at Louis XIV's court to the Dutch change of heart was vitriolic. Louvois, the brilliant young Minister of War, delivered the chilling verdict that 'the only way to conquer the Spanish Netherlands successfully is to humble the Dutch and, if possible, to destroy them.'

Despite clear warnings that the French were preparing to attack, the Dutch took no effective counter-measures. They were hamstrung by their internal politics. The Amsterdam merchants, led by Johann de Witt, held effective power and by tradition were pro-French. When Louis led his troops into the Dutch Republic in the summer of 1672, it seemed that nothing could prevent the French capturing Amsterdam. One town after another fell in what rapidly came to resemble a military procession. But there was one last power which, in desperation, the Dutch decided to summon. At the end of June, the dykes were opened and thousands of acres flooded. The French army ground to a halt.

In the respite, the Dutch people took their bloody revenge on de Witt. He had resigned in July, and on 20 August an Orangist mob hacked him and his brother to death in the street. The Dutch again looked to the family who had provided leadership during much of the previous century. The House of Orange had been instrumental in winning Dutch independence from Spain and forging greater unity among the new Republic's seven provinces. After the fall of de Witt, the young head of the Orange family, the twenty-two-year-old

William, was invited to accept the office of Stadtholder, held by his forebears, and lead the Dutch resistance.

Another act of Louis XIV's, far away from the Netherlands, confirmed William of Orange as a bitter, personal enemy. In 1673, French troops occupied the principality of Orange, a small enclave in Provence, in southern France. Louis could not have chosen a more wounding slight. Orange was not simply William's land, but also bestowed princely status, giving William equality with the kings and princes throughout Europe.

The sheer might and ruthlessness of Louis XIV's attack on the Dutch spread alarm throughout western Europe. The French King was rapidly deserted by his allies, but strains soon developed within the anti-French coalition. Louis emerged from the war in an even more dominant position. 'France has already become the arbiter of Europe,' observed Frederick William, Elector of Brandenburg-Prussia, in 1679, 'henceforth no prince will find security or profit except with the friendship and alliance of the King of France.' Although William of Orange saw neither security nor profit unless Louis was checked the prospects for rebuilding a coalition against the French seemed bleak. No other ruler could match Louis's 200,000-strong standing army, the rest of western Europe was militarily weak and divided, and the Austrians, the Germans and the Poles were preoccupied by war with the Turks.

During the 1680s, Louis turned his attentions to his eastern borders with the German states. French troops occupied strategic territories in the Spanish Netherlands, Spanish Luxembourg, the Moselle valley and Savoy, and in 1681 Louis seized the imperial city of Strasbourg. The Turkish invasion of the Austrian Empire was seen by Louis as a further opportunity to strengthen his position, since he calculated that an Austrian defeat would leave the way open for him to lead his own crusade and emerge as the saviour of Christian Germany. When the Turks besieged Vienna in 1683, Louis refused to help his fellow Catholic, Emperor Leopold, and sought to dissuade another Catholic king, John Sobieski of Poland, from going to Austria's aid. At the same time, Louis encouraged the Turks, earning him the soubriquet the 'Christian Turk'. None of this endeared Louis to the Vatican. Sobieski's brilliant victory over the Turks and the relief of Vienna were a bitter disappointment for both Sultan and Sun King, an unholy alliance if ever there was one.

French dominance in western Europe was speedily reasserted. When the Spaniards attempted to recover Luxembourg they were quickly humiliated by Louis. At the peace of Ratisbon (or Regensburg), the French retained their recent gains, including Strasbourg and Luxembourg. Louis agreed to a twenty-year truce with Austria and Spain, designed to snuff out William's plans for an anti-French coalition.

By 1685, Louis was in an immensely strong position. The Spanish were beaten, leaving him well placed to secure the succession when the infirm King

Carlos II eventually died. The Austrians and Germans were preoccupied in the Balkans. William of Orange was constrained by the revival of pro-French support in Amsterdam and was isolated in Europe. The same year, a Catholic, James II, became King of England, Scotland and Ireland. His destiny, and the fate of his three kingdoms, would become inextricably linked with the struggle between Louis XIV and William of Orange.

II

William of Orange had strengthened his ties with the English, Scottish and Irish crowns by marrying James's eldest daughter, the fifteen-year-old Mary, on his twenty-seventh birthday, 4 November 1677. The marriage between these Stuart cousins would provide a crucial link between the power-struggle unfolding in Europe and the political crisis which developed in the three kingdoms of the British Isles.

Within a year of the marriage, James's position as heir to the throne came under serious threat. England was caught in the grip of anti-Catholic hysteria. Evelyn, visiting London on 1 October 1678, found Parliament 'now alarmed with the whole Nation, about a conspiracy of some eminent Papists, for the destruction of the King, & introducing Popery'. The wild allegations of Titus Oates were never substantiated, but the Popish Plot none the less had considerable political impact, and 'quite changed the genius and the motions of Parliament'. Between 1678 and 1681 the English Parliament repeatedly sought to exclude James from the succession on grounds of his Catholicism. His earlier conversion, according to Evelyn, 'gave exceeding griefe and scandal to the whole Nation; That the heir of it, & the son of a Martyr for the *Protestant Religion* should apostasize'. Charles II, however, successfully outmanoeuvred the exclusionists. Although the English feared Catholicism and absolutism, which they believed went hand in hand, they had direct and relatively recent experience of the horrors of civil war and Cromwellian-style military rule. By branding his opponents as rebels and republicans, Charles won moderate opinion to his side.

King and court had won a resounding political victory. With trade flourishing and state revenues buoyant, Charles set about consolidating his position. Borough charters were redrawn to strengthen supporters of the Crown. The discovery of a conspiracy to assassinate Charles and James as they returned from the races at Newmarket in 1683, the Rye House Plot, assisted the King's policies. 'The whole Nation was now in greate Consternation, upon the late Plot & Conspiracy,' noted Evelyn. 'The *Papists* in the meane while very jocond, & indeed they had reason, seeing their owne plot brought to nothing, & turn'd to ridicule & now a Conspiracy of Protestants . . .' That summer, Charles and James pointedly inspected their army at Blackheath, visible across the Thames from the City of London, a bastion of independence against the Crown. The recall of the regiments from Tangiers, with their professional officers, heralded the creation of a professional officer corps whose first loyalty would lie to the Crown. In 1684, the King sanctioned the commissioning of Catholics in the army in Ireland. For the last four years of his reign, Charles governed without Parliament, brushing aside the Triennial Act, which required a general election at least every three years.

On Charles's death in February 1685, the Crown seemed more secure than at any time since the restoration of the monarchy, a quarter of a century earlier. In the general election, the Tories, who were generally supportive of the Crown, won a large majority. James's position was further strengthened within a matter of months through the defeat of two armed uprisings, one led by the Duke of Argyll in Scotland and the other by the Duke of Monmouth in the English west country. It helped James, as a Catholic king, that both rebellions early in his reign were led by Protestants. The ruthless despatch of Monmouth's surviving raw recruits by the thirty-seven-year-old Judge Jeffreys at the 'Bloody Assizes' served as a salutary warning to the rest of the country. Under Monmouth's threat, James doubled the size of his standing army in England to 20,000. It was never reduced during his reign. James regarded it as an essential instrument in strengthening the Crown and centralizing authority, a process begun by his brother in his latter years and common across Europe. But whereas Charles had bolstered the Anglican–Tory establishment, James threatened to undermine it.

In the autumn of 1685, news reached London that Louis XIV had revoked the Edict of Nantes, which had conferred basic rights on the Huguenots, France's minority of nearly 2 million Protestants. Whatever Louis' motives, whether to meet a concern that the Huguenots were establishing a state within a state, or to impress the Pope, the impact on Protestant opinion in England was immediate. 'Here was such a real argument of the cruel and persecuting spirit of popery,' recalled Burnet, the Anglican clergyman, adding that 'the French persecution came very seasonably to awaken the nation, and open men's eyes to so critical a conjuncture: for upon this session of parliament all did depend.'

Reports of persecution of the Huguenots and alleged atrocities could scarcely have come at a worse moment for James. Evelyn noted that at the opening of the new session of Parliament in November 1685, James demanded the 'continuance of a standing force in stead of a Militia, & indemnity & dispensation to Popish officers from the Test [Act]'. As the diarist observed, these were 'Demands very unexpected & unpleasing to the Commons'. James's policies were touching raw nerves. Fears of military rule were compounded by the spectre of a Catholic king commanding a Catholic army. James was incensed at the reaction and prorogued Parliament.[10] It was never to meet again while he was in England.

The impact of 'that dismal tragedy', as Burnet described it, sent shockwaves the length and breadth of the Continent, 'and had no small influence on

PLATE I

James II. The maritime symbols signify the King's earlier naval career.

PLATE II

Mary of Modena, James II's second wife.

Princess Mary, James II's eldest daughter.

PLATE III

Prince of Orange, Dutch Stadtholder and later William III of England.

PLATE IV

Europe's Catholic adversaries, King Louis XIV of France (left) and the Emperor Leopold I of Austria (right).

PLATE V

The arrival of Princess Mary in England, February 1689. The large white flag at the masthead of her ship proclaimed in blue letters 'For the Protestant religion and the liberty of England.'

PLATE VI

Richard Talbot, Earl of Tyrconnel,
James II's Lord Deputy of Ireland.

PLATE VII

Patrick Sarsfield, a leading figure
in the Jacobite Irish resistance.

PLATE VIII

Contemporary print of the siege of Derry, 1689, showing
ships on the river Foyle and the Jacobite besiegers.

all men's minds'. Huguenots were effective propagandists. Diplomatically, Louis' action was extremely damaging. If he had hoped that his display of religious zealotry would impress the Pope, he signally failed. Innocent XI would have been better disposed towards him if he had assisted Leopold against the Turks. The Elector of Brandenburg-Prussia resisted any further French subsidies. In the Baltic, Sweden deserted its former ally and thereafter generally took an anti-French line. In England, Burnet acknowledged that James 'was very kind to the refugees', and ordered 'a charitable collection over the nation'. But there was a six-month delay in launching the collection, and the French Ambassador, Barrillon, was believed to have played a part in the delay. Barrillon claimed in his despatches that James would have liked to cancel the collection altogether if it had been possible.

In the Dutch Republic, the Orangist attitude towards Louis was vindicated and the pro-French faction were finished at a stroke. William's popularity soared and he was allowed to build up the Dutch army and navy. In the Principality of Orange, Louis had contrived to add injury to the insult he had inflicted on William in 1673. Orange had become a refuge for Huguenots from the surrounding areas, but when Burnet visited the principality he found that French soldiers had been billeted there to intimidate the people. 'This was done while the principality was in the possession of the prince of Orange,' noted Burnet, adding that its independence had been reasserted in 'an article of the treaty of Nimuegen [Nijmegen 1678], of which the king of England was the guarantee'. Its guarantor, James II, formally protested 'in very high terms', but 'nothing came of it'.

Worse was soon to follow for William, as 'the king of France did unite Orange to the rest of Provence, and suppressed all the rights it had as a distinct principality.' Again, nothing came of the English guarantee. Burnet arrived in the Netherlands from France at this time, and became a close confidant of William and Mary. James sought to explain his inaction to his daughter, but, as Burnet recorded, the King's reasoning would scarcely endear him to the House of Orange: 'The king [James II] writ upon it to the princess of Orange [Mary], that he could do no more in that matter, unless he should declare war upon it; which he could not think fit for a thing of such small importance.'

The increased hostility felt towards Louis across the Continent fell short of an effective anti-French coalition. William realized that if he was to counter the massive French superiority he had to ally Dutch sea power with the land power of the larger German states and the Austrian Emperor. This, however, seemed a forlorn hope. But when Louis attempted to make further inroads into the Rhineland by claiming part of the Palatinate for his sister-in-law, a Palatine princess, States in south and west Germany, including Bavaria and the Palatinate, formed the League of Augsburg in 1686. Austria, Spain and Sweden also enrolled, but the League initially remained ineffective as too many of its members were bogged down in the east fighting the Hungarians and the Turks. Within a couple of years, however, the scene was totally transformed.

III

As a Catholic, James II could not accept that only Anglicans were to be treated as truly loyal subjects. On the basis of this assumption, a framework of laws had been erected over the years which discriminated against Catholics and Protestant dissenters. Yet, if James was to introduce religious toleration and remove the handicaps imposed on non-Anglicans, he would need to move fast. At his age (fifty-one on his accession), he could not expect a lengthy reign, and any hope of further reform would vanish with the succession of his Protestant daughter, Mary. He would need to deploy his powers of royal prerogative to overcome the opposition, as his proposals would be strongly resisted in Parliament and were bound to stir a hornets' nest of controversy.

In the first test of the Crown's powers in his reign, James was triumphant. The judgement in *Godden* v. *Hales* in 1686 freed the way for the King to dispense with the Test Act and appoint Catholics to public and military office. This verdict was not wholly surprising, however, as James had already dismissed judges from the bench when he found himself in disagreement with their judgements.

James's dismissal of the Earls of Clarendon and Rochester, the Hyde brothers, from the Government in the winter of 1686–7 raised the political storm signals. Their sacking marked a break of continuity and loss of stability. The Earl of Sunderland, who became the King's new chief Minister, possessed a chameleon-like flexibility, having supported the demands for James's exclusion from the succession at the start of the 1680s. Tyrconnel's appointment as Lord Deputy of Ireland in early 1687 prompted widespread opposition, including that of the Catholic members of the English Privy Council, who were concerned at the political consequences in England. 'The noise of those innovations in Ireland', as Sir John Dalrymple later wrote in his history, 'filled England with alarms, as it is natural for the human mind to dread most those evils which it hears of, but sees not.' Anglicans feared that Tyrconnel was providing a foretaste of James's policies in England. Disgruntled Protestant officers returning to England spread damaging tales about the effects of Tyrconnel's transforming the Irish army into a predominantly Catholic force.

Although James did not commission unduly large numbers of Catholic officers in the English army, his efforts to establish a professional officer corps, dependent on the King and loyal to his policies, fuelled resentment among officers who suffered as a result. The King's tendency to view the army as an instrument to impose his political will, as with the enforced billeting of soldiers, created unease. Folk-memories of Cromwell's new model army were stirred, and there was a disturbing contemporary parallel with Louis' style of government.

In April 1687, the Declaration of Indulgence announced James's intention to suspend the penal laws and dispense with the Test Act in appropriate cases, pending Parliament's repeal of the legislation. The next day, James instructed the Fellows. of Magdalen College, Oxford, to elect a Catholic, Anthony Farmer, to the recently vacated presidency of their college. Magdalen's defiance in electing their own candidate, John Hough, indicated that a section of Anglican opinion was ready to resist the King. Hough was subsequently deposed by the Ecclesiastical Commission, established by James. It was clear that the Tory-dominated Commons would never agree to repeal the Test Act. James therefore planned to dissolve Parliament and ensure the return of a Commons which would support him. Although there was nothing new about Crown interference in elections, James displayed a rare zeal. Political arithmetic decreed that James needed the support of Protestant dissenters, but many feared that any new-found freedoms for themselves would quickly perish if Catholics once established a strong position in the state. Louis' persecution of the Huguenots was seen as an object lesson.

James set about demolishing Anglican–Tory power. He canvassed, pressurized, manipulated. Municipal officers and JPs were replaced, and town charters redrawn to give dissenters greater weight. After Parliament was finally dissolved in July 1687, James sent a questionnaire to local office-holders, former MPs and some voters, asking them three questions on the repeal of the penal laws. But this tactic backfired. Replies were orchestrated, prompting the first real attempt by the clergy and gentry to concert against James. As a correspondent informed Bentinck, one of the closest confidants of William of Orange, the questionnaire 'has angered and united the nation'.

IV

By the winter of 1687–8, English politics was ripe for intrigue. The news in the autumn that Mary of Modena was pregnant raised the possibility of a Catholic male heir and the founding of a Catholic dynasty. James's opponents could no longer console themselves in the confident belief that his reign was bound to be a brief interlude before Mary, his Protestant daughter, succeeded to the throne.

A small number of English dissidents and disloyal officers were already in contact with William. His membership of the Stuart family and his marriage to Mary occasioned William's close interest in English politics, but his overriding motivation lay in his determination to counter Louis XIV and his consequent desire to influence English foreign policy. He was anxious to prevent any Anglo-French alliance, and wanted at the very least to ensure English neutrality. But if at all possible, William would prefer to enlist English resources for the benefit of a Continental coalition, and so tilt the balance against France.

William had sent his envoy, Dijkvelt, on a fact-finding mission to England in

early 1687. In his talks with James, the envoy established that there was no
prospect of England collaborating with William against the French. But Dijkvelt also reconnoitred the political scene in England, and found a number of
people willing to provide intelligence for William. As Burnet later wrote of
Dijkvelt's mission:

> He desired, that those who wished well to their religion and their country would
> meet together, and concert such advices and advertisements, as might be fit for
> the prince to know, that he might govern himself by them. The marquis of
> Halifax, and the earls of Shrewsbury, Devonshire, Danby, and Nottingham, the
> lords of Mordaunt, the Lumley, Herbert and Russel among the admirals, and
> the bishop of London, were the persons chiefly trusted.

Later that year, after Dijkvelt's return, William despatched his trusted cousin
Zuylestein to maintain his contacts.

William's hallmark was highly effective propaganda. Timing and presen-
tation were all. In early 1688, as the prospects of a packed Parliament supporting the King and the creation of a Catholic dynasty preyed on the minds of
James's opponents. William intervened. In a pamphlet, issued under the name
of the Dutch Raadspensionary, or chief Minister, Caspar Fagel, William made
clear his position on the issue at the centre of debate in England. It was an
astutely judged appeal to moderate opinion, supporting freedom of worship
through a relaxation of the penal laws, a reform which many Anglicans were
able to contemplate, but opposing any repeal of the Test Act.

'Under all this disorder that England was falling into,' Burnet wrote,
'admiral Russel came to the Hague.' By April 1688, William's contacts in
England were anxious to discover his intentions. As Burnet reported,

> The prince answered, that, if he was invited by some men of the best interest,
> and the most valued in the nation, who should both in their own name, and in
> the name of others who trusted them, invite him to come and rescue the nation
> and the religion, he believed he could be ready by the end of September to come
> over.

In short, William would not commit himself to intervene in person unless there
was sufficient support in England, but if that support materialized he would
invade within a matter of months. The conspirators sought William's intervention to establish a 'free' Parliament, by which they meant blocking James's
creation of his own majority at Westminster. William believed that a show of
force would provide him with the leverage to shape English foreign policy.

The chief Williamite conspirator was Henry Sydney, 'in whose hands the
conduct of the whole design was chiefly deposited, by the prince's own order'.
Henry Sydney had entered the House of Commons in 1679, aged thirty-eight,
after a military career, and he was appointed Ambassador to the Dutch
Republic. At the Hague, he had:

> entered into such particular confidence with the prince [William of Orange],

that he had the highest measure of his trust and favour that any Englishman ever had. This was well known over England: so that all who desired to recommend themselves to the prince did it through his hands.

Sydney had been recalled when he reported Dutch criticisms of Charles II's policies. During 1688, Sydney approached prominent politicians about an invitation to William, including the Earl of Danby (formerly Thomas Osborne, Charles II's Lord Treasurer before being imprisoned in the Tower in 1679), the Earl of Devonshire, the Marquis of Halifax and Henry Compton, Bishop of London. Halifax, however, refused to take any part, arguing that 'it was a rash and desperate project'.

Among the most crucial figures approached by Sydney were 'three chief officers of the army, Trelawny, Kirk and the lord Churchill'. In Burnet's phrase, 'These all went into it.' As the historian John Childs reveals, these three senior officers 'had fought together in France during the Franco-Dutch war from 1672–1678, had seen service in Tangiers, and were very well known in military circles in England and the United Provinces'. Churchill's part in the conspiracy was crucial, for although very few were involved it struck at the heart of James's army and reached out to the navy, the court and the 'solidly Protestant Princess Anne'.

William began preparing his armada in the spring of 1688. Whether he sailed to England would depend on further assurances of support and events in Europe.

V

By the summer of 1688, events in Europe and England were fast coming to a head. Europe was in a flurry of diplomatic activity and military preparation. Dutch envoys were busily seeking troops to provide defensive cover for William's invasion force. At Vienna, William's ally, Count Waldeck, was negotiating for the Emperor Leopold's neutrality in the event of hostilities between William and James II. In the Netherlands, the covert preparation of William's armada proceeded apace, camouflaged as defensive measures. Upstream on the Rhine, imperial troops reinforced the strategic German garrison at Philippsburg, as the French threat became increasingly menacing.

Following their successes against the Turks, the Austrians and Germans were likely to turn their attention to western Europe, and seek to regain the Rhineland territories ceded to France at Ratisbon four years earlier. The Elector of Brandenburg, a former ally of Louis', died in spring 1688. A couple of months later, the death of the old Archbishop Elector of Cologne robbed Louis of an important ally in the Rhineland. With Louis sensing that he risked losing control of events in the German states, the election of a successor to the see of Cologne was vital.

As Europe waited on the outcome, England was embroiled in a new political

crisis. James had ordered that the Anglican clergy should read his Declaration
of Indulgence from their pulpits on two successive Sundays. The clergy
resisted. When seven bishops, including the Archbishop of Canterbury, Sancroft, petitioned the King, James engineered their arrest on a charge of
seditious libel. On 8 June, they were imprisoned in the Tower of London
pending their trial. Two days later, James's wife, Mary of Modena, gave birth
to an apparently healthy son and heir. It had been assumed for some years that
the Queen would never bear a fit child, prompting rumours that the pregnancy
was bogus. It was even alleged that a baby had been smuggled into the Queen's
bed-chamber in a warming-pan. The birth of a new heir to the throne was
traditionally cause for ecstatic celebration. Yet 'the rejoicings over England
upon this birth were very cold and forced,' according to Burnet's account.
'Bonfires were made in some places, and a set of congratulatory addresses
went round the nation. None durst oppose them. But all was formal, and only
to make a shew.' The muted reception of the royal birth was thrown into sharp
relief within days by the scenes when the seven bishops were released on bail
and on 30 June when they were finally acquitted. 'Bon fires made that night, &
bells ringing,' reported Evelyn, 'which was taken very ill at Court . . .'

In the excitement generated by the bishops' acquittal, friction between
Catholic and Protestant soldiers exploded in an ugly incident at the army's
summer camp on Hounslow Heath. An Irish captain and English soldiers were
involved in a fracas. One of the soldiers was stabbed and the Captain was
hanged for his murder. When Feversham told James that the trouble had been
caused by nothing more than the shouts of soldiers on the acquittal of the
bishops, James is said to have replied, 'Do you call that nothing?'

On the day of the bishops' acquittal, the Williamite conspirators completed
their formal invitation to William. He had insisted on this two months earlier.
'Your Highness may be assured', the conspirators extravagantly claimed, 'there
are nineteen parts of twenty of the people throughout the Kingdom, who are
desirous of a change.' Written in Sydney's hand and signed by Danby, Devonshire, Shrewsbury, Lumley, Russell and Compton, the Bishop of London, the
'Immortal Seven' as they would later be mythologized, pledged that 'we who
subscribe to this will not fail to attend upon your highness upon your landing.'
They added that 'this is a season in which we may more probably contribute to
our own safeties than hereafter,' but had to admit that other influential figures
did not agree.

William received the invitation on Friday 6 July. By the end of the month, he
was determined to go ahead with his invasion. There were further reassurances, notably from John Churchill, the military commander. Sydney, the chief
organizer of the Williamite conspiracy, arrived in the Netherlands on 17
August. He brought with him a draft manifesto, which would be central to the
massive propaganda campaign planned to accompany William's invasion.
Danby, who had drafted the manifesto, advised that the invasion should be

postponed till the following spring. William was in despair at both Danby's advice and his draft, telling his advisers that the draft 'needs considerable changes. You will see that by the conclusion I throw myself entirely at the mercy of a parliament. Although I am afraid it cannot be otherwise, nevertheless handing over one's fate to them is not without hazard.' William's only concern for parliamentary rights was the extent to which they might impinge on his ability to influence foreign policy.

By late August, the scene was extremely menacing. Louis persisted in supporting his candidate in Cologne, although Fürstenberg had failed to win sufficient votes and seemed unlikely to secure the Pope's backing. The French King came to the conclusion that he had to launch a pre-emptive strike and defeat the League of Augsburg, otherwise he risked losing any remaining influence in Germany. He had, however, given little attention to his northern flank, the English Channel. Yet despite the failure of his belated attempts to negotiate a naval treaty with James and to ward off William from any aggressive action at sea, Louis decided to invade the Rhineland. He was aware that William would seize the opportunity and sail for England, but he much preferred to see the Prince of Orange heading across the North Sea rather than leading his troops up the Rhine towards Cologne. The Dutch were not members of the League of Augsburg, and Louis hoped that they would remain neutral. William, for his part, had been convinced that the French would try to disrupt his invasion plans, and was sceptical of a report that Louis planned to attack the Rhineland.

James was woefully under prepared to counter any invasion, having been ill-served by his incompetent Ambassador at the Hague, the Marquis d'Albeville, and reluctant to heed warnings from the French. On Tuesday 11 September, just days before Louis gave the final orders for his German offensive, the English King wrote to William saying how much he deprecated the prospect of war on the Continent, 'nobody wishing more the peace of Christendom than myself'. James would have every reason to regret the coming of European war. When d'Humières, the French General, marched his troops from the southern Netherlands to join the invasion of the Rhineland, he set in train the events which would bring war to the British Isles. As Evelyn noted,

> The French arm & threaten the Election of the Elector of Cologne. The Dutch make extraordinary preparations both at sea and land, which . . . puts us to many difficulties. The Popish Souldiers commit many murders & Insolences; The whole Nation disaffected & in apprehensions: what the event will prove God onely knows.[11]

CHAPTER THREE

FRIGHT AND FLIGHT

I

On Tuesday 25 September 1688, eleven days after Louis XIV had ordered his troops into the Rhineland, Tyrconnel received an urgent demand from London to send four regiments of Irish troops to England. This was no routine request. James had at last recognized the imminence of William's invasion. In all, nearly 2400 soldiers and 400 officers, comprising half the Irish army, were summoned to England. The suddenness of the order revealed more than a whiff of panic.

The intervention of Irish, and also Scottish, troops played into the hands of the Williamite conspirators. James would find it more difficult to rally English patriotic sentiment when he apparently had so little trust in the English army. He had unwittingly revived memories of the civil war, when his father Charles I called on Irish Catholic support against the Parliamentarians in 1643–4. It was an unhappy precedent.

The Irish reinforcements began arriving at Chester, Liverpool and neighbouring ports in early October 1688. The Irish Guards, under the command of William Dorrington, an Englishman, Butler's Dragoons and the infantry regiments of Lord Forbes and Anthony Hamilton, marched through the Midlands, arriving at their quarters in and around London by the end of the month. Forbes, incidentally, was Protestant, and his regiment included a couple of hundred Protestants, more than in any of the other Irish regiments. Justin MacCarthy, a senior Irish officer who had recently returned from Ireland and had reported to James on the state of the Irish army, was put in command of all the Irish troops.

Referring to the King's reinforcements, Evelyn wrote of the '5000 Irish' and '4000 Scots' – the English consistently exaggerated the numbers involved – and added that James continued 'to remove protestants & put papists in to Portsmouth & other places of Trust'. Amid fears of a French invasion, it was rumoured that the Irish had been sent to let in the French. The Portsmouth garrison, commanded by the Duke of Berwick, James's eighteen-year-old son by Arabella Churchill, included MacElligott's Regiment, which was substantially Irish in composition. Roger MacElligott had previously served with the English Brigade in the Dutch Republic, and his regiment was one of three in the English army briefly funded by Louis XIV. There were serious clashes between the Irish soldiers and both Berwick's troops and the local townspeople.

James's approach was entirely counter-productive, since it enabled William to present himself as the deliverer of Protestant Englishmen. This perception would be crucial, as the Williamites fully appreciated. In Evelyn's view, James's handling of the crisis:

> gave no satisfaction to the nation, but increasing the universal discontent, brought people to so desperate a passe as with uttmost expressions even passionately seeme to long for & desire the landing of that Prince, *whom they looked on as their deliverer from popish Tyrannie*, praying incessantly for an Easterly wind which was said to be the onely remora [delaying factor] of his expedition, with a numerous Army ready to make a descent. [My italics.]

Throughout the early autumn, the winds 'blew obstinately from the west', as was later noted by Macaulay, the nineteenth-century English historian. This 'prevented the Prince's armaments from sailing and brought fresh Irish regiments from Dublin to Chester'. In consequence, the prevailing westerlies 'were bitterly cursed and reviled by the common people. The weather, it was said, is Popish. Crowds stood in Cheapside gazing intently at the weathercock on the graceful steeple of Bow Church, and praying for a Protestant wind.'

Under threat of invasion, James promised elections to a new Parliament, as Evelyn noted, 'with greate professions of maintaining the Church of England: but without giving any sort of satisfaction to people, who now begin to shew their high discontent at several things in the Government: how this will end, God onely can tell.' James's concessions were too little, too late. In an attempt to shore up support, James urged the Anglican bishops to 'declare their abhorrence of this invasion'. But the bishops refused, in Burnet's words, 'with a courage that recommended them to the whole nation'. When James ordered them to compose a prayer against the invasion, their text was deliberately bland. 'Supporters of the Church of England then openly expressed in favour of the invasion and voiced their grief to see the wind so cross. They wished for an east wind, which on that occasion was called the protestant wind.'

The revival of the English myth of a 'Protestant wind' helps explain the astonishing success of 'Lilliburlero', which reappeared in the latter half of October 1688. When the ballad had first appeared at the time of Tyrconnel's appointment as Lord Deputy in early 1687, it had fortuitously included the verse, 'Oh, but why does he stay behind, Ho by my shoul 'tis a Protestant wind'. The myth of a 'Protestant wind' itself dated from 1588 and the defeat of the Spanish Armada, a centenary much in Protestant English minds as they perceived themselves to be once again at risk from the dual threat of Catholicism and despotic government.

The new-found popularity of 'Lilliburlero' was further evidence of the reaction in England against the sudden influx of the Irish regiments. New verses were added which mocked Irish Catholic soldiers in England as they prepared to defend a Protestant country from a Protestant invasion. 'A foolish ballad was made at that time,' Burnet recalled, 'treating the papists and chiefly the Irish in a very ridiculous manner, which had a burden said to be Irish words, "lero lero, lilli burlero".' Appealing to English prejudice, 'Lilliburlero' 'made an impression on the army that cannot be imagined by those who saw it not. The whole army and at last the people, both in city and country, were singing it perpetually.' In Portsmouth, a sailor was killed by some of MacElligott's Irish soldiers for singing 'Lilliburlero', prompting a vicious revenge attack on the Irish by a group of English sailors. Thomas Wharton, who wrote the lyrics, was later to boast that 'Lilliburlero' 'sung a deluded Prince [James] out of three kingdoms'.

The distinctive dragon's head weathervane high above St Mary-le-Bow eventually swung round and signalled an easterly on Sunday 14 October, to 'the great sorrow of the Roman Catholics, and the Joy of the rest of the Nation'. It happened to be James's birthday. Evelyn wrote of the 'wonderfull expectation of the Dutch fleete' and even drew parallels with the omens which preceded an earlier invasion, referring to 'the signal for the Victory of William the Conqueror against Harold'.

II

On the morning of Tuesday 16 October, William of Orange bade farewell to his wife Mary and left to address representatives of the seven Dutch provinces at the Hague. The meeting was a moving occasion, the accent heavy on predestination. Burnet recalled that the Calvinist William 'did not know how God might dispose of him: to his providence he committed himself.' According to Burnet, an eye-witness, 'It was a sad, but a kind parting . . . Only the prince himself continued firm in his usual gravity and phlegm.'

With the wind at last set fair for England, William was about to embark on the biggest political gamble of his life. Yet he had not defined how he envisaged achieving his stated objectives of preventing an Anglo-French alliance against the Dutch and gaining English support in 'the restoring and maintaining of Peace and Tranquillity in Europe', in other words enlisting English resources in the coalition against Louis. His European allies were reassured that William had no intention of seeking the English throne.

When William joined his fleet off Hellevoetsluys on the Maas estuary, it was the culmination of months of secretive planning and a massive logistical operation. William's invasion force was a cosmopolitan collection, predominantly Dutch, but with large numbers of Huguenots, and also Swedes and Brandenburgers, and 300 Swiss, 200 Finns and 200 blacks from Dutch plantations in the Americas. Of great political significance, six regiments of the long-standing Anglo-Dutch brigade, comprising 3000 infantry under the command of the Scot Hugh Mackay. The Anglo-Dutch brigade dated from the sixteenth century, when English and Scottish soldiers supported the Dutch fight for independence from the Spanish Empire. It survived through the 1600s, paid and equipped by the seven provinces – the Irish soldier, Roger MacElligott, had served in one of its three English regiments. The English monarch retained the right to recall the brigade if the need arose, as James had at the time of the Monmouth rebellion in 1685, when Evelyn saw the English regiments 'all excellently clad, and perfectly disciplined' at their camp on Blackheath. But when James summoned British sailors and soldiers in Dutch service in March 1688, only a tiny proportion of the brigade responded.

The presence of so many British Protestants in William's invasion force would help persuade the English that he was not a foreign invader bent on military conquest, but was their deliverer. In his *Letter to the English Army*, directed at the officer corps, William cited Tyrconnel's purge of Protestants from the Irish army, suggesting that a similar fate awaited them under James. As a means of countering the officers' professional loyalty to the King, William reminded them of their obligations to 'God and Religion, Country, Selves, Posterity . . . of being the Instruments of serving your Country and Securing your Religion'.

The appointment of an English admiral, Arthur Herbert, as commander-in-chief of the naval operation would help minimize any conflict of loyalties among the British contingent if the armada came into contact with the English fleet. Herbert had been elected to the House of Commons in 1685, and served as Rear Admiral of England and Master of the Robes under James II, until his dismissal from office in early 1687 because of his opposition to repeal of the Test Act. He was an experienced commander, who had lost an eye in a clash with an Algerine ship in 1678, was fond of his drink and a notorious womanizer. In a pamphlet issued to coincide with the invasion, Herbert appealed to English sailors:

> I as a true Englishman and your friend exhort you to join your arms to the Prince for the defence of the common cause, that as the Kingdom has always depended on the Navy for its defence so you will yet go further by making it as much as in you lies the protection of its Religion and Liberties.

William's emphasis on psychological warfare reflected his determination to avoid any naval or military battle with James's forces. A battle at sea would risk exposing the vulnerable Dutch transports to attack. Spilling English blood would give James an opportunity to rally support in England and revive old Anglo-Dutch animosities. The same principles would guide William's approach once he had set foot on English soil.

If, however, the need to fight should arise, William would not repeat Monmouth's error of relying on English support to materialize. He would also avoid antagonizing the English by ensuring that his troops were not left to live entirely off the countryside. This necessitated a massive armada. The full complement of the invasion fleet consisted of 49 warships and 200 transports, including coastal trading ships and 60 flat-bottomed Scheveningen fishing smacks. On board were 15,000 troops – about 11,000 infantry, 4000 cavalry and some artillery – with their horses, and vast quantities of arms and ammunition, waggons, coaches, pontoons and stores. A smithy, a printing press and a mint were also loaded aboard.

After a brief delay, awaiting transport ships and further supplies, William finally boarded his new flagship, *Den Briel*, on Friday 19 October. His armada left port on a north-easterly, but during the night the wind shifted to the north-west and blew up a storm. As Burnet wrote, 'We wrought against it all that night, and the next day. But it was in vain to struggle any longer. And so vast a fleet run no small hazard, being obliged to keep together, and yet not come too near one another.' The bedraggled fleet, its sailors and soldiers cold and demoralized, was forced to return to port. Yet no ships were missing, nor any lives lost. The only serious losses were 400 horses, who had suffocated after the holds had been battened down in the storm. When exaggerated reports of the losses reached London, an emboldened James withdrew the promise of parliamentary elections, made under threat of invasion only the previous month. It seemed conclusive proof that the King would never mend his ways.

Ten days passed before the wind returned to a favourable quarter. Eventually, during the night of 29/30 October, 'the wind changed and turned east-north-east bringing joy to all the fleet with the expectation of a prompt departure.' At four o'clock in the afternoon of Thursday 1 November, William's armada weighed anchor and headed out from the Maas estuary.

Although James had 25,000 troops at his command, with a further 15,000 reserves, he tried to protect too many potential landfalls. He suspected that the Dutch might attempt a repetition of their tactics in 1667, when their fleet sailed up the Medway in Kent. Reports of troop movements immediately before the invasion show that James expected the armada to head for the north or east coast. Bridlington Bay was identified as a likely landfall. But East Anglia and the south coast were not neglected.

The English fleet, under the command of Lord Dartmouth, was stationed off the Essex coast, by the Gunfleet sands. Dartmouth believed that William would sail into the mouth of the Thames, and opted for Gunfleet because it would also enable him to intercept the Dutch if they headed for the north, as James's Ambassador at the Hague, d'Albeville, was predicting. There was, however, one serious problem: Gunfleet was a difficult station to leave in an easterly, as Dartmouth discovered even before William's armada had left its moorings. The English Admiral expected that the Dutch fleet would seek a battle to clear a passage for their transports. He planned to search out the Dutch fleet as they entered the North Sea, but the wind developed into an easterly gale, and the English fleet was unable to sail.

While William's fleet headed north-west across the North Sea, William remained near the Dutch coast, awaiting his cousin, Zuylestein, who was due to return from England with the latest intelligence. When he arrived on board *Den Briel*, Zuylestein reported that James had sent troop reinforcements to the north. At a hastily convened council of war, William decided that his armada should head for the English west coast. This had been Herbert's wish all along. During the night of 2/3 November, the armada suddenly changed course. With the wind staying in the east, it was as easy for the armada to sail south-west for the straits of Dover as it was to carry on heading north-west for the Yorkshire coast.

At dawn on Saturday, the sails of the Dutch rearguard were spotted by the English look-outs. Dartmouth's further disaster was that the east wind was reinforced by a floodtide. Later that morning, while the English were still stranded off the Essex coast, the Dutch were sighted far to the south, 'on the backside of the Goddwin'. With the English fleet trapped and no French ships on station at Calais or Dunkirk, William was assured a clear run through the straits of Dover. His vast armada stretched out across the seas for almost 19 miles, responding to the crowds gathered along the cliff tops by striking up music on some ships and firing salutes. William's flagship, *Den Briel*, and other ships flew streamers proclaiming the Orange motto 'I will maintain' and the slogan 'The Liberty of England and the Protestant Religion'.

Sunday 4 November seemed a propitious day for William to make landfall – it was both his thirty-eighth birthday and his wedding anniversary. But William was persuaded by his English advisers that the following day would have far more resonance. Each year, 5 November was celebrated as the anniversary of the discovery of the Gunpowder Plot, which the English viewed as their deliverance from a Catholic assault on their Government. Delaying the landing by twenty-four hours offered a propaganda coup which William, sensitive to the overriding importance of politics, knew he could not afford to spurn.

During Sunday the 4th, the armada passed Portsmouth and the Isle of Wight. William's new plan was to land at Dartmouth on Monday the 5th. Overnight, however, a pilot's error caused the van of the armada to overshoot Dartmouth and Torbay. Then, late in the morning of the 5th, the wind suddenly fell to a calm before shifting to the south and later the west. The fleet was able to land safely after all at Torbay.

The hapless English fleet was still trailing far to the east, off Beachy Head. The change in the wind proved as disastrous for the English as it was providential for William. Dartmouth was unable to make any real headway against the strong westerly which began blowing through the Channel and was forced to take shelter behind the South Downs. The English fleet was destined never to make contact with William's armada.

Once William had set foot ashore at the nearby fishing village of Brixham, he permitted himself the only joke he is recorded as ever having made. Greeting the Anglican Bishop, Gilbert Burnet, the Calvinist Prince commented, 'Well, Doctor, what do you think of predestination now?'

III

William's invasion force represented a military threat, but the pressures he exerted were political and psychological. The key question would be the reaction of James, his troops and his subjects. Propaganda was central to William's strategy and was the origin of Williamite mythology, which has lived on through the centuries. The legend has been transformed by the vicissitudes of Irish history, but the image of 'King Billy' has its roots in the powerful propaganda campaign first unleashed in England in 1688.

William had successfully avoided any battle at sea, and needed to do the same on land. He had based his bold attempt to shape English foreign policy on a show of force, but he had to be seen to be acting more in sorrow than in anger. James, after all, had an inestimable advantage as the legitimate monarch, whose problem was his subjects' indifference to his fate, not imminent insurrection. A combative approach by William might yet stir English patriotism. William's priority was to return to the Continent as soon as possible, and it was crucial that he should not let himself be bogged down in the British Isles, which would be a risk once any fighting started.

The presence of a printing press and a mint on board William's armada was not mere whim. Like the French propagandists who promoted the image of the Sun King, William and his advisers were as slick in their use of the technologies of their day as any modern politicians. The Dutch had been in the forefront of pictorial propaganda since the 1500s and their independence campaign against the Spanish. William was often depicted with the cap of liberty, which signified to the Dutch their fight for freedom from imperial Spain. Manifestos, broadsheets, coins and medals were the centre-piece of the Williamite political armoury, and the recent influx of polemical Huguenot émigrés had sharpened their edge.

William's views on the penal laws and the Test Act had been skilfully presented earlier in the year, and special declarations had been targeted at England's soldiers and sailors on the eve of the invasion. The centre-pieces after William's landing were the two 'Declarations', or manifestos, designed to show William's policies and intentions 'in the most favourable light'.

The *Declaration of Reasons* was a heavily revised version of the draft sent by Danby in August, carefully tailored for its target audience, Anglican majority opinion. Without the acquiescence of the 'Church party' all would be lost. The *Declaration* depicted William not as a conqueror but as the 'Dutch deliverer', who sought to rescue the Protestant religion and the Anglican Church, and to restore the laws and liberties of England's ancient constitution. William had been concerned that Danby's first draft would give Parliament too much say, but suspected that there was little alternative. He now pledged that he would 'concur in everything' that a 'free and lawful Parliament shall determine'. William would have preferred to avoid any such commitment. Henceforth, he was a prisoner of his promise.

The reigning monarch was not attacked directly. The blame for England's ills was pinned on James's 'evil counsellors'. English reaction against Tyrconnel's Catholic revival in Ireland was also exploited: 'the dismall effects of this subversion of the Established Religion, Laws and Liberties in England appear more evidently to us by what we see done in Ireland.' The use of dirty tricks was central to the campaign. Although William must have realized that the allegations about James's recently born heir were far-fetched, he none the less associated himself and his wife with the rumour-mongers: 'not only we ourselves', proclaimed the *Declaration*, 'but all good subjects of the Kingdom do vehemently suspect that the Pretended Prince of Wales was not borne by the Queen.' William and Mary's own place in the succession was highlighted. A parliamentary inquiry was promised, although in the event none was forthcoming. The effect on James was devastating. He was deeply distressed that his son-in-law and nephew (William was the son of James's sister, Mary Stuart), and by implication his daughter, should doubt his word over the birth of his son.

The *Declaration* was printed at Amsterdam, Edinburgh, the Hague, Hamburg and London, and published in four different languages – English, Dutch, French and German. Copies were handed to all foreign ambassadors at the Hague, except the English and French. According to Burnet, 'many thousand copies' were sent to Britain, for distribution only after William had landed and not before. After his landing on 5 November, the *Declaration* was read aloud and posted in towns and villages throughout England. James's attempts at censorship and his own counter-propaganda proved ineffective. Williamite propaganda became a blitz during the winter. Broadsheets were directed at James's army, promising rewards to those who joined William, provided they did so 'seasonably'. Within weeks of his landing, William was printing 'two gazettes a week', Evelyn noting that 'every day' he 'sets forth new declarations &c. against the Papists'.

The challenge to James's Government, which soon lost any semblance of control over the press, unleashed a flood of critical and satirical pamphlets and tracts. 'Every thing (till now concealed) flies abroad in publique print, & is Cryed about the Streetes,' observed Evelyn. Few of James's subjects had any personal grievance against the King, but Williamite sympathizers were able to tap a rich vein of English prejudice against Catholics and the Irish. The King's reliance on Catholic advisers and his evident dependence on his Irish army were mercilessly exploited. A flavour of this material is given by an early comic book, *The Roman Post Boy*, which pandered to English prejudices, presenting bawdy jokes about Catholics, Irish and Jesuits, and mocking the Irish accent.

A totally misleading image of William was peddled to make him appear 'kingly' to the English. He was portrayed as 'robust and healthy', was said to possess 'wonderful proportions and features', and in character was 'benign', 'affable' and 'of . . . sweet temper'. In fact, William was a chronic asthmatic, five feet five inches tall, painfully thin, with a slightly deformed back and crooked nose, and was renowned for being irritable, short-tempered and sullen. William's real character traits later became fully apparent to those who met him, and prompted comment by the diarist Evelyn. But by the time that disillusionment with William had set in, the propaganda had served its purpose.

James later admitted to the damage inflicted on him by 'all artes', which had made him 'appear as black as Hell to my own people'. As the King ruefully lamented in his memoirs, 'What effect that hath had at home all mankind hath seen, by so general a defection in my army as well as in the nation amongst all sorts of people.'

IV

Three days after William's landing at Torbay, an order arrived at Dublin Castle for a further infantry regiment to be sent to England. But Tyrconnel was allowed to use his discretion, and replied that he had too few troops as it was to maintain security in Ireland. He promised, however, that Mountjoy's Regiment would be despatched in due course. Although it was summoned from Derry to Dublin, it was never sent.[12]

The first deserters left James's army within days of William's arrival at Exeter, on Friday 9 November. Although they were few in number, those quitting the King's service included Lord Cornbury, son of the Earl of Clarendon. As a nephew of the King through James's first wife, Anne Hyde, Cornbury was virtually a member of the royal family. He was one of the circle close to James's younger daughter, Anne, and served as Master of the Horse to her husband, Prince George of Denmark. James was so shocked by Cornbury's desertion that he delayed still further his own departure from London.

By Saturday the 10th, the first detachment of James's troops had been ordered to Salisbury, including Patrick Sarsfield and Richard Hamilton. The Irish contingent travelled there at the same time as James, who eventually set out on Sunday the 18th. James's army at Salisbury numbered about 24,000 men, while a further 8000 reserves remained in London. Meanwhile, advance parties from the two armies had been involved in the first skirmishes. Sarsfield led a detachment which killed thirty Williamites at Wincanton. William's second-in-command, the veteran mercenary, Marshal Schomberg exacted revenge, slaying more than fifty of the King's soldiers on the Dorchester road.

Barrillon, the French Ambassador, who accompanied the King to Salisbury, urged James to fight. Also joining James's councils was another Frenchman, the Comte de Lauzun, who had just arrived in England. It was in the French interest to see William tied down in England for as long as possible. It followed that William wanted to avoid the risk of becoming embroiled in a civil war. Equally, however, he was reluctant to open negotiations for the time being, since talks at such an early stage would limit what he might ultimately achieve. He would keep the pressure on James.

Salisbury proved disastrous for the King. There was little intelligence about his enemy's whereabouts, the weather was foul and his plans to rally the troops were ruined by a recurrence of his nose-bleeds, a symptom, in James, of extreme physical and mental strain. According to William Pryme, an eye-witness, James:

> rode backward and forward continually with a languishing look, his hat hanging over his eyes and a handkerchief continually in one hand to dry the blood of his nose, for he continually bled. If he and his soldiers did not chance to hear a trumpet or even a post-horn they were always upon a surprise, and all fit to run away, and at last they did so. All the nights there was nothing but tumults and every question that was asked, 'Where are the enemy?' 'Where are the enemy?' 'How far are they off?' 'Which way are they going?' and such like.

James's commander-in-chief, Feversham, a French Protestant by birth, told him that his officers could not be trusted. News of the uprisings in the North and the east Midlands added to his sense of betrayal. Danby seized York and Scarborough, while the garrisons at Carlisle and Hull mutinied. Delamere and Devonshire occupied Derby and Nottingham.

John Stevens, the Catholic excise officer, heard that Chester was secured for James by a force commanded by the old royalist officer, Viscount Maryborough (Caryll Molyneux), and that 'there were lately 3000 men out of Ireland.' But his hopes that 'Chester still held for the king' were soon dashed by the news that the city was in the hands of the Williamites 'and the Irish recruits being only many ships full of women and children that fled from Ireland for fear of chimerical massacres'.

James lost his nerve. On Thursday the 22nd, the first orders to withdraw from Salisbury were issued to his troops. Late on the night of Friday the 23rd, John Churchill and the Duke of Grafton (an illegitimate son of Charles II), along with a number of other officers, deserted to William. The next day, James's other son-in-law, Prince George of Denmark, deserted. Princess Anne, accompanied by Churchill's wife Sarah, fled Whitehall to join the Williamite rebels at Nottingham, James learning of their abscondment when he returned to London on Monday the 26th.

In another reversal of policy, the King announced his readiness to call a new Parliament, to dismiss Catholics from their posts and to negotiate with William. But a third *Declaration* appeared on Saturday 8 December, allegedly

published on William's instructions. William, however, had no knowledge of it.
Authorship was later claimed by Hugh Speke, an extreme critic of James, who
had been gaoled in 1683 by Judge Jeffreys for seditious libel. The bogus
Declaration was virulently anti-Catholic. Its impact was immediate. Within
days, anti-Catholic riots swept the country.

James's army, which still outnumbered the invasion force, had regrouped in
the Thames Valley around Maidenhead. At Reading, the detachment holding
the town for the King included three troops of Irish Dragoons. The townspeople
managed to send messages asking the Dutch to free them from the Irish troops. It
was a measure of English prejudice and a tribute to the skill of Williamite propaganda, that the Irish soldiers, serving the King, were seen as intruders, whereas
foreign troops, serving a foreign invader, were seen as the liberators. In the confusion which followed the Dutch assault on Reading, fifty Irish soldiers were
killed and the rest fled. On 9 December, the Irish left Maidenhead, and the
following day withdrew after a final skirmish with the Williamites at Windsor.

James was a beaten man. The number of desertions were far fewer than
William had expected, but crucially the few officers involved were at the heart
of the army's command structure. Their loss was a shattering blow to James
and his army, both organizationally and psychologically. His Government was
fast crumbling. 'The Popists in offices lay down their Commissions and flie:
Universal Consternation amongst them.' Evelyn was drawn to the inescapable
conclusion that 'it lookes like a Revolution.'

The King was obsessed with fear for the safety of his son and heir, and also
for his own personal safety, which was understandable bearing in mind the fate
of his father, Charles I, less than forty years earlier. James ordered Dartmouth
to escort the baby prince to France, but the Admiral refused to be 'the unhap-
pie instrument of so apparent ruine to your Majestie, and my Country as an act
of this kinde will be', and added a plea of some prescience:

> Pray, Sir, consider farther on this weightie point, for can the Prince's being sent
> to France have other prospect than the entaileing a perpetuall warre upon your
> nation and posterity, and giving France a temptation to molest, invade, nay
> hazard the conquest of England which I hope in God never to see.[13]

Dartmouth's advice fell on deaf ears. In early December, the Queen and her
infant prince were despatched to France. Late on the night of Monday the
10th, James himself fled Whitehall, bound for France via the tiny port of
Emley Ferry on the north Kent coast.

V

With James's flight, his Government and army disintegrated. The country
stood on the brink of chaos. Credit collapsed, anti-Catholic riots escalated and
mob-rule threatened. It was probably at this stage that William finally decided
to seize the throne.

The *English Courant* reported, 'no sooner was the King's withdrawing known, but the Mobile [mob] consulted to wreak their vengeance on Papists and Popery.' On Tuesday the 11th the *Universal Intelligence* recorded, with a degree of hyperbole, that Protestants had destroyed all 'Popish chapels' in and near York, Bristol, Gloucester, Worcester, Shrewsbury, Stafford, Wolverhampton, Birmingham, Cambridge and Bury St Edmunds.

The violence reached its peak in the capital on the Tuesday night, the sky more brightly lit than at any time since the Great Fire of 1666. Among those manhandled by the mob was James's Lord Chancellor, Jeffreys, notorious for the penalties he had meted out to Monmouth's supporters at the 'Bloody Assizes'. The mob's principal targets were chapels, embassies and private homes.

In this highly charged atmosphere, the English were panic-stricken at the supposed threat from groups of Irish soldiers, who had either fled after William's arrival or had been disbanded and were heading from southern England through the Midlands to the north-western ports. Around 4000 of James's troops, many of them Irish, were disbanded at Uxbridge by Feversham, but not all of them were disarmed. Irish troops in London were disbanded on Tuesday the 11th, and marched to Hounslow Heath to lay down their arms. On the night of 12/13 December, there occurred one of the most extraordinary incidents of the crisis, the so-called 'Irish Fear', or 'Irish Night'. In London in the early hours of Thursday the 13th, 'a report was spread all over the town that a great number of Irish' were 'got together, that they had burnt Uxbridge and put all to the sword, and were marching up directly to London'. The capital's entire population were stirred from their beds by cries of 'Rise, arme, arme, the Irish are cutting throats.' Dread of an imminent massacre was so strong that within half an hour of the alarm about 100,000 men were in the streets ready to resist the Irish, the scene illuminated by candles placed in the street-windows. By about four o'clock, people realized that it was a false alarm, and began returning to bed.

Irish soldiers were alleged to have burnt a number of towns, including Kingston in Surrey, Birmingham, Nottingham, Doncaster, Huddersfield and Stafford. Many other reports appeared of rumoured outrages committed by the Irish. Catholics feared the consequences of the Protestant panic. John Stevens left Chester and travelled through the west Midlands to London 'and thence to follow His Majesty':

At the time the rumour of the Irish burning and murdering all before them, which had been maliciously spread on purpose for the destruction of the Catholics, had prevailed, and people dreamed of nothing but blood and massacres, the very forgers of the lie having told it so often they believed it themselves.

The young Huguenot diarist, Abraham de la Pryme, was in no doubt who

was responsible for causing the terror. He claimed that the rumours had orig-
inated in the south, before spreading to affect the entire country. 'Most certain
it is', he commented, 'that it was nothing but a polite alarm raised and set on
foot by the king [William] and council to see how the nation stood affected to
their new king.' There is no evidence to implicate William directly. More
probably, the rumours were spread by his more extreme sympathizers. But the
consequences were of undoubted benefit to William. The English were
encouraged to regard him not as a foreign invader, but as their saviour from an
external threat.

One of the strongest cards in William's hand was his command of the only
effective force in the land. The morning after James's flight, the aristocrats,
bishops and gentry, whom the King had summoned to discuss a settlement
with William, met at the Guildhall in London. With the King gone, they
assumed the role of a provisional government, Archbishop Sancroft taking the
chair in James's absence. The assembly condemned the King's 'desertion' and
resolved 'to apply themselves to the Prince of Orange, who had with great
kindness, vast expense, and much hazard' sought the country's salvation from
arbitrary government and Catholicism. They proclaimed their 'support of the
Protestant Religion and Interest over the whole world'.

King James, however, had not yet left the country. He had been captured on
the Kent coast on Tuesday the 11th and held at Faversham, where his
fishermen–gaolers at first thought he was a Jesuit in disguise. He was shown
scant respect by his truculent captors, a spokesman declaring that they would
not allow the King to go to France to obtain foreign troops in order to over-
power the country. The provisional Government sent a detachment of 120
guards and 150 grenadiers to Faversham to attend James and secure him 'from
the Insolence of the numbers of People who may presse to come neer Him
upon this occasion'.

James despatched Feversham with a letter to William, suggesting that they
meet. But it was too late to outwit William. Feversham was arrested, and
Zuylestein went to London to tell James that William was prepared to consider
a meeting, but could not come to the capital until it was cleared of James's
troops. At Windsor on Monday the 17th, William informed leading members
of the House of Lords of James's invitation, but ventured that James would not
be safe in London. When the peers suggested that the King should be advised
to withdraw, William shrewdly insisted that they, not him, should deliver this
advice: 'by your favour my lord, it is the advice of the peers here, and some of
yourselves shall carry it.' Nominating Halifax, Shrewsbury and Delamere as
the messengers, William brilliantly implicated the politicians in James's final
demise.

In pouring rain, at about ten o'clock that night, the peers finally arrived in
Whitehall, escorted by three battalions of guards under the command of
General Solms, William's senior commander. After a brief discussion, James's

sentries withdrew. The three peers entered the Palace at Whitehall at about midnight to deliver their fateful advice.

At nine o'clock the following morning, Tuesday 18 December, James departed by barge for Rochester, accompanied by hand-picked Dutch Catholic guards. Within a week, he had crossed the Channel and landed at Ambleteuse on the Picardy coast, accompanied by the Duke of Berwick, his natural son. From the day that James joined Mary of Modena and their young son at St Germain-en-Laye, where he set up a court-in-exile, he became a prisoner of French strategy, a pawn to be deployed whenever it suited Louis XIV's Continental ambitions.

Towards the evening of Tuesday the 18th, William entered London, greeted by a crescendo of church bells and exuberant crowds waving oranges impaled on sticks. In Dublin, Tyrconnel, still unaware of James's first flight, had written his letter to the Earl of Antrim about the crisis in England and the need to put an end to the revolt at Derry.

'All the world go to see the Prince at St. James's where there is a greate Court,' noted Evelyn. 'He is very stately, serious, & reserved.' William was preoccupied with the enormous political and military challenges ahead. Settling the English constitutional crisis and securing his position in Ireland and Scotland would distract him from his original purpose, countering Louis. 'He hath such a mind to France', wrote the Marquis of Halifax, 'that it would incline one to think, he took England only in his way.'

PART TWO

BATTLE FOR IRELAND

CHAPTER FOUR

IRELAND THE
BATTLE-GROUND

I

The collapse of James's Government and army in England, and the King's final flight, placed Tyrconnel in an almost impossible position. His policies had improved the lot of Catholics, but the Catholic revival was not yet guaranteed. Now it was threatened by the crisis in England. He faced an imminent collapse of law and order, trade was at a standstill and Government revenues had virtually dried up. Yet, if he did not submit to the new regime in London, Ireland faced the awesome prospect of a Williamite invasion. Already, Williamite frigates were patrolling the Irish Sea.

The despatch of half the Irish army to England had left Tyrconnel in an extremely weak position. His plans to levy extra troops would necessarily take time, and he was desperately short of arms. Following James's defeat, the Irish regiments in England were in disarray. On Friday 14 December, the great 'Irish fear' prompted the provisional Government of peers in London to make one of their first executive decisions, ordering the arrest of all Catholic officers, who were to be taken into custody as hostages for the Protestants in Ireland. All Irish soldiers were to be disarmed and put into new quarters: MacElligott's Regiment in Chichester; Forbes's Infantry in Hatfield; Hamilton's Infantry and the Irish Guards in Lewes; and Butler's Dragoons in East Grinstead. At Tilbury, the Irish Guards evacuated the garrison, were disarmed, overpowered by the local people and put under arrest. At Portsmouth, the Duke of Berwick and Sir Edward Scott, an Irish Catholic, at first resisted stubbornly, but eventually surrendered. Irish dragoons, who had been stationed nearby, marched away on foot.

By January 1689, 1500 Irish Catholic soldiers were incarcerated on the Isle of Wight, but many escaped. Many Protestant Irish soldiers were regrouped into Forbes's Regiment, which became an entirely Protestant force, and was ordered to the north country. William was anxious to see the remaining Irish Catholic troops removed from the country as soon as possible, and reached an agreement with his Catholic ally on the Continent, the Emperor Leopold, that a regiment of Irish soldiers should be formed to fight against the Turks.

Dennis McGillicuddy, who had been MacElligott's Lieutenant-Colonel, was to lead the regiment, but many of the soldiers escaped on reaching the Continent and entered service with the French.

Exposed militarily and vulnerable financially, Tyrconnel faced a Protestant backlash against his policies. Many Protestants in Dublin and the northern counties were armed, and in the capital were reckoned to outnumber Tyrconnel's weakened army several times over, estimates varying from around two to one, to twenty to one. A plot to seize Dublin Castle and arrest Tyrconnel was only abandoned because of lack of support from Lords Granard and Mountjoy, themselves Protestants in the Irish army's high command. Protestants in rural areas ganged together for protection. In Munster, the army had difficulty re-establishing control over local armed associations of Protestants. Ulster Protestants made overtures directly to William, and their armed associations openly supported the Williamite cause. Derry was in revolt, its Protestants fearful of the rumoured Catholic uprising and angered at the withdrawal of Mountjoy's troops, summoned to Dublin as possible reinforcements for England, and the attempt to replace them with the Catholic Earl of Antrim's regiment.

Tyrconnel responded to Ireland's crisis by ordering the levy of 20,000 troops, a massive increase on the total complement of 5000 before the crisis began. At the same time, however, he endeavoured to reassure Protestants, opening negotiations with them in Ulster. As a concession to Derry, its garrison would henceforth be maintained by Protestant troops of Mountjoy's Regiment.

Ireland, however, was in no condition to resist a Williamite invasion, a point made to Tyrconnel by members of the Irish Privy Council. In December, there was speculation that Tyrconnel would resign. Reports reached William that the Lord Deputy was ready to disband the Irish army and relinquish his office in return for assurances that Catholics would be no worse off than they were at the end of Charles II's reign. James later claimed that Tyrconnel was merely playing William along, with 'a prudent show of wavering': the Lord Deputy 'strove to amuse the Prince of Orange's agents with a feigned disposition of submission till he could put himself and the kingdom in a position not to be forced to do it'. Yet Tyrconnel was initially depressed at Ireland's predicament, and it was not until January that he began to be more optimistic.

But how would William respond? The magnitude of his success in England had brought fresh problems. Before he could return to Europe, a new constitutional settlement had to be reached with the politicians in London, and unless Scotland and Ireland were brought under Williamite control, there would always be a serious risk that Louis XIV would aid and abet a counter-invasion by James. William had long been conscious of the strategic significance of Ireland. Over a year earlier, Bonrepaus noted that according to d'Albeville, the English Ambassador at the Hague, 'the principal anxiety of the

Prince of Orange is lest Ireland shall be put in condition, before the death of
the King of England [James], to cut herself off from his dominion when he
shall come to the throne'. Now that William was poised to 'come to the
throne', Tyrconnel's continued presence in Dublin Castle created a risk that
Ireland would indeed 'cut herself off'.

William, however, was anxious to avoid military commitments which might
tie him down for months, if not years. Moreover, according to Burnet, William
faced additional problems. 'The truth was, he did not know whom to trust.'
There was discontent in the English army, and he was fearful of sending his
Dutch troops, since 'it was to them that he chiefly trusted, for maintaining the
quiet of England.' Raising new troops would take time, and there was also a
shortage of ammunition. Negotiation with Tyrconnel might yield a settlement
in Ireland without needing to commit too many troops. He therefore rejected
advice that he should send a detachment immediately to force Tyrconnel's
surrender and opted instead for diplomacy.

On the advice of John Temple, son of Sir William, a supporter of the coup
in England, Richard Hamilton was appointed as an intermediary with Tyrconnel. It was a bold move on William's part. Hamilton was a Catholic, who had
been one of James's most trusted officers. He knew Tyrconnel well, their
acquaintanceship reinforced by marriage: Frances, Countess of Tyrconnel,
was the widow of Hamilton's late brother, George. Following James's flight,
Richard Hamilton had ostensibly become a supporter of William, an
impression strengthened by his being a nephew of the Duke of Ormonde, a
former Lord Lieutenant and leading Irish Protestant. Temple also vouched for
Hamilton's trustworthiness, and his acquaintance with Tyrconnel seemed an
asset for his role as intermediary.

It would be an understatement to say that William's intermediary inspired
little confidence among Irish Protestants. According to Oliver St George, who
gave evidence to the House of Lords inquiry later in the year, 'the papists lit
bonfires when Dick Hamilton came over; they said he was worth 10,000 men.'
The fears of Irish Protestants were justified: Hamilton and Tyrconnel sided
with one another against William.

In London, Irish Protestants continued to press politicians to intervene, but
when Clarendon took up their call that a force should be sent to Ireland,
William appeared indifferent: 'it is certain the prince has very little curiosity, or
sets a very small value on Ireland.' William and the English politicians were
becoming fully absorbed in the business of thrashing out a new basis of
government in England. Ireland took a back seat. In his address to the Convention Parliament on 22 January 1689, William gave a nod in the direction of
the Irish Protestants, 'requiring a large and speedy succour'. But nothing was
done. James was later to claim that, had William sent troops to Ireland at the
very outset, he would have 'easily effected what afterwards cost him so much
blood and treasure'.

II

At the end of January 1689, the English diarist John Evelyn surveyed the bleak political scene. William's 'morose temper' was antagonizing English politicians, and the army was 'not so in order, & firme to his Interest, nor so weakened' that he could be sure it would not cause William trouble. The outlook was far from promising: 'Ireland is very ill posture, as well as Scotland; nothing yet towards any [constitutional] settlement: God of his infinite mercy, Compose these things that at last we may be a Nation & a church under some fixt and sober establishment.'

While London was paralysed by political stalemate, attention in Dublin and at Versailles was focused on the issues of diplomacy and war. Tyrconnel rapidly strengthened his position, skilfully dispensing with Mountjoy, the potential leader of Irish Protestant opposition. Mountjoy had left for Paris, under the impression that the Lord Deputy wanted him to seek James's approval to negotiate with William. But Mountjoy never reached the court of the émigré King. Acting on secret instructions from Tyrconnel, Louis XIV imprisoned Mountjoy in the Bastille.

William's recruitment of England into the European equation on his side was a severe setback for Louis. But Louis had a new pawn, James, in his hand. The question was, how should it be played to maximum effect? On 15 January, a French naval officer, the Marquis de Pointis, and an Irish officer, Michael Roth, arrived in Ireland from France. Pointis was sent by Seignelay, the Minister of Marine and son of Colbert, the Controller-General of Finances. But whereas Seignelay was keen to capitalize on the strength of the French navy, his rival, Louvois, the Minister for War, believed that French forces should be concentrated on the Continent. Louvois, however, was out of favour at court and disliked by the King's mistress Madame de Maintenon.

Roth brought a letter from James to Tyrconnel, in which the deposed King hoped that his loyal Lord Deputy would be able to hold out 'till the summer at least', but offered little hope of French support. Louis was only prepared to provide up to 8000 muskets, and any further aid would depend on intelligence from Ireland. Nor was there any indication as yet that James intended to go to Ireland. The deposed King appeared content to remain in Paris, passing his time praying and hunting.

Tyrconnel's reply to James, dated 29 January 1689, revealed further evidence of his political skills as he sought to procure more assistance from Louis and a personal intervention by James. He stressed that Ireland's 'greatest need' was 'money . . . without which this Kingdom must be infallibly lost'. He noted that 'the Citty of London hath already furnished the Prince of Orange with £300,000 sterling for the reduction of the Kingdome,' and that Williamite troops were already heading for Chester, Liverpool and Bristol, whence they would embark for Ireland. 'I have been as much deceived in the hopes with which hitherto I have flattered myself', Tyrconnel wrote, 'that the

King of France would spare nothing to preserve a Catholique Country, by which he, as well as your Majesty, might very well count upon great advantage in some reasonable time'. Judging his appeal with fine skill, Tyrconnel added,

> If, Sir, your Majesty will in person come hither and bring with you those succours necessary to support this country . . . I will be responsible to you that you shall be entirely the master of this Kingdom and of everything in it; and, Sir, I beg of you to consider whether you can with honour continue where you are when you may possess a Kingdom of your own.

Tyrconnel then presented an assessment of the position in each of Ireland's four provinces and informed James that he was raising 40,000 troops. Their officers would be paying for them until the end of February 'to the ruin of most of them', but 'after that day I see no possibility for arming them, clothing them or subsisting them for the future'. The most remarkable aspect of Tyrconnel's letter was contained in an addition, prompted by the arrival of mail from England. 'Confirmation of the great Preparations amaking there against us' led Tyrconnel to implore that 'Money must be sent out of hand, Sir, or all is lost,' and to urge that the soldiers who had fled with James should be sent to Ireland, 'for I want officers as much as money'. In return for assistance of 500,000 crowns from the French, which would sustain Ireland against the Williamites for one year, Tyrconnel offered Irish territory. 'For my part', he wrote,

> I could wish Gallway and Waterford or any other ports of the Kingdome were putt into the King of France's hands for the Security of repaying him his money which he shall expend upon us . . . and [he] may fortify those Places upon his owne Charge and keep them.

In the initial plans for a French-backed expedition to Ireland, prepared by Louvois, only a small intervention was envisaged. The French would bear arms and money, and transport the British and Irish troops who had fled into exile with James and who would serve under the command of the Duke of Berwick. There was no mention of James accompanying them. Further financial aid would follow by the end of July, and the French promised that if Tyrconnel held out till the winter of 1689–90 Louis would despatch an invasion force against Scotland or England.

The combination of Tyrconnel's persuasion and French pressure finally convinced James that he should raise his standard in the one kingdom which had remained largely loyal. The French expeditionary force would be commanded by Lieutenant-General Rosen, a German from the Baltic who had served in the French army for forty years. Accompanying James would be the Comte d'Avaux, since Louis was keen that the deposed King should receive good advice, and that he should be kept fully in the picture at Versailles.

D'Avaux was an excellent appointment. An experienced diplomat, he had formerly served as French Ambassador at the Hague, where he had observed William at close quarters.

D'Avaux was given charge of 500,000 livres (£40,000), with instructions that up to 300,000 livres could be spent on James's authority, but the rest was to be held in reserve. D'Avaux's treasure chest was urgently needed. Tyrconnel's shortage of funds meant that he often could not pay his troops. In consequence they fended for themselves, their acts of plunder provoking more Protestants to flee the country or set up armed associations.

As the French fleet prepared to sail, the English were preoccupied with the final stages of their constitutional settlement. On Wednesday 6 February 1689, Evelyn wrote of 'Forces sending to Ireland, that Kingdome being in greate danger, by the Earl of Tyrconnells Armie, & expectations from France', but there was further delay before Williamite troops were despatched. The European scene was equally menacing. Louis was 'busy to invade Flanders', and was set to 'encounter the German Princes'. As Evelyn observed, 'this is likely to be one of the most remarkable summers for action, as has happed for many Ages.'

On Thursday the 7th, the House of Lords approved the earlier Commons resolution asserting that James had abdicated. William and Mary were to be crowned joint monarchs, an acknowledgement of William's role in usurping James and his determination to keep a personal hold on power. Three days later, Mary sailed for England, arriving on Tuesday the 12th. The next day, William and Mary were declared King and Queen at the Banqueting House, Whitehall. At William's insistence, the *Declaration of Rights* was read aloud only after he and Mary had been crowned, thus emphasizing it did not represent the conditions on which they occupied the throne. Their investiture was greeted 'with wonderfull acclamation & general reception. Bonfires, bells, Gunns &c.' As Evelyn noted, the twenty-six-year-old Mary showed no regret at her father's demise, which had brought her and her husband to the throne, but instead 'came into Whitehall as to a Wedding'. William, by contrast, was 'wonderfull serious & silent'. The new King seemed 'to treat all persons alike gravely: & to be very intent on affaires, both Holland, & Ireland & France calling for his care'.

On 15 February, just two days after the coronation in Whitehall, James II left his French court-in-exile for the Brittany coast, whence he would embark for Ireland. Louis XIV bade him farewell with a fine turn of phrase: 'The best wish I can form for your service is, that I may never see you again.' Bad weather at Brest delayed James's departure, but eventually twenty-two ships set sail, carrying British and Irish Jacobites, supported by French officers, arms, ammunition and money. On board with James were his two natural sons, James Fitzjames, the Duke of Berwick, and Henry Fitzjames, the Grand Prior.[14] Among the Irish Jacobites were the soldiers, Patrick Sarsfield and

Roger MacElligott, and Judge Rice, a Catholic, who had accompanied Mount-joy on his ill-fated mission to France.

In London, on 22 February, William called on all Irish subjects to lay down their arms and submit to his authority by 10 April. Pardon and toleration was promised to all who obeyed. Military action and confiscation of estates were threatened against anyone who resisted. But William's attempt to assert authority across the Irish Sea was ignored. Effective power resided with Tyrconnel. The disarming of the Dublin Protestants had netted the Irish army several thousand weapons, and the haul was extended to the whole country. The main centres of Protestant resistance were concentrated in Ulster at Derry, Enniskillen and, in the east of the province, at Hillsborough, County Down. Richard Hamilton, the former Williamite envoy who had been appointed Lieutenant-General by Tyrconnel, was despatched northwards with 2500 troops. On 14 March, Hamilton won a notable victory at Hillsborough.

Tyrconnel was in almost complete command of Ireland, but the battle for its future was only beginning.

CHAPTER FIVE

'AN ANGEL FROM HEAVEN'

I

On Tuesday 12 March 1689, the French Admiral, Jean Gabaret, with fourteen ships of the line, eight frigates and three fireships, all flying English colours, entered the Bandon estuary on the County Cork coast, passing between James Fort and the recently constructed Charles Fort on the headland opposite. When James II stepped ashore at Kinsale, he became the first English monarch to set foot on Irish soil for nearly 300 years.[15] James was greeted, in his own words, 'with all imaginable joy by his Catholic subjects'. Yet in Williamite eyes James was no longer the legitimate King. He had abdicated and lacked all authority. Jacobites, however, saw William as the usurper. Their competing claims could be resolved only through war.

James received a preliminary briefing on the state of Ireland from those who had come to greet him, including Sir Thomas Nugent and Justin MacCarthy. Two days later, the royal party moved to Cork. On Friday the 15th, the King received and pardoned Protestants from nearby Bandon. They had recently surrendered to MacCarthy and had been the last rebels defying Tyrconnel outside Ulster. James seemed anxious to conciliate his Protestant subjects.

James was joined at Cork by Tyrconnel, accompanied by 'a hundred gentlemen on horseback, brought by their anxiety to see and pay their respects to His Majesty'. The King paid Tyrconnel the 'honour not only to make him dine at his table, but set him at his right and the Duke of Berwick at his left'. Tyrconnel was 'immediately created Duke, in recompense of his great services and successful endeavours towards the preservation of the kingdom of Ireland'. There was also recognition from Louis XIV, 'who so valued the merits' of Tyrconnel 'as to send him the Cordon Bleu and a casket containing twelve thousand louis'.

Tyrconnel was able to report to his King that Protestant resistance was limited to the north, and that he 'had sent down Lieutenant General [Richard] Hamilton with about 2500 men, being as many as he could spare from Dublin, to make head against the Rebels in Ulster'. But, although he was recruiting more men to the Irish army,

The Catholicks of the Country had no arms, whereas the Protestants had great plenty, and the best horses in the Kingdom; that for artillery he had but eight small field pieces in a condition to march, the rest not mounted, no stores in the magazines, little pouder and ball, all the officers gon for England, and no mony in cash.

As the Jacobites discovered, Louis' supplies of arms were less than had been promised and were of poor quality.

Around 200 British and French officers arrived with James. These included the King's illegitimate teenage sons, the Duke of Berwick, and the Grand Prior; his close advisers, John Drummond, Earl of Melfort, and Henry Jermyn, Lord Dover; his military commanders, Sarsfield, Wauchope and Dorrington; the French diplomat, Comte d'Avaux, his commander-in-chief, Comte de Rosen, Lieutenant-Generals Maumont and Pusignan, Major-General Léry, and the Marquis de Pointis.

James left Cork on Wednesday the 20th, accompanied by Tyrconnel, and headed for Dublin. The Jacobite observer, Plunkett, described the rapturous reception for James as the King made his way through the Irish countryside:[16]

All along the road, the country came to meet his majesty with staunch loyalty, profound respect, and tender love, as if he had been an angel from heaven. All degrees of people, and of both sexes, were of the number, old and young; orations of welcome being made unto him at the entrance of each considerable town, and the young rural maids weaving of dances before him as he travelled.

The royal party reached the capital on Palm Sunday, 24 March, just under a fortnight since he had first stepped ashore. He was greeted outside the city by two harpists on a stage, and below it some singing friars with a large cross, and 'about forty oyster-women, poultry- and herb-women in white, dancing'. At the city boundary, the corporation awarded James the freedom of Dublin while pipers played 'The King enjoys his own again'. To a tumultuous reception from the Catholic population, the King passed through the streets from St James's Gate to the Castle. In James's own account, the Dubliners' 'lowd and joyful acclamations made him some sort of recompense for the indignities he had suffer'd from his other subjects'. But a Protestant observer took a different view, claiming that James 'came in with far less splendour than the lord deputy was used to do; he was very courteous to all as he passed and it is said he wept as he entered the Castle.'

On Monday 25 March, the day after his arrival, James delivered several major policy statements. He summoned the Irish Parliament to assemble on 7 May, almost a quarter of a century since its last meeting, and declared freedom of religion for all his subjects as long as 'nothing be preached or taught which may tend to alienate the hearts of our people from us'. In another attempt to show genuine concern for his Protestant subjects, he called on those who had

fled Ireland to return within forty days, promising protection for them and
their property.

From the outset, however, the Jacobite high command was divided. The
French political and military advisers, d'Avaux and Rosen, were filing reports
bemoaning the severe shortage of money, horses, provisions and trained men.
Others were more optimistic: a Catholic government and a Catholic army were
in control of virtually the whole country and were supported by the vast
majority of the population. They believed that the limited Protestant resistance
in the north would be brought to a speedy end. Almost as soon as James and
his Scottish adviser Melfort landed in Ireland they were talking enthusiasti-
cally about pressing on to Scotland, and thence to England. Before James left
France, he had been in touch with his leading supporters in Scotland, Viscount
Dundee and Lord Balcarres, who had calculated on receiving help from
strongly Jacobite Ireland. MacCarthy, an experienced Irish commander, reckoned that James's only real problems in Ireland would be putting his troops in
shape and finding the means to transport them across the narrow sea passage
to the Scottish mainland, since Admiral Gabaret had left only three frigates at
James's disposal when he sailed from Kinsale to return to France.

The divisions within the Jacobite leadership, which were to prove a serious
weakness, were partly the result of differing perspectives. James was English,
Melfort Scottish, d'Avaux French and Tyrconnel an Irish Catholic aristocrat.
But there were also clashes of personality. D'Avaux, who was the shrewdest of
the Jacobite inner cabinet, thought Melfort 'neither a good Irishman nor a
good Frenchman' and a bad influence on James, whereas he regarded Tyrconnel as an ally. Tyrconnel had certainly made a determined effort to court
d'Avaux, lodging him in a 'fine house at the end of the town of Dublin', and
personally collecting the French Ambassador with 'twenty-six-horse carriages
and many other four-horse ones'. Melfort dreaded Tyrconnel's 'temper and
pride', and seemed set on opposing all his proposals. Tyrconnel, who knew the
situation in Ireland better than anyone and had prepared the ground for the
King's return, deeply resented James's confidence in Melfort.

As a result of ill-health, but also because of Melfort's influence, Tyrconnel
slipped into the background during the summer. 'I am assured', the French
officer, Pointis, wrote, 'that Lord Tyrconnel's discontent, as much as his indis-
position, has contributed to his retirement to a country house.'

II

'I need not take pains to tell you the deplorable Condition of Ireland,' William
told the English Parliament on 8 March 1689.[20] He blamed the 'zeal and
violence of the Popish Party there, and by the assistance and encouragement
they have from France', concluding that 'it is not adviseable to attempt the
reducing it, otherwise than by a very considerable Force, which I think ought
not to be less than 20,000 horse and foot.'[17] Two weeks later, the House of

Commons voted £302,361 17s 10½d 'for six months towards the reducing of Ireland'. A further £109,387 10s 7d was voted, principally to meet the costs of transportation and providing artillery. It was also envisaged that a second tranche of £302,361 17s 10½d should be paid for a further six months 'if the War in Ireland shall so long continue'.

How would James's Irish army match up to William's 'very considerable force'? When James arrived in Ireland, all that remained of his Irish army were three regiments of cavalry, one regiment of dragoons and five regiments of infantry. Since the previous December, however, Tyrconnel had been working assiduously with the leading Catholic gentry to levy a much bigger force. By the spring, it was reported that the Irish had raised 50,000 troops. Tyrconnel's achievement acted as a deterrent against any Williamite invasion, although the English Government was also deeply concerned at the risk of Jacobite insurrection in England and Scotland. To the surprise of many English politicians, William still seemed more interested in the Continental campaign, despite the news of James's landing in Ireland.

Although the numbers in the Irish army appeared impressive, the reality on the ground was far less so. The increased number of regiments, including thirty-five infantry regiments, and their inflated size were simply unmanageable. Many officers lacked any military expertise. The troops lacked equipment and even rudimentary training. Once James had been safely installed in Dublin Castle, Tyrconnel began reorganizing regiments and weeding out personnel. 'Whether this was a prudent action', noted Plunkett, 'hath long since been argued pro and con,' adding that 'the disbanded captains and subalterns were struck to the very heart by the breach.' What remained beyond dispute was that James stood no chance of withstanding the proposed Williamite invasion without a great deal more assistance from Louis.

The news that Richard Hamilton had routed the Protestant forces in eastern Ulster and driven them back to the Bann and the west of Ulster had encouraged the Jacobites. But they also heard that a Williamite force was being assembled at Liverpool for the relief of Derry, where the Protestants still held the walled city and were refusing to recognize James's authority. As long as the Protestant resistance in Ulster continued, William would have a toe-hold on the island and a potential base for invasion, while James would be deterred from making an early crossing to Scotland or England.

In March, the Scottish Convention Parliament had strongly backed William. The Scottish Jacobite minority naturally sought to combine with their allies in Ireland, who held the reins of power and were in command of an army. In early April, Alexander Maclean, an envoy from the Scottish Jacobite clans, arrived in Dublin to see Tyrconnel, and found, to his surprise, that James was in the capital. Maclean informed the King that if 2000 troops and supplies were sent from Ireland they would be joined by between 5000 and 6000 Highlanders. These figures for Highland support were based on an overestimate. Although

James and his advisers agreed to commit three regiments to Scotland they would not send them until Derry had been brought under control.

Derry's intransigence exacerbated the divisions within the Jacobite high command. D'Avaux advised sending a large army, accompanied by the French generals, but opposed James's heading north. James, however, demurred, and proposed sending only Berwick and the French commander Major-General Pusignan with the reinforcements. Although the King changed his mind, and accepted that his commander-in-chief Rosen and other senior generals should go, he insisted that overall command should remain with Hamilton. When the Jacobites set about gathering 'tools and other things necessary for a siege', they discovered that 'there was nothing at all of what was required.'

On Monday 8 April, James left Dublin and headed north. His excursion to Ulster was unrelievedly dispiriting. The disturbances of recent months had ravaged the countryside, the roads were virtually impassable and the weather was appalling. Eventually, on Sunday 14 April, a bedraggled James reached Omagh, in County Tyrone, where he was told of a report that thirteen English warships were sailing for Derry. He needed little persuasion to head back towards Dublin. When, however, he reached Charlemont, County Armagh, he received a letter from Berwick reporting that there was no sign of the English fleet.

The Jacobites had won control of the countryside between the Bann and the Foyle and, after forcing the Protestants back, had encircled Derry. About 30,000 Protestants were trapped inside the walls of the city. Their plight seemed hopeless. When the English relief ships bearing two regiments finally arrived in Lough Foyle on Monday 15 April, their commander, Kirk, had quickly concluded that nothing could be done. The Irish forces were in such superior positions that it was simply a matter of time before Derry fell. Waiting only to collect the garrison's leading officers, the ships returned to England. All further relief supplies for the city were cancelled.

Berwick made an enticing appeal to James to halt his return and head for Derry, suggesting that if James appeared in person the city would open its gates to him. It was a prospect which proved irresistible to his father. According to one Jacobite account of the period, James went 'in order to preserve his Protestant subjects there from the ill-treatment which he apprehended they might receive from the Irish'. Covering more than 60 miles in a day and a half, James arrived at Derry early on Thursday 18 April. But the exploit went disastrously wrong.

At ten o'clock on the Thursday morning, James and Rosen approached the city walls with their troops. The King and his commander-in-chief were unaware that Hamilton had offered terms for Derry's surrender, promising that his troops would not come within several miles of the city while the conditions were being considered. As James and Rosen approached, there suddenly roared from the battlements 'a terrific discharge of cannon and musquetry [which] continued with little or no intermission for the rest of the day'. The citizens were outraged that Hamilton's pledge to keep his troops back had apparently been flouted. To the sound of their gunfire was added the cry of defiance, 'No surrender!'

A Jacobite captain, Troy, fell dead at the King's side. Several others among the royal bodyguard were killed. A chastened James retreated out of the range of fire, and spent a rainy day in the saddle watching the gunners' display, having 'no better entertainment than bullets of 14, 16 and 22 pounds of weight'.

The Derry garrison apologized for firing on the King. The next day, James sent the Earl of Abercorn with a message inviting twenty representatives from Derry to the Irish headquarters to discuss terms for surrender. The city seemed on the brink of giving in, but in the end the militant faction triumphed. Abercorn returned with their reply of defiance.

James saw no point in remaining any longer at Derry. He left Maumont in command of the siege, with Hamilton, Berwick and Pusignan as his immediate subordinates, and returned to Dublin accompanied by Rosen and Melfort. There, he encountered d'Avaux, who had advised against his going from day one, and who found the King 'to be very mortified over his latest proceeding'. Plunkett, the Jacobite chronicler, reminded his readers of 'the return Londonderry made the King for all the pains he had taken in travelling so far in order to gain those rebels with lenity [leniency]', commenting that "tis what he always gets from Protestants generally.'

III

The Irish Parliament assembled in Dublin on 7 May 1689, against the backcloth of European and civil war. The previous week, the English and French fleets had clashed off Bantry Bay, County Cork, the largest sea-battle fought in Irish waters either before or since. At Derry, the Protestants continued their resistance. On the day of the state opening, England formally declared war against France and the Enniskillen Protestants defeated Jacobite troops at Belleek.

In this highly charged atmosphere, the Irish MPs and peers gathered at the old King's Inns, near the present Four Courts building.[18] They were summoned because James was short of money. His army was costing a fortune, but revenues were depressed and the subsidies from Louis only went so far. The solution was to raise more taxes, which required parliamentary approval. James would have to make some concessions, but Irish expectations far outstripped what any English king would be willing to give.

Tyrconnel had guaranteed that the Parliament would be his animal. Two hundred and thirty MPs were returned for a total 300 seats, the only recorded contest being fought in Dublin City. The counties of Donegal, Fermanagh and Londonderry and a number of boroughs, mainly in Ulster, failed to make any returns. About two-thirds of the Commons were members of 'old English' Catholic families, including Dillons, Fitzgeralds and Nugents. Among the Gaelic Irish were O'Reillys, MacNamaras, an O'Brien, an O'Neill from Tyrone and Charles O'Kelly from Roscommon, who was later the author of an oddly titled account of the period, *Destruction of Cyprus*. The soldiers Patrick Sarsfield and Justin MacCarthy were returned, the latter subsequently elevated to the Upper House as Viscount Mountcashel. Only six MPs were Protestants, and in the Lords only five of the thirty or so peers were Protestants, although four bishops of the Church of Ireland also attended.

An English king's attendance at the state opening of an Irish Parliament was unprecedented.[19] James's speech, which he delivered in his robes with a crown specially made in Dublin, included his long-awaited proposals on the vexed questions of religion and property. But his words did not measure up to Irish demands. He promised neither restoration of the Catholic Church to its position before the Reformation, nor repeal of the land settlement, refusing to go further than refer to 'relieving such as have been injured in the late Act of Settlement, as far forth as may be consistent with reason, justice, and the publick good of my people'.

From the outset, James's approach was that of an English King eager to be restored to his throne in London, with his powers and privileges preserved exactly as he had left them. For nearly 200 years, the most powerful constraint on the Irish Parliament's independence had been Poynings's law. This stipulated that every bill should first be approved by the King and his Privy Council in England. James was strongly opposed to its repeal. During the session of the Jacobite Irish Parliament, he upheld its principle by regularly considering proposed bills with his closest advisers, although this gave d'Avaux, Louis XIV's adviser, a say in Irish legislation.

Exactly a week after the state opening, a bill to repeal Poynings's law was introduced and subsequently proceeded through most of its stages in the Commons. As James's biographer later observed 'the Irish had talked much and earnestly desired the repeal of Poynings' law, it being the greatest sign and means of their subjection to England', but the bill was finally dropped. James's continued insistence on royal approval before any bill could be passed by the Irish Parliament had proved decisive. Irish MPs were less compliant over their relationship with the English Parliament, passing a Declaratory Act, which stated that laws passed by the English Parliament would not apply in Ireland unless they had also been passed by the Irish Parliament. Appeals from Irish law courts to courts in England were also banned.

The Irish hoped for sweeping religious reform, but were disappointed. Catholics wanted repeal of the Act of Uniformity, which recognized only the established Church of Ireland, the removal of the penal laws which discriminated against them, and return of Catholic clergy to their livings, churches and position in the community. Catholics won significant improvements, but the Protestant established Church remained. James had disappointed both sides: Irish Catholics were dissatisfied, the Church of Ireland felt threatened. James had sought to meet some Catholic demands, but would not go further for fear of alienating English Protestant opinion.

As the prospect of a bloody civil war daily grew more menacing, neither the Dublin Parliament nor their counterparts at Westminster were in any mood to spare those whom they identified as traitors. Around 2000 people were named in the Irish Act of Attainder. Depending on their degree of involvement in the rebellion, they were required to give themselves up by a certain date and stand trial. The penalties for most offenders were execution and confiscation of estates. James submitted to the wishes of his Irish Parliament only with reluctance. But Irish MPs suspected royal leniency and specifically barred James from granting any pardons after 1 November that year. The English Parliament was equally suspicious of William, and put a similar constraint on William in 1697. Oligarchies, whether Catholic or Protestant, often turned out to be more vindictive than monarchies.

Land reform was by far the most important issue facing the Jacobite Parliament. Although James had specifically ruled out repeal of the Restoration settlement in his King's Speech, just three days later a repeal bill was introduced in the Commons to general acclaim. Both MPs and peers were soon bogged down in acrimonious debates which occupied most of the session, despite the problems in the north and the growing threat of invasion from England. The Protestant Bishop of Meath warned his fellow peers not 'to dispose of the skin before we catch the beast'.

The Gaelic Irish pressed hardest for outright repeal, having lost most under Cromwell and gained least from Charles II, but some 'old English' Catholics had benefited under the Restoration settlement and took a more moderate line. James, himself a large landowner in Ireland, actively encouraged the opposition to outright repeal. James's biographer claiming that 'he saw the distraction it would breed, how it would inflame the Protestants, and rob him of his most serviceable Catholics, ruin the trade, and sink the revenue.' In the end, however, James's desperate shortage of money told against him. The Parliament was also debating a supply bill to provide a subsidy of £20,000 per month from a property tax and threatened to delay the first monthly instalment unless James allowed repeal. He initially resorted to debasing the coinage. On 18 June, he announced his intention to put into circulation brass coins, the notorious 'gun money'. Four days later, lack of funds forced his capitulation and he gave the repeal bill royal assent.

The repeal Act provided for the restoration of property rights to the heirs of 'all manner of persons' who owned land or buildings, held tenancies or enjoyed any other entitlements to property, 'in this kingdom of Ireland on the 22nd of October 1641'. Everyone who had gained property under the Cromwellian settlement, or who was an heir of one of its beneficiaries, therefore stood to lose his property without compensation. As the Rev. Robert H. Murray, editor of Stevens's Journal, commented 'Twenty-four years before, the expropriated landowners had received no equivalent, and they meted out the same treatment to the Cromwellians.'

Repeal did not stop at simply reversing the Cromwellian settlement. The Act also confiscated the lands of all Williamite sympathizers in Ireland. One of the most contentious land grants, the acquisition of Derry city and county by the London companies during the reign of James I, was also overturned. Catholics who had acquired land under Charles II's modest reforms, the so-called 'new interest', who now found it returned to the 1641 owners or their heirs, would be compensated from the stock of land confiscated from Williamites and the London companies at Derry. The Act also set up a special court to hear the claims of the dispossessed and their heirs.

The issue of land revealed a sharp difference in perspective within the Jacobite leadership. For the Irish, land was their prime motivation for supporting James, yet James had been against repeal, and his English and Scottish supporters regarded the issue as a dangerous diversion. Stevens, an English Jacobite, argued that

> Nothing could be more pernicious or a greater obstruction to the King's service than was this parliament. First it drew to and kept in Dublin all that time the nobility and principal gentry who before were dispersed at their posts, raising or encouraging and exercising their men or upon actual service. Secondly, the Act of Repeal being passed, private interest outweighing the public good, every one quitted his command to enter upon his estate, to settle his house, and improve his fortune.

James pithily concluded, in his biographer's words, that it would have 'been more generous in the Irish, not to have pressed so hard upon their Prince, when he lay so much at their mercy, and more prudent not to have grasped at regaining all, before they were sure of keeping what they already possessed'.

In the end, the English perspective was imposed. James adjourned the Irish Parliament and suspended the special court introduced to settle the land claims, 'because some may neglect the public safety of the kingdom upon pretence of attending their private concerns'. The war would settle who owned the land. Victory for James would principally benefit the 'old English' nobility and gentry. Defeat would inflict a Williamite land settlement on the country. The coming war was nothing less than the battle for Ireland.

CHAPTER SIX
A VERY SAD PROSPECT

I

The bad weather which had dogged James's wretched expedition to Ulster during April had delayed the departure of a second French convoy from Brest. The fleet, under the command of the Comte de Châteaurenault, was loaded with supplies of arms, ammunition, money and personnel, which were sorely needed in Ireland. French artillery officers, engineers and commissaries had embarked, along with about 1500 Irish, English and Scottish Jacobites who had gathered on the Continent after James's flight. Among the volunteers who had made their way to the Brittany coast was John Stevens, who wrote of their 'laying aside all worldly considerations, having only before their eyes their duty and love to their sovereign, resolved to follow him through all hazards, in hopes of being instrumental in regaining his just rights'.

Admiral Châteaurenault's fleet of twenty-four ships of the line, accompanied by frigates, fireships and two merchantmen, finally weighed anchor on the morning of Friday 26 April. Encountering fog at the start of the voyage, they sighted land to the west of Kinsale on the morning of Monday the 29th. Off Kinsale, however, the French also sighted two English warships. According to an Irish colonel contacted by a search party, a fleet of twenty-three English ships had been blockading the coast for a fortnight. The wind was unfavourable for Kinsale, but Châteaurenault was eager to find a suitable landing place before being engaged by the English. He therefore set sail for Bantry about 40 miles further west, beyond Cape Clear and the Fastnet Rock.

William had issued instructions to blockade the southern Irish coast on 11 March. But the political crisis had left the English fleet unprepared and the proposed merger with the Dutch fleet was not completed until late in the spring. A week after William's instruction for a blockade, Herbert found that only five ships of the line and one fireship at Portsmouth were ready to sail. He eventually set sail on Thursday 4 April and by Sunday the 12th was off the Irish coast, between Cork and Kinsale, where he heard rumours that the French were planning to send a 'considerable number' of reinforcements. But gales forced Herbert away from Ireland, and on Tuesday the 23rd he led his damaged ships into the Pembrokeshire port of Milford Haven.

The English ships left the Welsh port on the same day Châteaurenault set sail from Brest, Friday 26 April, but were delayed by 'Thick Fogg'. Herbert had originally intended to seek out the French near their own coast, but a shift in the wind caused him to 'steer away for Kingsale; judging that the likeliest place to meet them'. This also enabled him to join with reinforcements, which brought his complement to eighteen ships of the line. Towards evening on Monday 29 April, off Kinsale, 'one of our scouts made signalls that he discovered a fleet'. Although Herbert had prevented the French from entering Kinsale, he lost contact with them.

On the morning of Tuesday 30 April, the French fleet rounded the Sheep's Head (Dunmanus Point), and dropped anchor in Bantry Bay. It was an ideal place for disembarkation, although its location to the west of Kinsale would entail an even lengthier haul for passengers and freight across the poor Irish roads. Châteaurenault was aware that the English fleet was close at hand and the slow process of disembarkation began.

Herbert meanwhile was still desperately searching the extreme southwesterly coast-line for the elusive French fleet: 'In the evening our scouts got sight of them againe to the westward of Cape Clear. Wee steered after them and found that they were gott into the Bantry; we lay off that place that night.'

The next morning, Wednesday 1 May, both fleets prepared for battle, Herbert's the smaller – eighteen warships, a frigate and three fireships, a total firepower of 1062 guns, against Châteaurenault's twenty-four warships, two frigates and six fireships, bearing at least 1200 guns. The English entered the Bay past the Sheep's Head, and by eleven o'clock their vanguard was pressing Châteaurenault to engage.

The conflict lasted six hours in all, ship firing directly against ship for at least four hours. As the English commander wrote in his report on the engagement to the Principal Secretary of State, the Earl of Nottingham,

> soe continued battering upon a stretch till about five a clock in the afternoone that the French admirall tackt from us, but indeed had soe disabled us in our masts and rigging that I was not, nor half owr ships, in any condition to follow them or make any further attempt upon them . . .

Châteaurenault was facing the open sea, and hauled down his red flag. Herbert's 'bloody' flag was hauled down a little later.

The encounter was over. The English retreated to the Scillies. The French returned briefly to Bantry Bay, before sailing for France. Neither side lost any ships, but 96 of Herbert's men were killed and about 250 wounded; the French lost 43 men, with 93 wounded.

Although the engagement was inconclusive, the French had beaten the English blockade and achieved their objective. When d'Avaux informed James with evident delight that the French fleet had beaten the English, the King revealed the lasting loyalties of a former English admiral, with his retort: 'C'est bien la première fois donc' ('It is the first time').

The commanders were circumspect in their assessments. Châteaurenault blamed his junior officers for failing to turn French superiority to full advantage. They, in turn, blamed their commander. On the English side, Herbert ruefully acknowledged his enemy's achievement in an apologia to the Earl of Nottingham: 'Tis trew they have gained theyr poinct, for wee have not been able to hinder them from landing whatever they brought, though I can trewly say it has not been my fault . . .' In Herbert's book, neglect of the English navy during the winter of 1688–9 was the real culprit. Yet Herbert had no need to worry. William needed to claim victory 'to prevent the bad success of this first essay of his new arms from affecting the minds of the seamen'.

A week later, William honoured the fleet, dining aboard Herbert's flagship in Portsmouth Harbour. He promised each seaman who fought at Bantry Bay ten shillings, knighted two of his captains, Cloudesley Shovell and John Ashby, and elevated Herbert to the peerage as the first Earl of Torrington. 'Pleased with the attention,' Dalrymple observed, 'the seamen believed they had beat that enemy by whom a few days before they had acknowledged they were defeated.'

In Dublin, on James's instructions, Bantry Bay was celebrated on Sunday 5 May by the singing of the 'Te Deum' and a display of fireworks. To the astonishment of John Stevens, who had been aboard the French convoy, the most exaggerated claims were soon being made about the engagement:

Every day supplied us with fresh fables of the entire defeat of both English and Dutch fleets, and with hyperbolical and monstrous relations of the greatness of the French both as to the number and bigness of ships . . . The incredible number of arms reputed to be brought from France would have furnished Xerxes army and they, added to what were before in the kingdom, made not up 50,000 men. The millions of money spoken of would have impoverished Croesus and broken the bank of Venice . . .

In addition to transporting James and the 1500 Jacobite volunteers to Ireland, the two French convoys of the spring of 1689 had brought senior personnel and supplied an estimated 1 million livres (about £80,000), 3000 swords, 16,000 sabres, 1000 pairs of pistols, 500 carbines, 500 muskets, 500 flintlocks, and 100,000 pounds of powder. Later in the year, 4600 muskets and further supplies of arms, powder, lead and match would reach Ireland.

James sought to capitalize on French naval support, urging d'Avaux, Louis's adviser in Ireland, to ensure that Châteaurenault remained in Irish waters. He envisaged the French fleet establishing control of the northern channel in the Irish Sea, preventing Williamite reinforcements reaching Derry, carrying the Jacobites' heavy guns to the siege, and transporting James, with 10,000 Jacobite troops, to Scotland. The French could then return to Brest by sailing round the northern and western coasts of Ireland to avoid the threat from the English fleet. Châteaurenault, however, had already departed for the French coast.

James still hoped that the French fleet would return and enable him to invade England or Scotland. During the summer, the three French frigates which Gabaret had left at James's disposal transported 300 Jacobite dragoons from Carrickfergus to Scotland. But the French were reluctant to commit their fleet to the seas off northern Ireland without suitable docks or harbour facilities, and became even more wary after the signing of the Anglo-Dutch naval alliance in late May 1689.

Despite French assistance, the Jacobite army remained inadequately equipped. According to estimates prepared for James, the Jacobites' total field artillery amounted to twelve cannon and two little mortars. To make matters worse, it was soon discovered that the muskets sent with Châteaurenault were of poor quality, and almost all of Ireland's armourers were Protestants and could not be relied upon. Estimates of the strength of the Irish army were greatly exaggerated. When Stevens reached Dublin he found that the soldiers 'will follow none but their own leaders, many of them as rude, as ignorant, and as far from understanding any of the rules of discipline as themselves'. Despite his lack of military experience Stevens was presented to the Grand Prior, Henry Fitzjames, 'who immediately gave me the promise of a lieutenancy in his regiment, and a few days after delivered me the commission'.

Ireland's inability to support the war effort was graphically described by James's Chief Justice, Keating. Allowing for a certain degree of hyperbole, Keating described Ireland in the early 1680s as 'the most improved and improving spot of earth in Europe'. By May 1689, however, Ireland was 'reduced to the saddest and most disconsolate condition of any kingdom or country in Europe'.

II

'Matters publique went very ill in Ireland,' noted Evelyn in May 1689, summing up the disquiet felt in London.

> Confusion and dissention amongst ourselves, stupidity, unconstancy, emulation, in the Gouvernors, employing unskillfull men in greatest offices: No person of publique spirit, & ability appearing &c; threaten us with a very sad prospect what may be the conclusion.

William had not dared to commit his troops across the Irish Sea because he was alarmed at the threat of Jacobite insurrection in England and concerned at events in Scotland. Moreover, he was not at all confident of the loyalty of the English army.

The Williamite fears that James would invade from Ireland were heightened by what was seen as a potential fifth column in England. Many of the Irish troops disbanded in December 1688 had still not returned to Ireland. According to John Kelly, who had come to England in 1688, a group of 500 Irish soldiers were waiting in Lancashire to assist James. There were many other reports of Irishmen being involved in Jacobite plots. One of William's Secretaries of State, the Earl of Shrewsbury, sent orders to west-coast ports, from Cornwall to Westmorland, for the arrest of 'all such Irish papists as shall be found making their escapes into Ireland'. Shrewsbury was anxious to discover what had become of the Irish soldiers, and was surprised that magistrates had not taken notice of the collection of so many 'dangerous disaffected persons'.

Parliament had passed a bill in March 1689 temporarily suspending *habeas corpus* in the case of people arrested by order of the Privy Council or Secretary of State on suspicion of high treason. This was renewed until late May, when a further proposed extension led to heated exchanges in the Commons. Many MPs objected that the legislation threatened to undo the revolution and restore arbitrary power to the Crown. Others strongly supported the Government. 'In Lancashire, since the Irish were disbanded they meet in parties,' warned John Hampden, 'and you have no way to obviate this danger but by this bill.' The Government won the vote by 126 votes to 83, and the suspension was extended until 23 October 1689.

William's sense of insecurity in England was compounded by even more worrying problems in Scotland. Although the Rev. George Story, an English army chaplain, and an eye-witness from whom we shall hear more, acknowledged that he was 'a Stranger to Reasons of State', he none the less viewed developments north of the border as an important constraint on the expedition to Ireland:

> Lord *Dundee* had left the Convention at *Edinburgh* raising a powerful Faction for the Late King, in the North of *Scotland*, and the Castle of *Edinburgh* was not as yet surrendered by the Duke of *Gordon*; it might not therefore be thought prudent, to part with an Army out of our own Kingdom, till the Danger were over from that Quarter.

The Government were severely censured for their dilatory approach towards Ireland, Evelyn noting that 'the new king much blamed for neglecting Ireland, now like to be ruined by the Lord Tyrconnell and his popish party'. The House of Commons set up a committee to investigate 'the Occasion of the Delays in sending Relief over into *Ireland* and particularly to *Londonderry* . . .' On 5 July, MPs expressed their anger that Ireland was 'over-run by [His] Majesty's declared Enemies the *French*, in conjunction with *Irish* Rebels, occasioned . . . by the Neglect or ill Conduct of some Persons employed in the Management of the Affairs relating to that Kingdom'. When the Government repeatedly blocked the committee's access to official papers, the Commons voted without a division that those who had 'been the Occasion of delaying sending Relief to *Ireland* and who sought to prevent a full inquiry were 'enemies to the King and Kingdom'.

III

Following Derry's refusal to open its gates to James in April 1689, the commander of the garrison, Robert Lundy, a Scottish lieutenant-colonel in Mountjoy's Regiment, had advised its citizens that they were in no position to resist the Jacobite siege. Lundy's approach, however, which combined military incompetence and poor leadership, had already aroused Protestant suspicions about his true loyalties. In a citizens' revolt, the organization of Derry's resistance was made the responsibility of two military governors, a professional soldier, Major Baker, and a Protestant clergyman of English descent, George Walker.

Lundy was in fear for his life, and with the connivance of the new governors fled the city disguised as an ordinary soldier with a load of match on his back. After returning to Scotland, he was arrested and imprisoned in the Tower of London, but was later rehabilitated. To this day, however, 'Lundy' has remained a term of abuse among Ulster Protestants, and at the annual celebrations of the shutting of the gates of Derry an effigy of 'Lundy the traitor' is still burnt.

Derry continued to hold out. Baker and Walker were redoubtable figures, and behind them were even more resolute characters. When Baker was killed, he was replaced by the defiant John Mitchelburne, another professional soldier. Walker wrote a vivid blow-by-blow account of the siege, but, according to an alternative account written by John MacKenzie, the true hero was Adam Murray, a fellow Scots Presbyterian. Even in their most desperate struggle, the rivalries between the new English and the Scots Presbyterian settlers in Ulster could not be quelled.

The garrison at Derry, which included representatives from regiments throughout Ulster, outnumbered the Jacobite force of around 4000 and was able to inflict damaging blows. The French commander Maumont was killed, and his successor Pusignan was fatally wounded. The Jacobites lacked any suitable siege equipment, and although conditions inside Derry were atrocious the Irish besieging them were inadequately sheltered from the persistent cold, wet weather. During May, James again intervened, and again undermined the efforts of his commander on the spot, Richard Hamilton. Anxious to demonstrate his concern for all his subjects, whatever their religion, the King granted a pardon to Derry's citizens. About 10,000 took advantage of the offer and left the beleaguered enclave. James, however, became alarmed at the numbers who emerged, since this would enable a smaller number to defy the siege even longer. In a further reversal of policy, he instructed Hamilton not to allow any more to leave.

The Jacobites were caused further dismay by the news that a Williamite relief force of four regiments led by Kirk was on its way to Derry. James remembered Kirk for his desertion the previous autumn, but respected him for his ruthless suppression of Monmouth's rebellion in 1685. In an effort to block Kirk's task force, the French officer Pointis supervised the building of a boom across the River Foyle, about 2 miles from the city towards the sea. James again sent Rosen, his Marshal in Ireland, to Derry. Yet Hamilton was to be left in charge of the siege, a further source of confusion and resentment on the Jacobite side.

Rosen was determined to seize the initiative and conceived a dastardly plot which would finally bring Derry to its knees, rounding up all Protestants in the surrounding areas and driving them under the walls. Rosen assumed that their co-religionists inside the walls would take pity on them, allow them inside, and find themselves shorter of food than ever. Derry's leaders, however, responded by threatening to execute their Jacobite prisoners, a threat made vivid by the building of a gallows on the walls. At this point, Hamilton intervened and the Protestants outside were allowed to return to their homes uninjured.

By the end of June, Derry was extremely hard-pressed. The conditions inside the walls were disgusting. Many were dead or dying, dysentery was rife, and in order to survive the inhabitants were eating dogs, cats, even mice and rats, and tallow. The relief ships which had transported Kirk's regiments and supplies of food were tantalizingly close, visible from the city walls, as they lay at berth in Lough Foyle. The boom across the Foyle seemed to have done its job. Kirk showed an extraordinary lack of initiative, accepting that an attempt to break the boom was too risky and failing to investigate any further when his messenger, who had penetrated the Jacobite lines to reach the city, failed to return.

On James's instructions, Hamilton offered the city terms for a surrender in early July. Its citizens were promised a full pardon and guarantees of their property rights, freedom of worship and permission for anyone who wanted to leave for England or Scotland. The city was on the brink of accepting, the only issue at stake being the precise timing of the capitulation. But before this final detail was resolved, news reached Derry that Kirk and his regiments had landed at Inch island in Lough Swilly and were advancing towards the rear of the Jacobite positions. Despite their desperate plight, the city's representatives held out on their last demand, and the negotiations collapsed.

Which side would crack first was a question whose resolution was desperately close. Jacobite morale was extremely low. Dejected by the stalemate, James was telling Hamilton to force the issue, while at the same time advising how to handle a withdrawal.

But with Derry on the point of surrender, Kirk decided to return to Lough Foyle and make his much-delayed attempt on the boom. On 28 July the *Mountjoy* of Derry rammed the boom, but failed to break it and for a while was grounded on the shore and came under heavy artillery fire from the Jacobite guns. HMS *Swallow* sent a longboat to cut the boom's fastenings, and finally the *Phoenix* of Coleraine broke through. *Mountjoy* and *Phoenix* then sailed upstream with their cargoes of beef, peas, flour and biscuit, somehow evading the barrage of Jacobite cannon.

Although at least one Jacobite commentator alleged that 'those gunners lost Ireland through their neglect of duty,' the responsibility attached not to the ordinary Irish soldiers but to their political and military leaders. Lacking any effective siege equipment, the troops had been condemned for month after month to a frustrating, wearying experience in awful conditions. The handling of the operation had been lamentable, and prompted Plunkett to write of 'the ridiculous siege of Londonderry'.

Yet the raising of the siege at Derry was only one part of James's disasters in Ulster. Protestants based around Enniskillen and the Erne valley had harried his troops for months in an effective guerrilla campaign. Following their defeat of Jacobite forces at Belleek in early May, the Enniskilleners heavily defeated a Jacobite force led by Patrick Sarsfield. Although Berwick later scored a triumph for the Jacobites outside Enniskillen, he had to return north to counter Kirk.

In July, James sent Mountcashel (Justin MacCarthy) to the Erne valley, with three regiments of foot, sixteen troops of cavalry, dragoons and field-guns. Mountcashel was supported by Anthony Hamilton with a force of dragoons, and also the Ulster Gaels. But Kirk, by then based at Lough Swilly, provided the Enniskilleners with arms and ammunition, and the assistance of English officers. In the initial exchanges on 30 July, Mountcashel took the castle of Crom on Lough Erne, but the Enniskilleners recovered, and ambushed and massacred Hamilton's dragoons. Next day, Mountcashel came under fierce attack at Newtownbutler. As James later recounted,

> though the foot fought with great obstinacy and the general did all that could be expected from a brave and experienced officer, yet the king's horse soon giving way the rest were totally routed and my lord Montcassel [Mountcashel] very ill wounded and taken prisoner.

James's continued preoccupations in Ulster had prevented him sending stronger reinforcements to Scotland, let alone leading his own planned invasion of Britain. In the spring, the French had snubbed his plans to land 10,000 troops at Troon. The small force of 1200 Jacobites which landed at Cara on the west coast of Scotland in early May was defeated. In early July, with Derry and Enniskillen still resisting, James felt that he could only spare Purcell's 400 troops and sent the three French frigates left by Gabaret to Carrickfergus as transports.

During their crossing of the North Channel, the French frigates encountered two small Scottish Williamite frigates, the eighteen-gun *Pelican* and the twelve-gun *Janet*, which had been patrolling off the coast of the Mull of Kintyre in an effort to prevent any crossings by Irish Jacobites. Despite strong resistance by the Scottish sailors, their ships were captured and brought to Dublin.

The Scottish Jacobites were dismayed at the limited support they were receiving from Ireland. None the less, they defeated the Williamites at Killiecrankie on 27 July, only to suffer a shattering blow in their hour of victory. Viscount Dundee, their charismatic commander, had been fatally wounded. Although the Scottish Jacobites fought on, the demise of 'Bonny' Dundee was to prove an irreparable loss. Their fate would depend more than ever on the efforts of their King across the water.

In Ireland, Jacobite morale plummeted under the hammer blows suffered in Ulster. The explanation for the Jacobite tragedy lay in the incompetence of their superiors, their woefully inadequate equipment and their lack of professional training. In war, however, incompetence is rarely the preserve of one side. By the summer of 1689, the Williamites were exhibiting their share.

III

It was not until mid-July 1689 that Schomberg was finally appointed commander of the Williamite expedition to Ireland. He reached Chester on 20 July, and planned to head straight for Derry, where he would join forces with Kirk and the Enniskilleners.

Epic mismanagement added to the delays. There was lack of troops, lack of equipment and lack of ships to transport them. The army was reaping the consequences of the great political upheaval during the winter of 1688–9. Schomberg pinned much of the blame on the supply officer at Chester, Shales, whose spectacular unreliability prompted speculation about his loyalty and fuelled rumours that he was a recent convert from Catholicism.

By far the most serious problem, however, was William's lack of trust in the regular English army. He dared not send them to Ireland. They had ratted on James, and might rat on him. It was far safer to despatch them across the Channel, where they would bolster the coalition against Louis XIV, than risk them in a bloody civil war across the Irish Sea. Churchill, whose desertion from James had earned him the earldom of Marlborough, was therefore sent in command of 8000 regulars to the Netherlands, to serve under the command of the Prince of Waldeck. William's Dutch troops and his Huguenots, along with new English recruits, would be despatched to Ireland. Rather than trust an English officer in Ireland, William preferred to rely on one of Europe's foremost mercenaries, a commander who had fought for half-a-dozen different monarchs. During a long career, the seventy-three-year-old Duke of Schomberg had abided by the code of a seventeenth-century mercenary, ready to serve any monarch and never deserting during a campaign. Second in command to Schomberg was William's senior Dutch officer, General Solms, who had led his guards into London the night before James's flight and William's arrival at Whitehall Palace.

On 12 August, Schomberg was finally able to sail. He embarked at Hoylake with ten infantry regiments aboard a convoy commanded by George Rooke, consisting of five naval ships and eighty transports. The remainder of the foot and horse followed in another forty transports, along with arms, ammunition and stores. With Rooke's squadron protecting the Irish Sea, and backed by a favourable wind, the Williamite fleet put into Bangor Bay at the southern entrance to Belfast Lough the following day. There was no challenge on land from a force of 500 Jacobites, led by a Scottish brigadier, Maxwell, who retreated south to join Berwick at Newry. On 17 August, Schomberg's troops marched to Belfast, receiving an ecstatic welcome from the local Protestant population.

The main Jacobite stronghold at Carrickfergus, on the northern shores of Belfast Lough, was subjected to a major bombardment from land and sea. The Irish eventually surrendered a week later. Schomberg allowed the Jacobites to 'march out with their Arms, and some Baggage, and they were conducted with a Guard to the next *Irish* Garrison, which was then *Newry*.'

In a foretaste of the bitterness which would characterize the Williamite war, some of the local people and the Scots-Irish among Schomberg's troops violated the terms, abusing and humiliating the Irish:

> The Countrey people were so inveterate against them (remembering how they had served them some days before) that they stript most part of the Women, and forced a great many Arms from the Men; and took it very ill that the Duke did not order them all to be put to Death, notwithstanding the Articles: But he knew better things; and so rude were the *Irish Scots*, that the Duke was forced to ride in among them, with his Pistol in his hand, to keep the *Irish* from being murdered.

Eventually, by the end of August, William's target of 20,000 troops on Irish soil was achieved. This included the complements which Kirk had earlier brought to Derry and Enniskillen. Schomberg's army consisted of four cavalry regiments, eighteen of infantry, and one of dragoons. Of the infantry, two regiments were Dutch, three Huguenot, and the remaining thirteen comprised new English recruits. Two further regiments of cavalry and infantry followed in September.

The Jacobites had long dreaded the arrival of the Williamite invasion. Schomberg, however, faced no easy task. Quite how difficult it would become had not been foreseen.

IV

These were dog days for the Jacobites. Derry, Newtownbutler and Dundee's death at Killiecrankie were followed by Schomberg's invasion. James's

influential but highly unpopular adviser, the Earl of Melfort, was held responsible for the poor showing in Ireland. The former Scottish Secretary departed
for France, and was little missed.

In Ulster, only Charlemont, County Armagh, remained in Jacobite hands.
The Irish army was a fraction of its former strength. At the end of July, James's
commander-in-chief, Rosen, reckoned that the Irish army could not put more
than 6000 or 7000 in the field, a third of whom would be unarmed. Stevens
drew a pitiful picture:

> most of the men were very raw and undisciplined, and the generality almost
> naked or at least very ragged and ill shod. The only creditable and hopeful part
> of the army were the horse, who were for the most part good men, well moun-
> ted, but their number not very great.

Economically, Ireland was in a mess. Debasing the coinage sent prices soar-
ing. In early September, it was reported from Dublin that 'brass money falls to
seven pence per pound exchange, and thirty-eight shillings per guinea, and as
that falls so the value of the goods rise in proportion.' Desperate measures
were taken in the capital: 'and now the great brass gun that stood in the castle
was melted to make brass money; it weighed 7,321 lbs; and was the fourth or
fifth broke for the purpose.'

The remaining Protestants in Dublin had established contact with Schomberg. The Jacobite Government issued an array of emergency decrees to
counter the menace and Protestants were disarmed. The French generals
judged that defending the capital was beyond the capabilities of the Irish army.
They advised James to withdraw west to Athlone and try to hold the line of the
Shannon for the remainder of the campaigning season. But the King was
obdurate: 'he was resolved not to be tamely walked out of Ireland, but to have
one blow for it at least.'

A defiant James despatched Berwick to command the Jacobite troops at
Newry, and himself led a small force of 200 northwards, arriving at Drogheda
on 26 August. The French were still urging the King to withdraw, but Tyrconnel, risen from his sick-bed, where he had spent most of the summer, gave
James his strong support. As d'Avaux reported on 10 September, 'Fifteen days
ago we scarcely hoped to put affairs upon so good a footing; but my Lord
Tyrconnel and all the Irish have laboured with so much zeal that all is in a state
of defence.'

Schomberg was ready to march south, and left Belfast on 2 September. The
Williamite army headed for Newry, but storms in the Irish Sea had delayed
their provisions from England. The retreating Jacobite force under Berwick
made their march a misery by burning the town and devastating the
countryside. Five days later, Schomberg halted his troops just north of
Dundalk. The Williamites camped on low-lying, marshy ground, with a hill
rising behind them. It was a curious choice, as the hill attracted rain, which

then drained on to the marshy ground below. But with autumn already approaching (by the present-day calendar it was 17 September), Schomberg decided that he would not risk advancing any further south.

Encouraged by Schomberg's hesitancy and reports from a Williamite deserter of sickness and inadequate provisions, James was keen to move his troops forward, but the French were still advising him to withdraw to Connaught. Tyrconnel's intervention was crucial. As James later recalled 'the Duke of Tyrconnel and the rest of his own subjects were unanimously of his own opinion. The Duke, moreover, assured them that there was not corn enough in Connock [Connaught] to subsist twenty thousand men two months; upon which the King resolved . . . to advance . . . accordingly upon Holy Rood day, the 14th of September, they marched.'

James led his troops to Ardee, lying between Drogheda and Dundalk. On 16 September, the Irish army reached the River Fane, 5 miles south of Dundalk. Finally, the following day, James moved his troops within half a mile of the enemy camp. As Story recalled: 'About nine a Clock in the morning (it being a very clear Sun-shine day) our Camp was alarmed; the Enemy display'd their Standard-Royal, and all drew out, both Horse and Foot, bringing along a very handsome Field Train.' The Irish army was drawn into battle order. In the Williamite camp, 'It was reported, that several great Officers were for fighting,' but, as Story recalled, Schomberg's answer was, '"*Let them alone, we will see what they will do.*" He received several fresh Accounts that the Enemy advanced, and always bid, "*Let them alone.*"'

Schomberg rejected William's calls for him to fight, arguing that he was still awaiting further reinforcements and that his troops had been issued with inadequate equipment. He also wrote to William of the exceptionally difficult terrain, 'with bogs to the right and left: Such a country was never seen.' William's impatience grew as the weeks passed, but still Schomberg would not be drawn, or pushed, to engage the enemy. Responding to the King's anxiety that 'unless something is risked now, the war will draw out to length,' Schomberg replied that 'There is reason to fear, that if we had hazarded all for all, and had not succeeded, the enemy would have been immediately masters of all Ireland.'

The Jacobites were puzzled by Schomberg's behaviour. D'Avaux wondered if there was some plot for the Protestants in Dublin to rebel while the Irish army was being lured far away from the capital. Some of the Irish soldiers were keen to fight, and jeered at the immobile Williamites behind their defences. James, however, was content to score a moral victory. Although still badly short of weapons, d'Avaux reported to Louis that the Irish army was transformed. There was also news of a reversal of fortunes in the west of Ireland, where Patrick Sarsfield had marshalled a counter-attack against the Enniskilleners and eventually forced their capitulation at Sligo.

At Dundalk, Schomberg's problems were only just beginning. The Jacobites were near enough to his camp to circulate propaganda among the Williamites encouraging deserters. Incriminating letters were found among the French Huguenot regiments. On investigation, Schomberg discovered that these troops included Catholics who had come to England via the Netherlands, and were recruited without precautions being taken to discover their true allegiance. Six of the alleged conspirators were hanged, and about 200 French soldiers were weeded out and sent back to England. They at least were spared what was to follow.

As the rain persisted, the conditions in Schomberg's camp became atrocious. So marshy was the ground that huts were built to replace the tents. Overcrowding and sheer negligence persisted, as did the spread of disease and death. Story witnessed utter degradation: 'the living occupants seemed very sorry when the others were to be buried . . . whilst they had them in their huts they either served to lay between them and the cold wind or at least were serviceable to sit or lie on.' Leaving the Williamites to the misery of Dundalk, James withdrew on 6 October and led his army back towards Ardee. But the Irish troops were soon experiencing something of the Williamite agony, as an inadequate diet and the awful weather began to take their toll.

In November, as the winter set in, James returned to Dublin. Schomberg finally led his men away from the horrors of their camp at Dundalk and, as predicted by Tyrconnel, withdrew to the north. But there was no respite from their suffering. As Story observed, the quarters were indifferent, 'And then most of the Men being very weak before they left the Camp, and marching in the Cold and Wett to come to those Places, we had more that died when they came to Quarters, than died in the Camp.' Over 6000 men from the Williamite army died that winter, many at Dundalk itself, others either in hospital in Belfast or on the ships ferrying home the sick.

The Irish war was deadlocked. Neither the Jacobites nor Schomberg's depleted forces were capable of resolving the issue without some dramatic intervention from outside the island.

V

As the autumn of 1689 approached, William was concerned that the French might attempt to send more supplies to Ireland. He did not want any repetition of Bantry Bay. But he found, as with his army in Ireland, that while he urged action the commander on the spot resisted. The reports from Torrington (Herbert) were redolent of Schomberg's from Dundalk. In early September, the Admiral wrote that sickness among his men had left '599 dead and 2,588 sick'.

It was not only a matter of sickness, severe though that was, nor the weather at that time of year. The Anglo-Dutch fleet simply did not have enough seaworthy warships. Torrington stressed that although the Dutch were not afflicted by sickness four of their ships were defective and had been withdrawn, and there might be 'some reason to be doubtfull of the rest'. On 8 September, Admiral Russell, also at Torbay, was pleading with Nottingham that the fleet was in no state to obey the King's wishes.

William, however, proceeded to place extra burdens on his overstretched fleet. His Continental preoccupations took precedence. He was concerned to keep the Spanish committed to his great coalition against Louis. At the same time, he wanted to maintain access to Spanish ports since this would enable the English fleet to maintain a presence in the Mediterranean for trade and strategic reasons. He was therefore keen to capitalize on the opportunity offered by the proxy wedding of Anna Maria of Neuburg, a Palatine princess, to King Carlos II of Spain. Anxious to please the Spaniards, William offered the services of his fleet as a safe escort from Rotterdam to Santander, on Spain's northern coast.

Torrington and Russell continued to press their case against committing the fleet to sea, but by mid-September William would hear no more objections. Torrington was ordered to take the fleet to Brest. If the French fleet were at its winter moorings in Brest, Torrington was to return, but if the French fleet were at sea, he was to do 'what he shall judge best, with due regard to the season of the year'. Russell warned Nottingham on 18 September that he was 'realy under the greatest aprehension of our sucksess . . .', but he had to obey William's orders. A squadron of thirty ships was allocated to escort the new Queen to Spain, most of them continuing to the Mediterranean to show the flag, 'impress the Turk', and return with gathered trade. Another squadron would sail for the West Indies. This would leave 30 English and Dutch warships (40 if the ships in the Irish Sea were added) to guard against a surprise break-out by the fleet of 70 French warships and 100 fireships at Brest.

A squadron under Rear Admiral Lord Berkeley guarded the southern Irish coast and intercepted two French warships. But the second managed to escape, and brought the Marquis d'Albeville, James's former ambassador at the Hague, 'and gentlemen with money to pay some French ships' in Ireland, including Lord Dover (Henry Jermyn), into Kinsale on 6 November. Further disappointment for William followed when plans to seize Kinsale had to be abandoned because of bad storms. Berkeley concentrated on guarding Schomberg's supply lines further north, but this left southern Ireland unprotected. Rooke, who had been ordered south by Schomberg, raided the Skerries, to the south of Drogheda, and Cork harbour, but was then forced to withdraw his squadron to England for renovation and repairs.

William's ambitious plans for the fleet delayed the refitting of the Channel ships. Maladministration continued to dog the navy. Sailors and shipyard workers were caused untold distress by the irregularities in paying their wages. On 26 January, Admiral Russell, at winter anchorage at Spithead, issued a dire warning to Nottingham: 'For Godsake my Lord, cast your eye sometimes towards the next summer's fleet. I dread the French being out before us. If

they are, wee shall run the hazard of being undone, which is no good prospect.'
The Government would have been well advised to take heed.

VI

By the winter of 1689–90, James's moral victory over Schomberg had put
many of the Jacobites in a more optimistic frame of mind. But as Stevens, the
young English Jacobite serving in Ireland, opined, 'This too great confidence
of the good posture of our affairs produced in all men such a security as proved
without doubt very prejudicial to our interest in the end.'

James and his army were easily distracted from the rigours of war, 'Every
one laying aside the care of the public wholly devoted himself either to his
private affairs or to his pleasure and ease.' The recruitment and discipline of
the army were 'for a long time laid aside'. The pretence that regiments contained their full complement of men was maintained, although:

> the regiments continued really in the same posture of weakness they came from
> the camp. As an example may be produced the regiment of Colonel Thomas
> Butler of Kilcash which mustering always upward of 600 men could not at any
> other day bring into the field above 200.

James withdrew to Kilkenny, avoiding a capital overcrowded with his troops
and riddled with winter infections. He wrote confidently to his Scottish supporters of his plans, when the weather permitted in the spring, to despatch a
substantial Irish force under the command of the Duke of Berwick to Scotland. In January, Major-General Thomas Buchan, a Scottish commander with
the Jacobite army in Ireland, sailed from Dublin to Mull with several professional soldiers, ammunition and money. The Scottish Jacobites, however,
were bitterly disappointed, despite Buchan's efforts to reassure them that
Berwick would soon arrive with 8000 soldiers.

In Ireland, meanwhile, James's officers, spent their time pursuing their
private business, while 'the money ill gotten was as ill spent in all manner of
debauchery, luxury and riot'. O'Kelly echoed Stevens's sentiments, lamenting
that the winter season 'was idly spent in revels, and gaming, and other
debauches, unfit for a Delphinian [i.e. Roman Catholic] court'. Dubliners,
especially the capital's women-folk, were portrayed by Stevens as willing
accomplices:

> The women were so suitable to the times that they rather enticed men to lewd-
> ness than carried the least face of modesty, in so much that in every corner of
> the town might be said to be a public stew. In fine, Dublin seemed to be a
> seminary of vice, an academy of luxury or rather a sink of corruption, and living
> emblem of Sodom.

In the Rev. Robert H. Murray's edited version of Stevens's journal, which
appeared in 1912, the notes provide other accounts of the alleged 'licentious-
ness' in Ireland during the late 1600s. But the Reverend felt able to reassure

his readers that 'This lax state of morality has passed away,' and claimed to
glimpse a silver lining of sorts in even the darkest cloud: 'The effects of the
penal laws were evil, but perhaps the sufferings they involved purified morals.'

Tyrconnel, however, was unaffected by the winter's distractions and,
ensconced again in Dublin Castle, remained grimly aware of reality. Dublin's
defences were strengthened and Tyrconnel instigated a further weeding out of
the army, but little was done to sustain its morale, let along effect the much-
needed training. Tyrconnel reiterated the Jacobites' desperate shortage of
money and arms in his letters to Mary of Modena, pleading with the Queen,

> Madam, let 50 tuns of copper be sent us (besides the forty now a-coming)
> before the end of March, tho you pay for it, for we are undone if ever that mettle
> fails us, as I have often repeated, and ten tunns of steel, for we begin now to
> make firearms here, without which we cannot work.

As had been the case ever since James first arrived in Ireland, the country's
plight rendered his campaign unsustainable in anything other than the short
term, unless there was renewed French assistance. Tyrconnel was aware of
William's mounting political problems in England, brought on by the spiralling
costs of war and Schomberg's failure. In his despatches to Mary of Modena in
France, Tyrconnel argued that 'the people of England were never in such a
disposition to throw off the usurper [William] and receive their owne king
[James].' If, however, no attempt at an invasion was made and William was
allowed time 'he will by all sorts of wayes and meanes establish his tyranny over
those helpless people in one year's time more.' Tyrconnel repeatedly
bemoaned the inability of the French to see where their true interest lay:
'Otherwise, how could they refuse letting the King haveing their ships to waft
him over into England att this, when all things and men there lye soe well
disposed to receive him.'

Viewed from Versailles, there was everything to be gained from keeping
William tied down in a long and exhausting war in the British Isles, with the
crucial proviso that the French did not over-extend themselves. The possibility
of their sending a detachment of troops to Ireland had been mooted during the
early months of 1689, before James left St Germain for Ireland. From the
outset, however, the French offer was always envisaged as part of an exchange.
Louis was prepared to send help, but his European campaigns devoured
manpower and he had no intention of agreeing to a deal which would help
James without strings attached. In return for experienced French troops, Irishmen would have to fight on the Continent.

The enlistment of Irish troops into Louis' Continental campaign seemed an
odd way to strengthen the Irish army. To the French, as to William, the Irish
campaign was an adjunct of the wider European war. Louvois, the French
Minister of War, had made clear to Mountcashel in early 1689 that French
commitments in Europe would prevent any possibility of French troops being

available for service in Ireland until the following winter (1689–90). Mount-cashel was invited to lead the Irish troops on the Continent, an offer which was accepted without any apparent thought about whether troops could be spared from the hard-pressed Jacobite army, or about the effect of his generous offer to select only soldiers of a high calibre from among the Irish ranks.

James was far from sanguine about the proposed exchange. But he was persuaded by d'Avaux that the Irish army would benefit from better trained and more experienced troops. In the summer of 1689, the plan for an exchange had hit a further hitch when Mountcashel was captured at New-townbutler. A suggestion from the French that Sarsfield should be sent in his place provoked James into a fury. James also flatly rejected the proposal that 5000 French infantry were worth 6000 or 7000 Irishmen, and remained insistent that equal numbers of troops should be exchanged.

PART THREE
SUMMER 1690

CHAPTER SEVEN

'OUT OF KNOWLEDGE
OF THE WORLD'

I

On 27 January 1690, William prorogued Parliament in order to forestall the mounting opposition in both Houses. In his speech in the House of Lords, he confirmed his intention to intervene personally in Ireland:

> It is a very sensible affliction to me, to see my good people burthened with heavy Taxes; but, since the speedy recovery of Ireland, is, in my opinion, the only means to ease them, and to preserve the peace and honour of the nation, I am resolved to go thither in person, and, with the blessing of God Almighty, endeavour to reduce that kingdom.

William's decision was taken with the gravest misgivings. 'It is a terrible mortification to me,' he confessed to his Continental ally, the Elector of Bavaria,

> to be able to do so little to contribute to the common good this year, and that I am obliged to go to Ireland, where I shall be as it were out of knowledge of the world. If I can soon reduce that kingdom I shall afterwards have my hands free to act with all the more energy against the common enemy [Louis XIV].

English politicians were deeply divided. Many were alarmed at the thought of William's absence while British Jacobites were plotting James's invasion of the mainland and the French fleet was poised at Brest, ready to exploit the short-comings of the Anglo-Dutch fleet in the Channel. Others, however, argued that there was little prospect of security for England as long as James was based in Ireland. As Sir Thomas Littleton MP commented, 'if the king be not master of Ireland this summer, we shall not hope to keep England long.'

The English House of Commons had been increasingly concerned at the cost of fighting the war on all fronts – Schomberg and William in Ireland, Marlborough with the regular army on the Continent, and the fleet on the high seas. In October 1689, William had asked the Commons 'That what they thought fit to give towards the Charges of the War for the next year might be done without delay.' MPs responded by voting a 'Supply . . . not exceeding . . . two millions to be added to the Public Revenue.' Crucially, however, strings were attached to the extra funds. Dissatisfied with the mismanagement of naval finance, MPs appropriated, or earmarked, £400,000 raised through a new Land Tax Bill specifically for the navy, itemizing how that sum was to be spent by the Government: £200,000 of it allocated to the speedy payment of sailors, £100,000 for victualling and £100,000 for stores.

A precedent had been set. William frequently returned to Parliament to finance his wars, but there were no more blank cheques. Money was only voted for specific purposes. William's wars thus established the two key principles of parliamentary government – regular meetings and parliamentary control of government spending.

When Tyrconnel heard the news in February 1690 of William's plan to intervene personally in Ireland, he observed prophetically, 'we are likely to have a great work on our hands this summer.' Writing to Mary of Modena, he reiterated his belief that unless James mounted his own invasion of England 'this country [Ireland] cannot possibly hold out longer from falling into the Prince of Orange's hands than this year.' But the French remained unwilling to commit their fleet to such a venture, and Tyrconnel was forced to conclude, with a prescience which James would never acquire, 'we are only destined to serve a present turne and be sacrificed at last to our enemies.'

II

Despite William's decision to go to Ireland, it was the French fleet, not the Anglo-Dutch, which made the first major landing of 1690 on the Irish coast. On 12 March, a year to the day since King James II had landed at Kinsale, Lieutenant-General Marquis d'Amfreville sailed his fleet of thirty-six warships, fifteen smaller vessels and twenty-five merchant ships into Cork and Kinsale harbours. On board was the Comte de Lauzun at the head of more than 6500 troops, accompanied by officers, artisans, engineers and hospital personnel, and carrying arms and ammunition, brass, steel, brandy, flour, grain, wine, carts, tools, hospital supplies, tents, cloth for tents, flags, shirts and shoes. Not all of Lauzun's six regiments were French. One was German under the command of Zurlauben, and another consisted of Walloons. Many of the Germans were Protestants, much to James's annoyance. James asked Louis XIV in the future to send him only 'thorough-paced Roman Catholics'.

The French had planned to sail from Brest in December 1689, but had postponed their departure until the following March when the Anglo-Dutch fleet was preoccupied with William's European diplomacy. As Story noted, 'Our Fleet was then attending the Queen of *Spain*, which made this Undertaking very easy to the *French*.' On Friday 7 March, the same day that d'Amfreville had set sail from Brest, the English fleet left Torbay, Admiral Russell heading for Spain, Captain Killigrew eventually bound for the Mediterranean and Captain Wright for the West Indies. Their late departure would prevent Killigrew's Mediterranean fleet from returning in time to strengthen the Anglo-

Dutch patrol of the Channel for the early part of the 1690 campaigning season. As a result, de Tourville's large French fleet at Brest would enjoy a considerable advantage for much of the spring and summer.

Neither d'Amfreville nor Russell was aware of the other's movements. On Monday 10 March, however, a Dutch privateer had contacted Russell and reported '30 sail of men-of-war and 20 other ships about 20 leagues westward.' As the *London Gazette* was later to observe, it 'must have been the French going for Ireland', although at the time London remained ignorant of d'Amfreville's landing at Cork. Sir Cloudesley Shovell, commanding the English squadron in the Irish Sea, only learnt of the French success towards the end of March.

Awaiting the French fleet's arrival on the Irish coast were d'Avaux and Rosen, released from their secondment to Ireland. Also waiting were more than 6000 Irish soldiers, whose embarkation would fulfil James's part in the exchange deal with Louis. When d'Amfreville's fleet weighed anchor and sailed down the Lee estuary in early April, bound for France, the Irish troops aboard would form the nucleus of the legendary 'Irish Brigade' who would fight for a century under the flag of the French King. After landing at Brest and La Rochelle, the complement of five incomplete and poorly trained regiments were regrouped into three under the command of Mountcashel, O'Brien and Dillon.

The English Jacobite, John Stevens, compared the Irish soldiers who left for France unfavourably with Lauzun's regiments. The French were 'well clothed, armed, and disciplined, in return whereof they received a like number of unarmed, ragged, and inexperienced men'. Yet there is no doubt that it was France, not Ireland, which had the better of the deal. The Irish fought wholeheartedly for their new patron, whereas the primary concern of Louis XIV and his commanders was to preserve intact the regiments sent to Ireland, ready to recall them to the Continent whenever this would best suit French strategy.

D'Amfreville's orders to return immediately to France with the Irish soldiers meant that there was no prospect of his engaging Sir Cloudesley Shovell's small squadron in the Irish Sea. Shovell went unchallenged and the Williamites' vital supply lines to the north of Ireland remained intact. The day after Lauzun's arrival at Cork, Schomberg was at Belfast, greeting the first reinforcements for the 1690 campaigning season, as Story reported: '400 *Danes* from *Whitehaven* to *Belfast*, and the Week following all the Foot arrived from *Chester*, with the Prince the [sic] *Wittemberg* their General'. The full complement of the King of Denmark's troops consisted of about 6000 infantry and 1000 cavalry under the command of a German aristocrat, the Duke of Württemberg-Neustadt. Negotiations for hiring them had begun the previous summer, but the Danish convoy of eighty ships transporting them had not reached Britain until November. William's envoy to the King of Denmark, Molesworth, who had arranged the terms for their service, noted that few of the infantry were Danes, and were 'for the most part strangers of all countries whom choice or fortune brings there: Germans, Poles, Courlanders [Latvians], Dutch, Swedes, Scotch, Irish, and now and then an English seaman whom they make drunk after a long voyage'. Inevitably, with such a polyglot force, a number were found to be Catholic, just as James had discovered Protestants among Lauzun's troops.

The disembarkation of these troops under the King of Denmark's colours stirred folk-memories among the Irish of the Norsemen, 'the old invaders of our country'. Schomberg was overjoyed at their arrival following the disastrous loss of about 10,000 men at Dundalk in the autumn and in Ulster during the winter: 'The Duke [Schomberg] went down to see them, and was very well pleased, for they were lusty Fellows, and well Cloathed and Armed.'

Throughout the spring, the Williamites amassed an army which would be about half as big again as the Jacobite force. Reinforcements and supplies poured into Belfast, Story noting that:

> there came Ships every day from *England* with whatever was needful for the Army, and in the second Week of *May* there landed a Regiment of *Brandenburgers* with three *Dutch*, and a great many *English* Regiments; and by this time all the Recruits were come, and the Regiments cloathed, so that we had an excellent Army . . .

III

Sir Cloudesley Shovell's control of the Irish Sea provided Schomberg with valuable intelligence. In March, Shovell captured two small ships and interviewed their occupants. According to his report, 'These people say that the brass money is mightily out of request at Dubline and 'tis common to give forty to fifty shillings of it for a guiney and that every thing is so excessive dear that 'tis almost incredible to report it.' The arrival of the French in Dublin exacerbated the problem. As Stevens noted, they 'were paid in silver, which was no small damage and discouragement to the rest of the army who received none but brass money, for by that means this sort of coin lost much of its former value'. Revenues were so low that 'a subsidy granted when the parliament sat was near lost in the very collecting.' James was driven to further debasement of the coinage:

> Not only all the old brass and copper that could be found in Dublin or the country was consumed, but many of the largest brass guns were melted down, and the want still continuing it was to be feared all the cannon of that sort of metal in the kingdom were in danger.

The Jacobites' problems went deeper than the economy. Although the French had arrived, in Stevens's words, 'to the great satisfaction of all good men . . . they being the very flower of the foot of the army', Lauzun's presence was soon generating new difficulties. Tyrconnel wrote to Mary of Modena in early April, reporting that the French commander 'complaines of the ill order taken for the reception of himselfe and his troops'. On his arrival in the capital, Lauzun's insistence on possession of the Castle and city for his troops caused considerable resentment. The Irish army, already poorly quartered and barely living at a subsistence level, was moved to the outskirts in order to accommodate the French. It did not help that around 500 of the new troops were reportedly attending Protestant churches.

Lauzun was a poor replacement for either d'Avaux or Rosen, lacking the diplomatic qualities of the former and unable to offer the military skills of the latter. He had participated in James's war councils at Salisbury, and had ingratiated himself with Mary of Modena, after escorting her and the baby Prince of Wales to France. He was in his mid-fifties, a short fair man, vain and prone to intrigue. Within a month the friction exploded into violence at a meeting of James's inner cabinet. On 16 April, as a Protestant Dubliner reported, 'Great debate happened in Council about the French, and it was said that Lauzun, the French General, struck our City Governor, Simon Luttrell, a box on the ear, and Dorington threatened to lay down his command.' There were also reports of 'discontents among the Irish about the measures of governing'. Tyrconnel's alleged willingness to serve the interests of the French was said to be antagonizing Sarsfield, 'and each have partys dependent on them'.

Jacobite spirits were further dampened by Sir Cloudesley Shovell's daring Easter raid on Dublin harbour. According to a Protestant eye-witness, 'Five ships and four yachts' anchored in the bay at 'about seven in the morning'. As the tide came in, the yachts, accompanied by one of the ships, weighed anchor, sailed into the harbour and seized 'Bennett's ship, a vessel of twenty-two guns, laden with Protestants' goods for France', which 'was to sail in a day or two'. The ship in question was the *Pelican*, which had originally formed part of the Scottish Williamite patrol off the Mull of Kintyre, and which the French frigates had captured the previous July, since when she had been refitted by the Jacobites. According to Tyrconnel's account of the incident in his despatch to Mary of Modena, the ship was loaded with 'wool, tallow and hides of the King's', which would have been sold in France 'and the product to bee disposed of as your Majestie should direct for the supplying of us with what we need most'.

Resistance to Shovell's raid was ineffectual: 'The captain and all the men fled after firing a very few shots, and losing about five or six more killed in the ship, in the sight of the king and all the army that was in town.' As Tyrconnel recounted, 'had those gentlemen not been very civill or fearfull, they could have burnt all the vessells in the harbour, in spight of all we could do to hinder them.' Insult was added to injury. It was not only the loss of the ship and its valuable cargo which 'fretted the King's party much' but also 'the insolence of the attempt, for it was said a shot flew pretty near the King, which made him remove'. A Jacobite officer who was chasing a Williamite landing party had his horse shot from under him and was forced to wade across the muddy shore. The Williamites 'then played up and down the river Lallibolero'.

The humiliation wrought by Shovell seemed to symbolize the Jacobites' wasted winter and exposed their vulnerability through insufficient naval support. There was at least a little consolation in the success of the *Janet*, sister ship of the ill-fated *Pelican*, in evading Shovell's attentions and successfully crossing from Ireland to Scotland. Aboard the small frigate was Seaforth, the Scottish commander, accompanied by officers and Irish grenadiers, and a cargo of corn and ammunition. Despite all James's assurances during the winter, however, Berwick and his force of 8000 never materialized in Scotland.

In mid-May, at about the same time as the *Janet* crossed to Scotland, 'an open Boat' arrived at Belfast, carrying eight or nine refugees. Its occupants gave Schomberg 'a more exact Account than any he had formerly, how all things went with the *Irish*'. They recounted the problems suffered by Protestants under the Jacobite regime, and reported on Lauzun's insistence on 'possession of the Castle'. Monthly quotas were required from clothiers, hatters and shoemakers for the army, and there were 'considerable Stores of Corn and other Provisions at *Drogheda*, *Trim*, *Navan*, *Dublin*, *Cork*, *Waterford*, *Kilkenny*, *Athlone* and *Limerick*'.

Most striking was the refugees' insight into the Jacobite state of mind. It was revealed as highly defensive, dependent on an uprising in England or the efforts of the French fleet, as Story noted:

> The Method they [the Jacobites] proposed to deal with K. *William's* Army, was, to make good the Passes upon the *Newry* Mountains, and at *Dundalk*, to Spin out the War, as by Order from *France*, and dispute their Ground without a general Battel till they came to the *Boyne*, and there to defend the Pass but still without a Battel, if they could help it, they hoping in a small time to hear some extraordinary thing from a Party of K. *James* in *England*, and from the *French* Fleet.

IV

'Summer drawing on,' observed Stevens in Dublin, 'the preparations for the campaign began to be hastened.' On Monday 19 May, the infantry regiment led by the seventeen-year-old Henry Fitzjames, Lord Grand Prior, 'was drawn up in Oxmantown Green, where it was first viewed by the king, and then marched away towards the north'.

The Grand Prior's foot regiment marched to Drogheda, via Swords, Balrothery and Jenkinstown Bridge. War had transformed the town: 'Since this rebellion it is totally ruined, its trade lost, most of the inhabitants fled, and the buildings ready to fall to the ground.' North of Drogheda, the Jacobite army began to assemble for the summer campaign. Leaving the town on

Saturday 24 May, the Grand Prior's men were joined within the next few days by other regiments, including James's Horse Guards, Lord Dungan's Dragoons, Colonel Sutherland's Horse, Colonel Parker's Horse and Colonel Roger MacElligott's and the Earl of Tyrone's Regiments.

The next day, Wednesday the 28th, Stevens and the rest of the Jacobite force marched further north and set up camp at Ardee. Maxwell's Dragoons, the Earl of Antrim's and the Earl of Westmeath's regiments joined them over the next few days. On Saturday the 31st, 'in the morning two women were hanged as spies by order of Major-General Léry.' Food was scarce, 'the badness of the weather contributing much thereto, by reason of the country about us was bare . . .'

Reconnaissance parties scoured the countryside towards the north, but despite rumours of sightings there was no sign of the Williamite army. Further reinforcements continued to join the Irish army. But new arrivals did not always herald good news. Among them was Teague O'Regan, the veteran Irish soldier, and the garrison of Charlemont, on the Fermanagh–Tyrone border, which had been the last significant Jacobite position in Ulster. They had held out against the Williamites through the winter, but by the spring faced starvation. O'Regan capitulated on honourable terms. At the surrender, the Irish garrison of about 800 marched out in two battalions, accompanied, according to Story, by about 200 women and their children. They were led by Teague O'Regan riding his 'very lame' but 'vicious' horse, and wearing:

> a plain Red coat, an old weather-beaten Wig hanging down at full length, a little narrow white Beaver cock'd up, a yellow Cravat-string but that all on one side, his Boots with a thousand wrincles in them; and though it was a very hot day, yet he had a great Muff hanging about him, and to crown all, was almost tipsy with Brandy.

James was so impressed with O'Regan's defiance that he knighted him and sent him to defend Sligo, a task he would perform with some success.

As regards the Jacobites' prospects, Tyrconnel believed that although their position:

> bee not as good as I could wish, yet it is not soe bad but that if the Prince of Orange should come (as wee believe he will immediately), we hope by God's assistance to make a good defence. The army we have are not soe numerous as his, nor soe well armed, but our men are in good heart, wee have a great many brave men att the head of them, that will, I am perswaded, not quitt their master nor their friends in the day of tryall.

As James's own subsequent account reveals, he was in a quandary about his best strategy as the Williamites prepared to move south. When James left Dublin in mid-June, he seemed in two minds whether to adopt a defensive or an aggressive approach. Recalling the success of his tactics against Schomberg, he 'only proposed to himself, since the inequality of numbers was so great, to try if by defending posts and rivers he could tire and waste the enemies' forces, having experienced by the foregoing campaign that nothing could be more fatal to them than delays'. On the other hand, 'his own universal wants made that a hard game to play too,' since it would bring him no nearer to recovering his English throne. For the time being, therefore, James 'thought fit to advance with his troops as far as Dundalke and eat up the forage there about, and preserve his own country behind him'.

V

On Wednesday 11 June, as both sides finalized their preparations for the new campaign, 'The weather till now having continued very cold, wet, and raw, became on a sudden extreme hot.' William had left Kensington on Wednesday 4 June, and spent three nights on the road to Chester. Throughout the journey, people turned out to cheer him, and groups of women ran alongside his coach, demanding to kiss his hand. Travelling with him were his brother-in-law, Prince George of Denmark, his close adviser, Bentinck, the former Viceroy of Ireland, the Duke of Ormonde, and his Secretaries of State for Ireland, Sir Robert Southwell, and for the War in Ireland, Sir George Clarke. The Williamite party subsequently joined Shovell's fleet of 6 warships and 288 transports at Hoylake. Also aboard for the crossing were 15,000 troops, including the Dutch artillery, and £200,000, which would be welcomed by Schomberg's unpaid soldiers.

William first sighted the Ulster coast on the afternoon of Saturday 14 June. Southwell reported to Nottingham that the King and his advisers were 'extreamely delighted to see three or four hundred ships overspreading the spatious bay of Carig-fergus. All of them fired to express their joy . . .' According to Story, after landing at Carrickfergus, William proceeded to Belfast, where 'he was met also without the Town by a great Concourse of People, who at first could do nothing but stare, never having seen a King in that part of the World'. William's Irish Secretary was heartened that the celebrations carried on through the evening, 'and not only here at Belfast the numerous resort of officers, the fireworks and bonfires concluded the solemnity of the night, but the neighbouring hills and villages adjoyning had their bonfires alsoe'.

Although the next day was a Sunday and this was Belfast, work none the less came first. More reinforcements were sailing into Belfast Lough by the day. Something of its appearance towards the end of the seventeenth century was captured by Gideon Bonnivert, a soldier of Huguenot descent in an English regiment. To the left, the village of Bangor, 'which is butt a small one but very fitt for vessels to come to the very sides of it, both sides are very rocky . . .' and to the right, 'the Castle of Carickfergus which is a strong place; we took it last yeare and lost no great quantity of men.' As to Belfast itself, Bonnivert and his fellow soldiers 'saw on our arrival great nomber of poor people', although it was 'a large and pretty town and all along the road you see an arm of the sea upon your left, and on the right great high rocky mountains which tops are often hiden by the clouds'. Close by the King's Custom was 'a very long stone bridge which is not yett finished'. The people were 'very civill' and spoke 'very good English'.

William was soon fully occupied with all the administrative and political chores of government. Among those summoned to meet him was the young Colonel, Thomas Bellingham, who recalled his first meeting, on Monday 16 June: 'A hott, close day. I was sent for by 2 this morning, and before 6 I came to Bellfast. I was kindly receiv'd by ye D[uke] and Kirke, and favourably recommended to ye K[ing], whose hand I kiss't and he promis'd to remember me.' The promise was kept. Bellingham was duly appointed William's aide-de-camp for the campaign.

When Presbyterian ministers sought William's 'favour and protection', partly because of their resistance to the Jacobites at Derry, the Williamite Secretary for War, George Clarke witnessed something of the friction among Ulster's Protestants. At the meeting was the Rev. George Walker of the established Church of Ireland. As Clarke noted, '... Mr Walker, who had been Governor of Londonderry, and with whom I was talking, could not contain himself, but contradicted what they said with a good deal of warmth, though not loud enough for the King to hear.' The Presbyterians were rewarded when William doubled the annual sum previously paid them by the monarch to £1200 – James had withheld the payment, which had been set at £600 by Charles II.

Friction also existed within the Williamite high command. William had been bitterly disappointed at Schomberg's failure the previous autumn, and behaved in an off-hand manner towards the Duke, showing total lack of respect for Schomberg's experience of Ireland, his opinions, or even for his feelings. So open was William's display of disdain for his nominal second-in-command that Clarke commented:

> I can't omit in this place to take notice of the little regard the King showed to that very great man, the old Duke of Schomberg: all the countenance and confidence was in the Dutch General Officers, Count Solms, Mons. Scravemore [Scravenmoer] etc., insomuch that the Duke, who commanded next under his Majesty, was not so much as advised with about the march of the army, as he complained to me himself while we were at Belfast.

Schomberg's resentment as 'these slights and ill-usage' caused him to confide in Clarke, 'in the hopes of putting an end to his uneasiness'.

Five days after landing, an impatient William left Belfast, dining at Lisburn on Thursday the 19th. According to Story, William, with characteristic bluntness, made known his annoyance about the time it was taking to organize his campaign: 'And seeing that things did not go on so fast as he desired, he exprest some Dissatisfaction, saying, *That he did not come there to let Grass grow under his Feet.*' As Story added, William 'made his Words good, for the whole Army now received Orders to march into the Field'.

In Dublin on 19 June, the day of William's departure from Belfast, a panicky Lauzun effectively imposed martial law on the capital's remaining Protestants.

And an order of the General's was published by beat of drums in all quarters of the town, that all Protestants in town not inhabiting in it three months should depart in twenty-four hours on pain of imprisonment; that no Protestant be in the street from ten at night to five in the morning, nor out of their houses, if an alarm be beaten, on pain of death, and all Protestants to deliver up their arms and ammunition, both offensive and defensive, on pain of death.

The summer's campaign was starting with a vengeance.

CHAPTER EIGHT

ON THE EVE

I

By midsummer 1690, the fate of Europe, no less than that of Ireland, hung in the balance. Two great European battles were fought in the last ten days of June – one on the Continent, the other at sea – before William and James would engage in the third, on Irish soil. Yet Ireland's combatants would not know the outcome of those first two battles until they had fought their own.

On Saturday 21 June, as James and William prepared their armies on either side of the Mountains of Mourne, their Continental allies were locked in combat in the Netherlands. The Battles of Fleurus would be the first of many occasions over the coming century when the Irish Brigade, fighting in the service of the French King, would encounter the English army. The coalition suffered a crushing defeat, Marshal de Luxembourg's 45,000-strong army overwhelming an English, German and Spanish force of 37,000 under the command of Prince George Frederick of Waldeck. The French lost 2500 dead, the allies lost 6000 dead and 8000 prisoners. Fleurus opened up the prospect of a drive by the French army deep into the Netherlands and Germany.

By the time that news of the defeat at Fleurus reached London, there were already reports of a major French challenge at sea. On Sunday the 22nd, Queen Mary was told that the French fleet was off the Devon coast, between Falmouth and Plymouth. She wrote to William warning him of the threat, but his Irish campaign had begun in earnest on the same day and contact became intermittent.

As the first reports of the threat from the French fleet reached Whitehall, around 60,000 men in two great royal armies were harrying and skirmishing along Ireland's eastern seaboard. After a wretched spring and early summer, Ireland was experiencing a heatwave. Day after day throughout the latter part of June, Colonel Sir Thomas Bellingham wrote in his diary that it was 'a hott, close day', 'very hott' or 'excessive hott'.

William 'marched at the head of 20,000 men by Hillsborough and Dromore to Lochbriclan', leading his men south. At Loughbrickland, Schomberg received an intelligence report that 'the Irish had quitted Newry and set it on fire,' and duly 'sent a detachment of dragoons, who extinguished it, and saved part of the town'. Showing characteristic deference to the formalities of seventeenth-century warfare, the old Duke 'despatched a drum to General Hamilton to give him notice that if the Irish Army committed any more such barbarities he would give no quarters'.

From Newry, a Williamite reconnaissance party of dragoons and foot under Captains Crow and Farlow headed 'towards *Dundalk* to discover the enemy'. As Story noted, however, 'We had sent out several Parties before, and the Enemy had notice of it,' a view later confirmed by James's comment, 'It being observed that every night the latter [William] sent a party to a pass called the Half-way Bridge . . .', a contingent from the Irish army, commanded by Lieutenant-Colonels Dempsey and FitzGerald, laid an 'Ambuscade'. The Jacobites claimed that they had killed 'above sixty', while they suffered only 'a few wounded and fewer killed', though the losses included Dempsey. According to Williamite sources, however, only around twenty of their men were lost and Farlow was taken prisoner, 'but the Enemy lost more, as we understood by some Deserters that came off next Day.'

Deserters were endemic to the Irish war, the product of the many different parts of Europe from which both the Jacobite and Williamite armies were drawn, and the chopping and changing of alliances and allegiances. The previous autumn at Dundalk, Schomberg had been alarmed to discover Catholics among the Huguenot regiments. Now, also at Dundalk, the Jacobites found reason to worry. On the day of the skirmish south of Newry, Stevens recounted the capture of 'one who received pay as sergeant in our regiment, deserting to the enemy and hanged at the head of the battalion'. Three others, however, likewise recruited in France after serving in Lord Dumbarton's regiment in the English army in Flanders, 'went away to the rebels, which caused a reasonable suspicion that they and some of the same stamp that were among us came over as spies rather than to serve'.

While Stevens was witnessing the deserter's public execution, Story observed a no less effective way of setting an example. At Loughbrickland, William reviewed his army accompanied by 'Prince *George*, the General, the Duke of *Ormond*, and all the great Men', but it was the manner of the King's inspection which impressed his troops:

> the Weather was then very dry and windy, which made the Dust in our Marching troublesome; I was of Opinion, with several others, that this might be uneasy to a King, and therefore believed that his Majesty would sit on Horseback at a distance in some convenient Place, to see the Men march by Him, but He was no sooner come, than He was in amongst the throng of them, and observed every Regiment very critically: This pleased the Soldiers mightily, and every one was ready to give what Demonstrations it was possible, both of their Courage and Duty.

This impression of William's genuine rapport with his troops was soon confirmed. On his return the next day from reconnoitring south of Newry, William
was handed a requisition for his own wine, 'but He was dissatisfied that all
things for the Soldiers were not so ready as he desired, and with some heat
protested, that He would drink Water rather than his Men should want.'

Later on Monday the 23rd, Major-General Kirk's reconnaissance party
reported seeing 'a great Dust towards a place called *Knock-bridg*, by which he
understood that the Enemy were marching off towards *Ardee*'. Two more
Jacobite deserters informed the Williamites that 'the Body which then was
removed from *Dundalk* was about 20000. It was the discovery of our Advance
Parties which made them draw off, and they gave it out that they would stay for
us at the *Boyne*.'

The Jacobites had withdrawn from Dundalk at about noon, 'but it being
known the King [James] designed to abandon that place, the soldiers in a
disorderly manner fell to plundering the stores.' As they moved south, their
commanders failed to restore discipline: 'We marched back about nine miles
in such manner as looked more like a flight than deliberate retreat, and
encamped on the north side of Ardee.' The Jacobites were to stay three days at
Ardee, where Stevens 'spent the last two days in exercise, and teaching the
men to fire, which many of them had never been accustomed to before'.

While James's army regrouped at Ardee, the Williamites began their disciplined march south. On Tuesday the 24th, 'His Majesty set out a Proclamation to be read at the Head of every Regiment, That no Officer or Soldier
should forcibly take any thing from the Country People and Sutlers, nor press
any Horses that were coming to the Camp.' Justice was summary. The next
day at Newry, 'a Deserter of Sir *Henry Bellasis's* Regiment was shot.'

As Bonnivert headed south 'over the high hills to Newry', he was astonished
that the Jacobites had surrendered their advantage in the mountain passes.

Tis not to be imagin'd how strong naturally many passages are that way; and
besides that many strong tho' small forts made by King James, which made me
admire many times what should have made him quitt those passages, which
might have ruin'd most part of our army with the loss but of few of his own.

Equally striking was Bonnivert's impression of William: 'That day was the first
of my seeing the King rideing in Irish Land, and he had then on an orange
colour sash.'

The troops sweltered in the heat-wave. As the Williamites pressed on
towards Dundalk, 'we heard great Shooting at Sea, which we once look'd upon
to be the *French* and *English* Fleets, but it was only our own Fleet coming
towards Dundalk'. It was an impressive show of force by Sir Cloudesley
Shovell, but his squadron was sorely missed by Torrington and his inferior
Anglo-Dutch fleet in the English Channel. As Shovell cruised off the Irish
coast, Tourville's powerful French fleet met Torrington's allied fleet on

Thursday the 26th off the Isle of Wight, where the two admirals then began manoeuvring for position.

At about six in the morning of Friday the 27th, Thomas Bellingham entered Dundalk and found the town 'wholly deserted, but strongly fortify'd. No inhabitants left but Capt Bolton and his wife who are both stript. Our army encamp'd about a mile south from Dundalke, being now entire, Douglas' party having joyn'd ours.' Lieutenant-General Douglas had led about 10,000 men southwards by a different route, further inland, via 'Armagh, Blackbank, Ball's Mills'. This parallel advance threatened to outflank the Jacobites, forcing them to withdraw south from Dundalk towards the Boyne, in order to protect Dublin. Douglas's troops rejoined William at Dundalk, where another significant arrival was observed by Bonnivert: 'The Inniskilling Dragoons came there to us. They are but middle siz'd men, but they are never the less brave fellows, I have seen 'em like masty dogs runn against bullets.'

By Story's reckoning, the '*English, Dutch, Danes, Germans,* and *French*' now encamped with William at Dundalk made 'in all not exceeding 36000, though the World call'd us a third part more'. None the less, the Williamite army was still 'a third part more' than the Jacobite force encamped at Ardee. Bellingham now found time to go with a colleague 'as farr as Lurgan race, and sate there some time eating bread and cheese', but in Dundalk there was harsh evidence of the hardships of the war. As Story reported, 'as we went through the Town, we found several of the *Irish* that lay dead and unburied, and some were alive, but only just breathing.'

As the Williamites were assembling at Dundalk, James led his troops from Ardee, a town which 'fared no better than Dundalk, being plundered by our own men and left desolate'. The following day, Saturday the 28th, they 'marched again about five miles and encamped within three of Drogheda, near a small village, along cornfields, gardens, and meadows, the river Boyne in the rear'.

The armies were now very close, James's a couple of miles to the north of Drogheda, William's about to move south to Ardee. Scouting parties were continually reporting back, each side watching the other like hawks. Nerves were getting frayed. At about midnight on Saturday, James's officers suddenly ordered the hasty removal of the ammunition and baggage, tents were hurriedly taken down, and 'the whole army drew out without beat of drum and stood at their arms the whole night, expecting the approach of the enemy.' But there was no enemy: it had been a false alarm.

At daybreak on Sunday the 29th, James's army again moved on:

> no enemy appearing, the army began to march in two columns, the one through Drogheda, the other over the river at Oldbridge, and encamped again in two lines in very good order on the south side of the Boyne, between two and three miles from Drogheda, the river running along the whole front . . .

As the Jacobites entered the Boyne valley and crossed the river, William's army 'marched in three lines beyond *Ardee*, which the Enemy had likewise fortified, especially the Castle'. Neither in the mountains near Newry, nor at Dundalk, and nor now at Ardee, had James mounted any real resistance. General James Douglas later wrote to his brother, the Duke of Queensbury, that the Williamites trooped through 'the mountains and straight passes of the Nury [sic], Dundalk, and Ardie; all of which the enemy did very civilly leave to our possession'.

William's army pressed on southwards, Story noting that: 'we marched within sight of the Sea a great part of the day, and could see our Ships sail all along towards *Drogheda*, which certainly must be a great Mortification to the Irish.' During their march, 'there was a Soldier hanged for deserting, and a Boy for being a Spy and a Murderer.' Passing through Ardee, 'a *French* Souldier happ'ned to be very sick with drinking water, and despairing to live, pluck'd out his Beads and fell to his Prayers, which one of the Danes seeing, shot the *French* man dead, and took away his Musquet, without any further Ceremony.' The ravages of war on the local people were all too plain: 'There were none of the *Irish* to be seen, but a few starved Creatures who had scraped up some of the Husks of Oats nigh a Mill, to eat instead of better Food.'

None the less, William 'observed the Countrey as he rid along, and said it was worth Fighting for'. James would have to decide whether to give him the opportunity.

II

With the enemy hard on his heels, James held a council of war. He had retreated before William's advance, from Dundalk to Drogheda. Should he continue to play for time or should he make a stand at the Boyne?

The River Boyne, which rises west of Dublin and runs to the north-east, entering the sea at Drogheda, is of immense symbolic and strategic importance. The neolithic burial mounds at Dowth, Knowth and Newgrange mark the valley as the birthplace of Irish civilization. Traditionally known as Brú na Bóinne, 'the palace of the Boyne', legend has it that these monuments were the home of Aengus, the Irish God of love. His mother Boan, who gave her name to the river, was swept to the sea by the waters from Trinity Well, the river's source, and supposedly the secret well of the King of Leinster. The Hill of Tara was the seat of the most powerful kings in pre-Norman Ireland, while the valley's monasteries and castles bear witness to the early Christian and Norman settlements.

Strategically, the Boyne was the last natural barrier of any significance before Dublin, some 30 miles to the south. If James chose to avoid a battle, the Irish capital would be abandoned, to all intents and purposes, to the Williamites. The French interest lay in prolonging the Irish war, not precipitating a head-on clash between the two opposing armies. Lauzun's orders were to give battle only when there was a reasonable chance of success. The French commander therefore argued against fighting at the Boyne, and advocated abandoning Dublin, strengthening the garrisons held by James, and heading west to the Shannon.

By the time that Tyrconnel joined the Jacobite camp at Ardee in late June, he had come to agree with Lauzun.[20] As he wrote to Mary of Modena, the Jacobites believed that William had assembled an army 40,000-strong.

> and has since been hard att worke to loose noe time to come up with us, for as it is his businesse to force us to a battle, soe it is ours to avoid it all we can but in case of the last extremity, or that we may att least see a great probability of beating him, which I confess I doe not yet nor any body else I converse with.

In his analysis of the Jacobite debate, Tyrconnel played devil's advocate, summarizing the argument of those who were in favour of making a stand at the Boyne:

> Will you suffer the Prince of Orange to march up to your capitall citty of Dublin and possesse himselfe of it, which will so dishearten your own army, and which will loose you all your reputation abroad as well as att home, and where the small magazins you have will be left, and a thousand other things that will sound noe better than the rest?

Against this, however, there was a strong case for not risking any decisive battle during the summer of 1690. William had a superior army, but if he failed to 'make himselfe master of this kingdome before November next', Tyrconnel argued that his position in England would grow worse,

> that he must bee ruined and deserted by his allies abroad; that . . . this next winter [1690–1] will bring the same distemper amongst them [the Williamites] that Monsieur Schomberg had the last; [and] that if the French fleet should beat the Dutch they may transport the King [James] into England, or att least soe supply him here.

'By all this, madam,' Tyrconnel explained, 'you will guess I am for the last opinions, tho' the King bee not,' and he added:

> To conclude, if you venture the battle and loose it, you are ever lost to all intents. England, France, and all the world will desert and dispise you, and you will bee blamed for your conduct, bee it never soe good; whereas if you can preserve the small army from being beaten, you have an hundred chances for you, and whoever has time has life, sayes your country proverb.

In response to his advisers, James acknowledged that he had 'not above twenty thousand men' while William had 'between forty and fifty thousand'. Against that, the Boyne offered 'an indifferent good' position, 'indeed the Country afforded none better'. But, as he later explained, the decisive argument in favour of fighting at the Boyne:

> was, that if he did it not there, he must loos all without a stroke, and be obliged

to quit Dublin and all Munster, and retire behind the Shannon, and so be reduced to the Province of Conough, where haveing no magazines, he could not subsist very long, it being the worst corn Country in Ireland.

The effect on the morale of his troops of continually retreating also had to be considered:

> besides his men seem'd desirous to fight, and being new raised would have been dishearten'd still to retire before the Enemie, and see all their Country taken from them, without one blow for it, and by consequence be apt to disperse and give all for lost, they would have reproached the King with not trusting to their courage, and have assured him of wonders had he but try'd them.

James was impatient to force the issue and return to the English throne as soon as possible, not wait on what others were doing at sea or in England. Even Tyrconnel had expressed a suspicion that any naval victory by the French over the Anglo-Dutch fleet would not be turned to the advantage of their Irish allies. As he had surmised in his last letter to Mary of Modena before leaving Dublin Castle for the Jacobite camp at Ardee,

> It's to bee feared their [the French] fleet will only tryumph in the English Channell, for some dayes shute a great many cannons into the English shore, and soe returne in August into their owne ports. Pray, madam, what good will that doe us, or harme to our enemies?

At the end of the day, James remained an English king through and through. Viewed in this perspective, the prospect of withdrawing to the west of Ireland and conducting a war of attrition while waiting on events elsewhere was ultimately seen by him as being too 'hard a game to play'.

III

On Sunday 29 June, as William marched south towards Drogheda and James crossed the Boyne, the Secretary of State in London, the Earl of Nottingham, was drafting a despairing letter to the Earl of Torrington, commander-in-chief of the Anglo-Dutch fleet in the Channel. Nottingham argued that Torrington's tactic of withdrawing eastwards 'will infallibly expose the Plimouth ships and [cause] Sir Cl. Shovell to be taken or destroyed by the French . . .' Such inaction would also jeopardize the Mediterranean trade being transported to English shores: 'Besides, Vice-Admiral Killigrew must needs be in the Channell by this time, with a great fleet of rich merchant men . . . so that should you avoyd a battle, we must lose more than we can possibly by one . . .'

Torrington, however, estimated that de Tourville's fleet was stronger than his own. His fleet consisted of thirty-four English and twenty-one Dutch warships under the command of Admiral Evertsen, against Tourville's seventy-seven ships of the line. Killigrew's Mediterranean fleet and Shovell's squadron in the Irish Sea were still too far away to offer Torrington support against the immediate threat. Yet when Torrington first stood to, the French had refused

action, which suggested to the English Admiral that de Tourville was acting
with considerable caution. Torrington reasoned that as long as the Anglo-
Dutch preserved 'a fleet in being', the French would not dare risk an invasion,
whereas the consequences of any engagement 'may not only endanger the
ruine of the fleet, but at least the quiet of our country too . . .'. Ministers were
left in no doubt of the Admiral's anger: 'lett them tremble at the consequence
whose fault it was the fleet is noe stronger.'

Government intelligence sources claimed that de Tourville's fleet was
weaker than Torrington estimated. Nottingham implored the Admiral, 'you
have certainly more capitall ships than they have, tho' their number of others
may exceed you, and others must every day come in to you, and before the
battle can be ended . . .' In fact, the intelligence sources were wrong and
Torrington's estimate was correct. Nottingham also warned the Admiral of the
political storm building up: 'I assure your lordship all men here are impatient
to hear of an engagement, and wonder it has been so long delayed.' Evelyn's
exaggerated account of the dominance of the French fleet gives a sense of the
public mood: 'The whole Nation now exceedingly alarm'd by the French fleete
braving our Coast even to the very Thames mouth: our Fleete commanded by
debauched young men, & likewise inferior in force, giving way to the Enemy,
to our exceeding reproch.' In the panic, the Government rounded up suspected Jacobite sympathizers. Even the elderly Samuel Pepys, former Secretary to
the Admiralty, and the Earl of Dartmouth, former commander-in-chief, were
sent to the Tower.

With both admirals under instruction from their governments to fight, the
long delayed engagement finally began off Beachy Head, near Eastbourne, on
the morning of Monday 30 June. The Dutch squadron was in the van and
immediately attacked the French vanguard under the command of
Châteaurenault, the veteran of Bantry Bay. While Evertsen pressed ahead,
Torrington was slowly manoeuvring the English fleet opposite de Tourville's
centre and rearguard. The wind shifted, and the Dutch and English ships were
separated. By early afternoon Evertsen's squadron was encircled by the
French and came under heavy fire. As the afternoon wore on the battle became
a confused mêlée. By the evening, the French had inflicted a shattering defeat
on the allied fleet. Ten Dutch and seven English ships were destroyed, and
two Dutch admirals killed. Tourville lost no ships, though about 400 of the
French were killed and another 500 wounded. The Anglo-Dutch fleet retired
eastwards to seek shelter in the Thames estuary. The French were masters of
the Channel.

In the immediate aftermath, recrimination was rapid. Torrington tried to
exonerate himself and place the responsibility on the politicians. The Government distanced themselves from their commander-in-chief. Nottingham, in
his letter of 3 July telling William about the débâcle, was uncompromising on
the Admiral's culpability: 'my Lord Torrington deserted the Dutch so shame-

fully that the whole squadron had been lost if some of our ships had not rescued them . . . I find it is believed by all men that we should have ruin'd that fleet which is now pursuing us, if my Lord Torrington had done his duty.' Torrington was imprisoned in the Tower. It was not until December that he was eventually tried by court martial and acquitted.

After Torrington's defeat, London and the south of England were in panic. Invasion by the French was expected any day, yet the regular army was away on the Continent and William's army was engaged in Ireland. The authorities in Kent were ordered to muster and arm the entire militia, horse and foot in the county. Lords Lieutenant in every other county were told to prepare half their mounted militia ready for action, and to round up Catholics and anyone suspected of being a Jacobite.

If Louis XIV were to extend his mastery of the seas round the Irish coast, William would be 'shut up' for months in Ireland. Burnet later claimed that 'England might have been lost before he could have passed the seas with his army.' Killigrew's fleet would not return from the Mediterranean until mid-July, and in any case was much smaller than the French fleet. Shovell's squadron would be no match if de Tourville sent a detachment into the Irish Sea.

Yet none of the combatants in Ireland had any means of knowing the outcome of the naval engagement for almost a week – it was not until 4 July, four days after Beachy Head, that William approved the Queen's order for Torrington to engage the French fleet. By that stage, the whole complexion of the war in Ireland had been transformed.

CHAPTER NINE

A BRUSH WITH DEATH

I

By the end of June 1690, as Dalrymple later wrote:

> the eyes of all Europe were now fixed upon Ireland, in which two warlike kings
> were to contend, as upon a public Theatre, for empire, and where the singular
> spectacle was to be exhibited, of a Nephew fighting against his Uncle, and of two
> Sons against their Father in law.

It was an exceptional conflict. James II and William III, both crowned Kings of
England, Scotland and Ireland, were close relatives, by blood and through
marriage. Not only were they uncle and nephew, they were father and son-in-
law. Accompanying William was Prince George of Denmark, the husband of
James's younger daughter Anne. Both royal armies were cosmopolitan: British,
French, Germans, Irish and Walloons fighting for James; British, Danes,
Dutch, French, Irish, Latvians, Poles, Swedes and Swiss fighting for William.
As the historian J. G. Simms observed, 'The drama of two kings fighting at an
Irish river for an English throne was in itself sensational. The fact that they
represented the major power-groups in Europe and were supported by inter-
national armies gave the Boyne a wider significance.'

On Sunday 29 June, James's troops had crossed the Boyne in two columns,
at Drogheda and at the stone-built hamlet of Oldbridge, which no longer
exists today, 3 miles upstream. The bulk of the Jacobite army encamped on
Donore ridge, high above the valley to the south. James set up his headquarters at the strategic vantage point afforded by the old church on Donore
hill. From there, he watched his officers choose their positions on the slopes
stretching down to the river and his men dig in along its southern banks.

At two o'clock in the morning of Monday the 30th, 8 miles to the north of
the Boyne, William's army struck camp and marched 'in three Lines' towards
the valley. William gained his first sight of the River Boyne shortly before
noon, as Jean de la Fouleresse, the Danish Ambassador, reported:

> As we descended the small hills with which the northern part of this kingdom is

studded, we discovered a very fine plain watered by the Boyne. A few hours later we came in full sight of the enemy, encamped on the further side of the little river. On drawing nearer we perceived that, on the enemy's side, the bank was high and steep in several places.

William observed the Jacobite army through field-glasses from 'ye hill of Tullaheskar'. It was here, to the north of Drogheda and to the east of the Jacobites' main camp, that 'his Majesty had a great deal of discourse with the Prince [George of Denmark], Duke *Schomberg*, Duke of *Ormond*, Count *Solmes*, Major General *Scravemore*, my Lord *Sidney*, and other great Officers, who were all curious in making their Observations upon the Enemy.' William and his commanders found it difficult to estimate the true strength of the Jacobites. Probably only part of the army was visible. But it was impossible to say how many were in Drogheda and how many were encamped beyond the hill to the south-west.

Across the valley James's officers were observing the arrival of William's vanguard and finding it equally difficult to judge the extent of the opposition forces. The Jacobite Captain, Stevens, noted that:

Early in the morning the enemy appeared on the tops of the hills beyond the river, some of the poor country people flying before them. They marched down and spread themselves along the sides of the hills where they encamped, but so as we could not discover them all, a great part being covered by the higher grounds.

Several hundred miles away the ships' cannons boomed off the southern coast of England. The sounds of war were about to impose themselves on the peace of an Irish valley. Buoyed though William was at the prospect of battle, Monday was commonly held to be an unlucky day. He would not run the risk of an immediate full-scale assault, but while his forces gathered on the hills to the north he sent an advance party of cavalry and dragoons down the slopes towards the river. Bonnivert was one of those who rode down to the river:

There we saw the enemy and were so neare them that we could heare one another speak, there being nothing but the river between us. As we were drawn up we had order to dismount and every man stand by his horse's head. We had not been there long but some of the King's Regiment of Dragoons were detached and sent to line the river side. So they begun to shutt at the enemy and those of King James's army at 'em . . .

The manoeuvre proved a costly exercise. Jean de la Fouleresse recalled that William 'sent a party of his cavalry to line the bank. King James did the same on his side. He moreover caused a small battery to be thrown up, and its fire to be directed against our cavalry.'

William had exposed his highly valued Dutch guards to the Jacobite field-guns before his own artillery had arrived. To describe it as a puzzling move would be generous to William. According to the Rev. Rowland Davies, the Dean of Ross, who witnessed the incident,

> We stood open during at least twenty shot, until, a man and two horses being killed among the Dutch guards, we all retired into a trench behind us, where we lay safe while much mischief was done to other regiments, and in the evening drew off and encamped behind the hill.

William's Secretary of State for Ireland, Sir Robert Southwell, reporting to the Earl of Nottingham, the chief Minister in London, reckoned 'near 200 balls' were fired, 'and perhaps we lost thereby about half a score horse and four or five men'. Without resolving the mystery of why William allowed his troops to be fired on, Bonnivert's account does not mince words about its consequences:

> Indeed 'twas a madness to expose so many good men to the slaughter without neede, for we had no artillery yet come to answer their. Ours not commencing till 3 in the afternoon. We did retire confusedly behind the hill at the sight of the Ennemy, when it might have bin better manadged.

Yet this costly manoeuvre was not the only reckless action of William's on the banks of the Boyne. That same afternoon there occurred an incident which almost ended the battle before it began and came within an ace of transforming the course of history. To the dismay of his advisers, William decided to take a closer look at the enemy. He headed down the northern slopes of the valley and 'rode in full view of the Irish army which are ranged upwards on the other side', as Southwell reported in his letter to the Earl of Nottingham the following day. From close beside the river, William calmly proceeded to survey the entrenchments on the opposite bank and their positions among the half-dozen stone houses and walls of Oldbridge.

William and his generals had already been in the saddle for more than twelve hours that day. It was understandable that they should feel a break for refreshment was long overdue, but William's choice of picnic site was reckless in the extreme. With complete disregard for the proximity of the enemy, he dismounted a little way along the bank, where a stream from the northern hillside enters the Boyne after rushing through a deep ravine, known today as King William's Glen.

What followed might have served as a warning. The Williamite chaplain, George Story, recalled the scene: 'whilst his Majesty sate on the Grass (being about an Hour) there came some of the *Irish* with long Guns and shot at our Dragoons, who went down to the river, and some of ours went down to return the Favour.'

The Jacobites could scarcely fail to notice William and his generals. As Southwell wrote, 'The enemy soon discovered that it must be his Majesty who was so attended.' Initially this did not seem to pose any direct threat to the picnickers. Story's account relates that 'a party of about forty Horse advanced very slowly and stood upon a ploughed Field over against us for nearly half an Hour.'

But the Jacobites' apparent passivity was misleading. Story recounted that 'This small party, (as I have heard from their own Officers since) brought two Field-pieces amongst them, dropping them by an Hedg, in the plow'd Land, undiscover'd.' In Southwell's account, the sight of William so near at hand 'made them draw downe two pieces of six pound ball from the foord a little higher, and plant them opposit to the place where our horse were drawn'.

Some Williamites believed that their leader had walked straight into a Jacobite trap. Robert Parker, a captain in the Williamite Lord Meath's Regiment of Foot, wrote in his memoirs of the 'rising ground on our side which overlooked their whole situation: to this place they concluded the King would come to make his observations: whereupon they planted four field-pieces in a place proper for their purpose, under covert of some bushes, which prevented them from being discovered.' William had come 'to the very spot' the Jacobites had expected, yet remained oblivious to the deadly threat.

As William and his high command mounted and began to ride 'softly the same Way back', two six-pound shots thundered from one of the cannons hidden near the Jacobite group. The first came desperately close to killing one of William's most senior commanders. As the Rev. Davies, observed, it 'struck off the top of the Duke of Wurtemberg's pistol, and the whiskers off his horse'. According to Story, it 'kill'd us two Horses and a Man, about 100 Yards above where the King was'.

The Jacobite gunner's second shot came within inches of killing William. In Story's words,

> immediately comes a second, which had almost been a fatal one, for it Graized upon the Bank of the River, and in the rising slanted upon the King's right Shoulder, took out a piece of his Coat, and tore the Skin and Flesh and afterwards broke the head of a Gentleman's Pistol.

Eye-witness accounts differ on the precise impact of the two shots, but there is little doubt that, had the second one varied only fractionally in its trajectory, William might well have been killed. His brush with death caused 'the greatest consternation imaginable'. As Burnet wrote, 'It cannot be imagined, how much terror this struck into all that were about him.'

William's own reaction was, to put it mildly, stoical. The Danish Ambassador reported that:

> Those about His Majesty thought he was dangerously wounded, but he said with great coolness, 'it is nothing, but the ball came very near' (*ce boulet est venu bien près; ce n'est rien*). The King then asked for his cloak in order to hide the hole burnt in his coat and went on further.

General James Douglas claimed that William's immediate comment was in Dutch: '*T'hoobt niet naeder*' (it's well it came no nearer).

Lord Meath, commanding his own infantry regiment at the Boyne, later wrote to a lady friend and described how immediately after being hit, William 'called for a napkin and an other coat; and after yt was settled upon him he stretched out his arme 3 times and sayd without ye least passhion; The enemy designed to prevent his fighting next day; But sartanly I'll be tomorrow amongst ye thickest of them.' It had been a remarkable escape.

The buff coat worn by William on the eve of the battle, perforated at the spot next to the shoulder in which King William received his wound, survived into the Victorian age. The dimensions of the coat proved that William was a man of small stature.

The immense relief felt by William's immediate entourage was expressed by Southwell, William's Secretary for Ireland, who wrote to the Earl of Nottingham that 'Your lordship will easily beleive the dread and concerne we all have been in at this accident.' Southwell added that he hoped that 'his Majestie will prevaile on himself to be more carefull hereafter, for he is not to be moved thereto by the persuasion of others'. But as Dr George Clarke later wrote of William's comment when he finally reached his tent later that evening, to the effect that 'his hurt would be of one advantage to him, for he should not wear armour the next day . . .' There was no question of William sitting out the battle.

II

The loss of William on the eve of battle would have had a devastating effect on his army. As Story recalled, 'it would have been of fatal consequence to the Army at that time, if he had fallen, since, instead of our going to them, the *Irish* would have been ready to come to us next Morning, and how we would have received them there's none can tell.'

News that William had been hit, and even that he had been killed, spread through his army. William immediately set about squashing any rumours that he had been killed, or incapacitated, by the blow, as the Danish Ambassador reported: 'he remained two or three hours longer on horseback, lest the report that he was wounded should spread through the camp and alarm the troops'.

Many simply would not believe, until they saw him with their own eyes, that William could survive the blow. Even those soldiers who had seen the King since the incident by the river wondered if he had been hit again. William donned a fresh coat, and rode out among his troops: 'So great was their joy at beholding him appear on horseback, that the whole camp rang with acclamations and with cries of "God save the King!"'

'At the same instant', noted the Danish Ambassador, 'similar shouts were heard in the hostile camp' across the river. The Williamites were later 'informed that they were occasioned by a speech which King James had delivered to his troops', but another eye-witness claimed that the Jacobites were cheering a report that William was dead. According to Robert Parker, the

Williamite infantry Captain, when the Jacobites first realized that William had been hit, 'observing some confusion in those about the King, [they] concluded he was killed; and this news soon flew to Dublin, and from thence to Paris, where they had publick rejoicings for it.'

The news of William's injury reached London on 6 July. Nottingham was called from his bed. Later that day, a distraught Mary wrote to her husband, 'Your letter came just before I went to chapell; and though the first thing Lord Notting. [sic] told me was, that you were very well, yet the thoughts that you expose yourself thus to danger, fright me out of my wits.' The Queen pleaded with William 'to take more care for the time to come'. This was more than natural concern for her husband. Mary urged him to 'consider what depends upon your safety; there are so many more important things than myself, that I think I am not worthy naming among them.'

In Paris, the rumour spread that William had been killed and was greeted with wild celebration. In August 1690, the monthly periodical *The Present State of Europe* reported:

> It was about midnight that the Court (of France) receiv'd the news of King William's *death* (on the report of one of King James's lackeys). Yet tho' it is not usual to make bonfires for the death of an Enemy before he is defeated in battle, the Emissaries nevertheless immediately ran about the streets, awaking up the people of the City, and crying out to them, *Rise and make Bonfires*.

Reaction in Rome, varying from one extreme to the other, reflected those throughout Europe. The French Embassy was ecstatic, the Austrians in despair, while the Vatican was subdued. As *The Present State of Europe* commented, had the news of William's death been true it would have been the end of the French King's most determined adversary.

III

During the afternoon, 'about three Clock' according to Story, the Williamite artillery arrived, 'and we lost no time, but took two or three of them down towards the River, and planted them on a Furry-bank over against the Pass.' The valley reverberated to the sound of cannon and mortar. In Bonnivert's account, as the Williamite artillery began 'to play upon theirs stoutly, then the ennemy shew'd they had many other batteries beside the first.'

James too had a narrow escape. Although he was not hit, it was too close a shave for the Jacobites' liking. Southwell's report to Nottingham recounted that 'one of our bombs beat down severall tents that were next adjoyning to that of King James and Count de Lausoon [Lauzun].' Story later heard that in the incident 'a Horseman that stood Sentinel' by James's tent had been killed, and 'they then removed their Counsel to some other Place . . .'

That afternoon, a French soldier among the Williamite troops suddenly broke ranks and 'ran through the River' to join the Jacobites: 'when they saw him coming, a great many of them came down to receive him, and crowding about him to hear News, our Cannon threw a Bullet amongst the very thickest of them, which killed several, and 'twas said the Fellow himself.'

Southwell reported to London information received about the Jacobites from a Protestant deserter: 'they have sent away some of their grosse baggage ... they are about 25,000 men, talking hautily that they will fight us, and even retreat six miles back, that we may freely come over to fight them.' Southwell commented that 'we are of the opinion the Boyne is the walls of Dublin, and if they defend not this they'l do little with that citty.'

As the sun was setting over the hills of Meath, the roar of the great guns was stilled. Councils of war were called in both camps. On the outcome of their decisions would depend the morrow's battle, and much else besides.

Both armies shared a common background. Their infantry contained musketeers and pikemen, though by this time the introduction of bayonets enabled the musketeers to act as their own pikemen. In battle, the musketeers generally formed in six ranks, the first three firing, then filing off to the rear and reloading as the next three took up position and fired. Pikes were used mainly to resist cavalry charges. Some foot regiments without pikes carried with them long pieces of wood, with sharpened spikes of iron and wood, which were known as *chevaux-de-frise*, the 'Friesian horse' or 'Swedish feathers'. These were driven into the ground, their spikes and sharpened ends pointing at the oncoming cavalry. The cavalry's main form of attack was to charge home with the sword, using the weight of their horses to cut through enemy troops, their carbines and pistols serving as auxiliary equipment.

The Irish war was also characterized by the deployment of the more recent innovation of dragoons, who fought on foot but rode small horses to increase their mobility, and grenadiers, both on foot and horse, who carried small, hollow iron, wood or ceramic spheres, packed with gunpowder, which could be ignited with a slow fuse before being thrown into the enemy's ranks. Twelve years earlier, Evelyn had observed the army on Hounslow Heath, and wrote of 'a new sort of souldier called *Grenadiers*, who were dextrous to fling hand granados, every one having a pouch full, & had furr'd Capps with coped crownes like Janizaries, which made them looke very fierce'.

William had a larger army, better equipment and more professional soldiers. In particular, the Williamites had more of the newer flintlock type of muskets, sometimes known as firelocks, fusils or fusees, which improved their rate of fire. William's Huguenot regiments, most of his Danish troops and a fair proportion of the English infantry were issued with flintlocks. By contrast, most of the Jacobite infantry were still using matchlocks, although some of their troops, notably those guarding the artillery and powder supplies, had flintlocks. Above all, William's troops, and especially his Dutch Guards and the foreign mercenaries, were far better trained and more professional than the Irish army. The crack troops on the Jacobite side were the French.

The terrain, however, would be critical to the outcome of the battle. James appeared to have the stronger position. According to Captain Parker, serving in the Williamite Earl of Meath's Regiment of foot, when William first saw the Jacobite positions he observed that they 'were strongly posted and drawn up to great advantage; and saw plainly it would be a difficult matter to force them from their ground'. This 'difficult matter' became the central issue of debate at William's eve-of-battle council of war. William's two most senior commanders, Count Solms and the Duke of Schomberg, were deeply divided. Solms argued for a massive frontal assault across the River Boyne at Oldbridge. Schomberg wanted to commit the bulk of the army to a major outflanking manoeuvre, leaving only the smaller part to hold the line on the northern banks of the Boyne.

The River Boyne provided James with a formidable first line of defence. His army was drawn up on the southern slopes of the valley at Oldbridge and the stretch of river running just below, a few miles inland from Drogheda. In those days the Boyne was tidal along this stretch, and, although it was fordable in a few places at ebb tide, its banks were generally either boggy or steep, and often both. The main crossing was at Oldbridge, with another at Drybridge a mile or two downstream, nearer Drogheda. Both fords were defensible, but not impregnable. The stone walls and houses of Oldbridge were all situated on the southern bank and would give excellent cover from which to defend the crossing. But the steeper northern hillside assisted the Williamite artillery to pound the Jacobite front line and the hamlet – it was here that they killed a Jacobite officer during Monday afternoon's bombardment. A deep ravine in the northern hillside opposite Oldbridge would provide shelter for any Williamite troops preparing to attempt a crossing.

James, however, was well placed to hold the crossings. The field fences and dips and ridges on the hillside rising to Donore provided good cover and offered the opportunity to mount fresh stands against any attack. The gentle slopes leading down to the southern banks of the Boyne were ideal for the cavalry to charge any Williamites who might scramble across the river. Beyond the dominating hill of Donore lay a direct line of retreat south to the village of Duleek and, once across the River Nanny, to Dublin.

The strong Jacobite advantage at Oldbridge strengthened Schomberg's case for attempting to outflank them. Lord Iveagh was sent to defend Drogheda for the Jacobites with a detachment of 1300 men. It would thus be difficult for the Williamites to turn James's right flank, as any attack there would prove costly, and would allow James time to retreat before William took the town. The greater danger for James lay upstream, to his left. The Jacobites had broken the bridge at Slane, but when Lauzun reconnoitred the river during Monday he discovered that it was fordable everywhere.

According to Story, at Monday night's council of war, the Duke of Schomberg initially 'advised to send part of the Army that Night at 12 a Clock, to pass the River at or near *Slane*-bridg, some three Miles above, and so get between the Enemy and the Pass at *Duleek*, which was about four Miles behind them'. The terrain would hinder any crossing, since the riverside slopes were generally steeper than at Oldbridge, particularly on the western side of Donore hill. If, however, the Williamites could cross the river at Rosnaree, they would be nearer to Duleek than the Jacobites, cutting their line of retreat and able to reach Dublin before James.

James later wrote that he realized the Williamites 'might march by their right up towards Slane to pass the river there', and then either engage his army on their left flank or seek to exploit the superiority of their horse and send a detachment to the capital. James therefore:

> sent Sir Neale O'Neal's Regiment of Dragoons to Slane with orders to defend that pass as long as he could, without exposeing his men to be cut to pieces, believeing the Enemie would endeavour to pass there, and then either offer the King battle, or march straight towards Dublin . . .

But there was an added danger for James from any Williamite thrust to his left. Again, the terrain was critical. From Rosnaree, the river flows in a northerly direction for a couple of miles, then meanders around a long horse-shoe bend, before reaching Oldbridge and turning to flow eastwards. Oldbridge thus lies in a loop of the river, towards the downstream end of the long horse-shoe bend. The bulk of James's troops were positioned in the loop, with the hill of Donore to their rear. If the Williamites outflanked them by crossing the Boyne upstream, and did so in sufficient strength, the Jacobites might rapidly find themselves encircled. The river was their first line of defence, but it might rapidly become a death trap.

Faced with complete disagreement between Solms and Schomberg, William opted for a compromise. He was keen to minimize the Jacobites' territorial advantage, and sought 'some measures . . . which might oblige them to break the order they were drawn up in'. He would not therefore concentrate his attack entirely at Oldbridge, as Solms urged. Neither would he commit the bulk of his army upstream, as Schomberg advocated. Instead,

> it was resolved that Lieutenant-General Douglas should march by break of day, with about 8000 men to the ford of Slane, two miles up the river, in order to pass there, and fall on the left flank of the enemy, while the King with the main of the army charged them in front.

Overnight, final preparations were made on both sides of the valley. In the Williamite camp,

> Orders were given out, that every Souldier should be provided with a good stock of Ammunition, and all to be ready at break of Day, to march at a Minutes warning . . . All the Baggage, with the Souldiers great Coats, were to be left behind with a small Guard in every Regiment to look after them.

James meanwhile decreed that the camp-site on Donore hill was to be cleared before battle was joined, ordering 'the baggage to be loaden, and be ready to march that the ground might be clear on which it camped by morning'.

With a variety of uniforms, and regiments on opposing sides wearing similar colours, the armies wore their identification in their headgear. 'That day we had all some green in our hatts, to know one from the other,' recalled Bonnivert, respecting the order to every Williamite to display 'a green Bough or Sprig in his Hat, to distinguish him from the Enemy (who wore pieces of Paper in their hats)'. The colours of identification were a link with the Continental war, of which the Boyne was part. Green was appropriate to the Williamites since it was also worn by the Dutch and their Spanish allies, while the white cockades of the Jacobites were traditional to the French army.

CHAPTER TEN
TUESDAY 1 JULY 1690

I

Before daybreak on Tuesday 1 July, Count Schomberg, son of the old Duke, led a Williamite party of cavalry, infantry and dragoons from their camp westwards towards Slane. They were looking for a suitable river crossing to the Jacobite's left. Gideon Bonnivert's regiment was among the detachment: 'we were up at two of the clock and we march'd to gain a passage two miles off about 5 in the morning. The passage was a very steep hill and a shallow river at the bottom.' The 'passage' was the ford of Rosnaree, and lying in wait on the 'very steep hill' opposite were Sir Neill O'Neill's regiment of dragoons 'with four or five pieces of Artillery ready to receive us'.

The overnight mist had not yet lifted as the day's first engagement began. The 'continuall fire' from O'Neill 'did not daunt' Count Schomberg's troops, of whom the 'Grenadiers and Dragoons were the first' across to the opposite bank. James recounted that, in the fierce fighting which followed, 'Sr Neale O'Neal's Dragoons did their part very well and disputed the passage with the Enemie almost an hour till their cannon came up.'

The Williamites eventually forced their way up the steep hillside, Schomberg's greater numbers overcoming O'Neill's superior position – some idea of just how remarkable their feat was can be gained by viewing the gradient of the hill from today's road along the Boyne's southern bank to the west of Donore. O'Neill's Dragoons 'then retired in good order with the loss only of five or six common men, but their Collonel was shot through the thigh and an officer or two wounded'. O'Neill died from his wounds some days later.

From their main position on Donore hill, the Jacobites had heard the drum beat which signalled Count Schomberg's march to the west, beginning under cover of darkness and a heavy mist. But it was not until Count Schomberg's party had crossed the Boyne, at around six o'clock, that William ordered General Douglas to follow with a larger detachment of infantry and a brigade of cavalry.

As the dawn sun began to break through the early-morning mist over the valley, James 'saw their right wing march towards Slane followed by a line of foot'. Stevens reported that 'We had this morning received advice that the enemy marching by night had beaten off a regiment of our dragoons that guarded the bridge of Slane and possessed themselves of it, and now we saw them marching off from their right towards it.' More important than the confusion about the precise location of Count Schomberg's crossing, which occurred at Rosnaree, not Slane, was the misjudgement about the Williamite right wing. James recalled:

> No sooner had the Enemie [Count Schomberg] passed there, but they stretched out their line to the right as if they designed to take us in the flank, or get between us and Dublin, which Monsr de Lausune seeing marched with the left to keep up with them, and observe their motion.

The mistake made by James and Lauzun was to assume that 'the main body of the Enemie's Army was following their right which had passed at Slane'. The French General, la Hoguette, had argued against committing too many troops to the left, and instead wanted the force defending Oldbridge strengthened. Apparently Lauzun had agreed with him on the eve of the battle. But in the morning a decision was delayed for about three hours, and when the order finally came it was to move to the left.

As Douglas led his troops towards the crossing at Rosnaree, the Jacobites 'on the other side marched from the left, the river being between both'. Stevens was among the Jacobite left wing now moving to check Count Schomberg and Douglas: 'for a considerable space we marched under the enemy's cannon, which they played furiously without any intermission, yet but did little execution.'

James meanwhile rode to his centre and right wing at Oldbridge 'to hasten up the troops to follow Lausune' and help block the Williamite assault to their left. In all about 10,000 Williamite troops, or around one-third of their total strength, made the crossing at Rosnaree during the morning. James was convinced, however, that this would represent the enemy's main thrust across the Boyne. He had to guard against them cutting his line of retreat and therefore urgently began committing even more of his troops to strengthen his left flank, in all approaching one-half of his (smaller) total strength.

When James reached Oldbridge, seeking reinforcements, he:

> found the Duke of Tyrconnel with the right wing of hors and Dragoons, and the two first brigades of the first line drawn up before the old bridg, from which post he did not think fit to draw them, the Cannon and baggage not being far enough advanced on their way to Dublin; however the rest of the foot march'd by, their flanks towards Lausune, and the King took the reserve, consisting of Purcel's hors and Brown's foot, with which he marched till he came up to that rear of the foot that follow'd Lausune.

Among the Jacobite troops moving to meet the challenge on their left were two regiments of horse, including Sarsfield's Cavalry Regiment, Lauzun and all six of the French infantry battalions, and a large number of Irish infantry. They were spotted by the Williamite detachment, as Bonnivert recalled: 'After some houres we saw the ennemy coming down a turneing between two Hills, which we knew by the rising of ye dust, and by and by they shew themselves in their best colours.'

The two sides drew up facing each other. Although the Jacobites were protecting their left flank in order to secure their line of retreat, they were doing so at the expense of their centre and right wing. They would be far less able to withstand any attack at Oldbridge.

As James returned from gathering reinforcements for his already sizeable wing, 'he found Lausune and the Enemie's Right drawn up in battle [lines], within half cannon shot, faceing each other: the King did not think fit to charge just then, being in expectation of the troops he had left at old bridg.' It was at Oldbridge, however, that William was to unveil the next stage in his battle plan.

II

As the morning wore on it became 'excessive hott', a 'very clear' day, 'as if the Sun it self had a Mind to see what would happen'. At 'about eight or nine o'clock', according to the Williamite Secretary of State for War, Sir George Clarke, 'our cannon began to fire upon two houses, with yards walled about, that stood on each side the road on the other side the Boyne.' William 'was then standing att ye Battery, seeing his cannon play att ye house of Old bridge'.

While the bombardment was softening up the Jacobite defensive positions guarding the ford at Oldbridge, the Dutch Blue Guards gathered in the ravine near the Williamite gun battery, shielded from view of the Jacobites. The guards were under the command of Count Solms, as they had been when they escorted him into Whitehall and triggered James's flight over eighteen months earlier. If everything now went according to plan, they were about to play a decisive part in the Irish war. William was biding his time. He was giving Douglas and Count Schomberg maximum opportunity to distract the Jacobites from the slopes opposite and cut their line of retreat. Crucially, he was also waiting until low tide when the crossing at Oldbridge would be at its shallowest.

At ten o'clock, the Dutch Blue Guards emerged from the ravine. They 'beat a March till they got to the Rivers side, and then the Drums ceasing, in they went, some eight or ten abreast, being presently almost up to the middle in the Stream (for they stopp'd the Current by their sudden Motion, and this made it deeper than usual)'. The Jacobites posted at Oldbridge held their fire until the Dutch Guards were about halfway across, 'then a whole peal of Shot came from the hedges, Breast-works, Houses, and all about, yet we could not perceive any fall except one, and another stagger'd.'

First across were the Dutch grenadiers. They quickly established a footing, causing the Jacobite infantry to retreat hurriedly from Oldbridge. All the while, more Dutch Guards were crossing the Boyne, followed by Huguenot regiments led by Caillemotte and Cambon, and also English regiments. Facing the Williamite assault were two Irish infantry regiments (Antrim's and Clanrickard's), along with five further battalions ordered to the scene from Donore, the Duke of Berwick's Life Guards, three cavalry regiments (Tyrconnel's, Parker's and Sutherland's) under the overall command of Major-General Dominick Sheldon, and, guarding the ford at Drybridge further downstream, Lord Dungan's dragoons.

In all, however, the Jacobites were only able to muster around 6000 troops along the front from Oldbridge to Drybridge. James, Lauzun and many of their troops had marched off to the left, where they would find themselves forlornly staring across ditches and a bog at the Williamite detachment who had crossed earlier at Rosnaree. The smaller Jacobite force who remained downstream at Oldbridge thus had to face the brunt of the Williamite assault. They were only about one-third the strength of the forces attempting to cross the river from the northern bank.

The bitterest fighting of the battle on the southern riverbank was being watched intently by William from his vantage point on the northern hillside. Not for the last time at the Boyne, the Irish cavalry 'charged very bravely'. According to Clarke, William was showing 'great concern for his Blue Guards', who were positioned between the river and two houses at Oldbridge. The Dutch were:

> forming as fast as they could to receive a body of Irish horse that was coming towards them upon a full trot. The King was in good deal of apprehension for them, there not being hedge nor ditch before them nor any of our horse to support them, and I was so near his Majesty as to hear him say softly to himself: 'My poor Guards, my poor Guards, my poor Guards', as the enemy were coming down upon them, but when he saw them stand their ground and fire by platoons, so that the horse were forced to run away in great disorder, he breathed out, as people use to do after holding their breath upon a fright or suspense, and said he had seen his Guards do that which he had never seen foot do in his life.

The Dutch Guards had devised a highly effective defence against the cavalry charge, as the Rev. Davies witnessed:

> At the first push the first rank only fired and then fell on their faces, loading their muskets again as they lay on the ground; at the next charge they fired a volly of three ranks; then at the next, the first rank got up and fired again, which being received by a choice squadron of the enemy, consisting mostly of officers, they immediately fell in upon the Dutch as having spent all their front fire; but the two rear ranks drew up in two platoons and flanked the enemy across, and the rest screwing their swords into their muskets, received the charge with all imaginable bravery and in a minute dismounted them all.

According to Story, however, the Williamites were soon under the most intense pressure: 'One would have thought that Men and Horses had risen out of the Earth, for now there appeared a great many Battalions and Squadrons of the Enemy, all on a suddain, who had stood behind the little Hills.' The Duke of Württemberg, commander of the Danish force, reported that 'The Dutch Guards attacked but met with great resistance.' They were supported by the Huguenot battalions of Caillemotte and Cambon, but the latter 'were overwhelmed by the enemy cavalry because they had no *chevaux-de-frise*'.

Losses were heavy on both sides. Around 150 Irish Guards and more than 100 Dutch Guards lost their lives. 'Many of the two [Huguenot] regiments were killed and Col. Caillemotte was mortally wounded.' In this mêlée, the losses of the Williamites were among the most serious which they suffered in the entire Irish campaign.

The Duke of Schomberg was rallying the Williamites, who were desperately trying to consolidate their toe-hold on the southern bank, 'But the Duke had not above 300 behind him, when first the enemy's horse made a desperate charge, in which he received two cutts in the forehead, but not very considerable.' From behind, the Huguenots sustained a fierce salvo of gunfire against the Jacobites, 'yet one of them shott him [Schomberg] into the throat, and downe he dropped quite dead. This is told me by Monsieur Faubert [Foubert], gentleman of his horse, who leapt down after him to save his body, and received also two smale wounds.'

It was a tragic end for the veteran mercenary. Yet he was seemingly unmourned by his last patron. According to Sir George Clarke,

> The King had immediate notice of it by some of the Duke's aide-de-Camp, but did not seem to be concerned, whether it was that he really was not sorry or that his thoughts were employed about the regiment of Dutch Guards, whom he apprehended in some danger from a body of Irish horse that was coming to attack them, I will not determine.

Jonathan Swift's epitaph to Schomberg in the north choir aisle of St Patrick's Cathedral, Dublin, records the Dean's criticism that the Duke's family had been too mean to record his burial there themselves: 'The fame of his valour was more effective with strangers than his closeness by blood was with his kinsmen.'

Dr George Walker, one of the Protestants' heroes of the siege of Derry, was also killed by the riverside at Oldbridge. His body was 'stripp'd imediately', ironically, according to Story, by the *Scots–Irish* that followed our Camp . . . and took most of the Plunder'. William was unimpressed by Dr Walker's bravery. On hearing of his death, the King is reported to have commented, 'Fool that he was, what had he to do there?' Clergymen had no place as soldiers.

By now the intense struggle on the slopes near Oldbridge had raged for almost an hour 'and was so hot till past eleven, that a great many old Souldiers said, they never saw brisker work.' At about eleven o'clock, William widened his line of attack further downstream, ordering the Duke of Württemberg 'to cross with the Danish troops and Hanmore's [Hanmer's] and La Mellionière's brigades'.

This second assault across the Boyne involved an estimated 12,000 troops, but the cosmopolitan Danish force found that the crossing was by no means easy. As Württemberg reported to the King of Denmark,

> Some [Jacobite] squadrons at once appeared to dispute the crossing and charged us. We replied with a great volley which so astonished them that they retired. Where Your Majesty's Guards crossed, the water was so deep that it come up to their armpits. We marched across by divisions. The bottom was very boggy. While we were marching out of the water a squadron of dragoons came up and attacked the Guards. I allowed only the grenadiers and some platoons to charge, on which the enemy was repulsed . . .

The Jacobite defence had held against the first assault at Oldbridge, but more and more Williamite troops were now scrambling, wading and virtually swimming across the river. The Jacobites were increasingly outnumbered, and as they moved along the banks from Oldbridge to counter the new assault their line of defence was spread increasingly thinly.

The Jacobite infantry began to fall back through the sheer weight of the Williamite attack, and the troops who crossed at Oldbridge were at last able to make further progress. As Württemberg's troops found, however, the Irish cavalry and dragoons were putting up an effective fight:

> When we had crossed the river and were mounting the hill we found the enemy dragoons and troopers more inclined to fight than the infantry, which hurried away before us so fast that our men could never engage them. The enemy horse advanced on our Guards, but as they found there were chevaux-de-frise and vigorous firing they retired again. They were actively pursued by our cavalry who were, however, unable to achieve anything of importance.

On the Jacobite right, Sheldon's Horse, less than 1000-strong, displayed immense bravery, and succeeded, for a while, in blocking the Williamite advance. 'It was Tyrconnell's fortune to charge first the blue regiment of foot-guards to the prince of Orange, and he pierced through.' As Stevens observed, James's 'horse guards and Colonel Parker's Regiment of Horse behaved themselves with unspeakable bravery'. The Irish horse continually charged down the slopes at the enemy, then regrouped, and charged down the slopes again and again. The Duke of Berwick later wrote 'Nous ne laissâmes pas de charger et recharger dix fois.'

Throughout the battle, Sheldon's Irish Horse maintained a resistance which has become legendary. They caused chaos in the Williamite vanguard, but lacked sufficient support.

III

At about midday, William extended the line of battle still further downstream. On the eve of the Boyne, he had told Lord Meath, 'sertanly I'll be tommorrow amongst ye thickest of them,' and now he led the third main assault, leading the remainder of his cavalry, Danes, Dutch, English and Ulstermen, across the river at Drybridge. William's bravery, bordering on recklessness, had not been diminished by his narrow escape the previous afternoon, as his Irish Secretary, Sir Robert Southwell, reported: 'He wears his Star and Garter, and will not disguise what he is; nor is he made ever the more cautious by the wound in his shoulder.'

The crossing at Drybridge was deep and William found himself in serious difficulty, 'for his Horse was bogg'd on the other side, and He was forced to alight till a Gentleman help'd him to get his Horse out.' The struggle aggravated William's asthma, as Southwell noted: 'the landing was so boggy, that he was fain to walk 3 or 400 paces, so as to be near out of breath . . .'

William was soon in the thick of the fray. Efforts to restrain him were all in vain. According to Southwell, the Earl of Scarborough (formerly Richard Lumley, one of the earliest Williamite conspirators in 1688) tried to prevent his leader being drawn into the front line:

> There were a party of the enemys horse drawn up at a little distance from him [William], where he gott over. He would have downe right have gon upon them, had not my Lord Scarborough as a sort of desperate cure forbid any to follow him, so that his Majestie looking behind, and being alone, seemed with reluctance to turn about his horse . . .

But, as more cavalry crossed the Boyne, William was soon rallying his horse to Scarborough's aid, 'and no sooner did others come in, but his Majesty pusht on, and put the enemy to flight.'

Initially, the Jacobites fought back against the new wave of Williamites surging across the river. 'Although', according to a Danish account, 'the enemy rallied several times and defended himself against our men, he was driven back each time. In the end, as his infantry were more inclined to retreat than to defend themselves he had to quit the field altogether.'

As the Jacobite foot began to withdraw towards Donore, the battle was increasingly dominated by the clashes between the Williamite cavalry and Major-General Sheldon's Irish Horse. In the Williamite account of Robert Parker,

> The enemy being now prepared, charged our first line, and broke through some of them: And some of ours in their turn obliged some of theirs to scamper off. By this time our whole army having passed the river, we charged each other alternately with various success.

Gradually the Williamites began to inch forward up the southern slopes. In the heat of battle, the fighting became confused. Determined Irish resistance

PLATE IX

FREDERICK Duke of SCHONBERG, Marquis of Harwich, Earle of Brantford, Baron of Tays, Gen.ll of all his Ma.ties Forces, Master Gen.ll of his Ma.ties Ordnance, One of his Ma.ties most hon.ble Privy Council, Knight of y.e most noble Order of the Garter, Count of y.e Holy Empire, & Mertola, Grandee of Portugal, Gen.ll of y.e Elector of Brandenburgs Forces, Stadtholder of Prussia &.
G. Kneller pinx.   I. Smith fe. et ex.

Duke of Schomberg, William's commander in Ireland during 1689.

PLATE X

The Battle of the Boyne, 1 July 1690. King William is in the right foreground on a dark hor

PLATE X

aring the star and garter, flanked by some of his cavalry.

PLATE XI

Detail from a print of the Battle of the Boyne by Theodor Maas, showing the Williamite gunners in action.

PLATE XII

The flight of James II from Ireland. The defeated King is seen embarking at Duncannon fort.

PLATE XIII

The Williamite commanders, John Churchill, Earl of Marlborough (left), and General Ginkel (right, detail).

PLATE XIV

Fighting at Sligo, on Ireland's north-west coast. This strategic town changed hands several times during the war.

PLATE XV

THE USURPERS HABIT

Caricature of Louis XIV relinquishing
Limerick, represented by his hat.

before the village of Donore caused renewed chaos in the Williamite ranks. William was not only exposed to the Jacobite gun-fire, but was also in mortal danger from the Enniskilleners, who mistook the Dutch Guards for their enemy. According to Southwell,

> Here his Majestie led up some Dutch troops, but before they had got in, the Inniskillingers had made an assault on the other side, and did very bravely at first, but espying another great party whom they took for the enemy, just ready to surround them, they began to fly; and did actually put in disorder the Duch horse and all others that stood in their way. The place was unfortunately full of holes and dung pitts, and the passage narrow; but above all the dust and smoak quite blinded them. His Majesty was here in the crowd of all, drawing his sword, and animating those that fled to follow him. His danger was great among the enemys gunns, which kild thirty of the 'Iniskillingers' on the spot. Nay one of the 'Eniskillingers' came with a pistol cockt to his Majestie, till he cald out, what, are you angry with your friends?

In the dust and mêlée mistakes were inevitable. 'The truth is', commented Southwell, 'the cloathes of friends and foes are alsoe so much alike.' Story reported that later the Williamite commander, Lieutenant-General Ginkel, stationed at the rear of his troops 'was in some Danger by our own Dragoons; for the Enemy being close upon him, they could not well distinguish'. Nor was the incident at Donore William's only narrow escape during the afternoon. A little later, 'he stood so neer the enemy when drawn up, that a bullet from a long gun touched his boot, and shot a horse that was next him in the legg.'

At its first attempt on Donore, the Williamite horse was driven back. 'His Majesty then came up,' wrote the Rev. Davies,

> and charged at the head of the Enniskilling horse, who deserted him at the first charge, and carried with them a Dutch regiment that sustained them; but the King's blue troop of guards soon supplied their place, and with them he charged in person and routed the enemy . . .

Story observed the fall of Donore: 'Some of Duke *Schonberg's French* Horse were here also, who behaved themselves well, and took one or two of King *James's* standards.' The Jacobite line was broken. The Irish infantry were in full retreat, overwhelmed by superior numbers.

Among the Jacobites taken prisoner was Lieutenant-General Richard Hamilton, the man whom William had entrusted to negotiate with Tyrconnel just under eighteen months earlier, but who had promptly thrown in his lot with the Jacobites. Hamilton was duly brought before William, who asked him, 'Whether the *Irish* would fight any more? Yes, (said he) an't please Your Majesty, upon my Honour I believe they will, for they have a good Body of Horse still.' Story gives a revealing account of William's reaction to Hamilton:

> The King look'd a little aside at him when he named his Honour, and repeated it once or twice, *Your Honour*: Intimating (as He always says a great deal in few

Words) that what the other affirmed upon his Honour was not to be believed, since he had forfeited that before in his siding with my Lord *Tyrconnel*; and this was all the Rebuke the King gave him for his Breach of Trust.

William would have needed little warning about Sheldon's Horse after their valiant performance throughout the battle, first on the slopes by the river, and subsequently at Plattin Hall, where they turned again and charged on the Williamites. The heaviest losses were suffered by Berwick's Regiment, of whom only 16 of 200 emerged unscathed, and Parker's, with just 30 left unwounded. 'Ye enemyes horse of Tyrconnell's Regiment behav'd themselves well,' commented William's aide-de-camp, Thomas Bellingham, 'but our Dutch like angells.' It was no small tribute to Sheldon's Horse that, in his thanks to the Dutch Blue Guards, William singled out their resisting 'the fury of the enemy's horse'.

The Irish cavalry had 'fought so well', as a Danish report acknowledged, 'that their infantry gained time enough to save themselves'. The time they gained was a vital half-hour, which 'saved King James's army from annihilation'. The Irish Horse had also prolonged the war which, but for that crucial thirty minutes, would have ended there and then.

As the Irish headed south for Duleek, they were left to wonder whatever became of the much-vaunted French troops. There had been no sign of them where the fighting was heaviest, at Oldbridge or on the southern slopes of Donore hill.

IV

While the battle raged at Oldbridge, the Williamite detachment which had crossed at Rosnaree and the Jacobite left flank were drawn up facing one another. James and his French commander-in-chief, Lauzun, were discussing tactics on their left flank, when:

> an Aide de Camp came to give the King an account that the Enemie had forced the pass at old bridg, and that the right wing was beaten; which the King, wispering in Lausune's ear, tould him, There was now nothing to be done but to charge the Enemie forthwith, before his troops knew what had happen'd on the right, and by that means try, if they could recover the day.

There was even worse news. Two of James's senior commanders, Sarsfield and Maxwell, had reconnoitred the ground between their left flank and the Williamite detachment, and reported that 'It was impossible for the hors to charg the Enemie, by reason of two dubble ditches, with high banks, and a little brook betwixt them, that run along the small Valley that divided the two Armys.'

The impassable terrain was a disaster for James. He had committed almost half his troops, including all the French regiments to his left flank. The Williamite advance at Oldbridge renewed the threat to his line of retreat, and now he was not even able to attack the Williamite force which had crossed at Rosnaree. La Hoguette, the French General, later claimed that he had told Lauzun that, in fact, the terrain was not impassable, and that they should attack. Lauzun allegedly replied that they would have to withdraw to Dublin. La Hoguette's claim appears to substantiate the view that Lauzun was determined all along that the French should not fight. But the General was anxious to defend his own role and shift any blame for the defeat on to his commander. Moreover, the terrain had been reconnoitred by two brave Jacobite officers, and it was on the basis of their advice that Lauzun decided not to commit his troops. Lauzun, however, was in an entirely defensive and negative frame of mind at the Boyne, when James urgently needed a more experienced and decisive commander.

As the Jacobites realized their plight, the Williamite dragoons in Douglas's detachment began a fresh attempt to outflank them. James feared that his line of retreat to the capital would be cut, deducing 'by the dust that ris' as they headed behind a nearby village that 'they seem'd to endeavour to gaine the Dublin road.' The main Williamite army was also in pursuit from Donore, and, to the astonishment of the Jacobites, some of Douglas's troops were ploughing straight through the deep bog which had separated the two armies. Since James was unable to attack, he 'thought fit to march also by his left towards Dublin road too, to pass a small brook at Duleek which was impracticable higher up by reason of a bog'.

James had been determined before the Boyne 'not to be walked out of Ireland without having at least one blow for it'. But the 'one blow' was badly bungled. The bulk of his army had played no part in it but were now in retreat. Moreover, James himself, undeniably a brave man, as his earlier military exploits had demonstrated, had allowed himself to be sidelined with many of his most effective troops on his left flank. In marked contrast, William had been in the front line, an inspiration to his army.

The bitterness felt by many Jacobites at their defeat 'without having at least one blow for it' was voiced by Stevens:

> I thought the calamity had not been so general till viewing the hills about us I perceived them covered with soldiers of several regiments, all scattered like sheep flying before the wolf, but so thick they seemed to cover the sides and tops of the hills. The shame of our regiment's dishonour afflicted me before; but now all the horror of a routed army, just before so vigorous and desirous of battle and broke without scarce a stroke from the enemy, so perplexed my soul that I envied the few dead, and only grieved I lived to be a spectator of so dismal and lamentable a tragedy.

Stevens was fiercely critical of the poor leadership and the behaviour of parts of the Jacobite army, who had conducted themselves in marked contrast to the 'unspeakable bravery' shown by the Irish Horse. As Story observed from the

Williamite side, had the French guarded the crossing at Oldbridge, instead of being posted on the Jacobite left, 'we had found warmer Work of it.'

Even James's promise to distribute brandy to each regiment was badly mis-managed. The intention had been that each soldier 'might receive a small proportion, in order to cheer them for the fatigue of the day'. But the brandy did not arrive till the army was on the march, with the result that the soldiers rushed to take as large a share as they could, 'drinking so extravagantly' that many were drunk – though Stevens is surely exaggerating in his claim that 'above 1,000 men were thereby rendered unfit for service, and many were left dead drunk about the fields.'

'There is no place of excuse for the dragoons,' Stevens wrote, 'especially the Earl of Clare's, commonly known by the name of Yellow Dragoons, being the colour of their clothes, who were the first that fled having scarce seen the enemy.' Some fled so fast that they allegedly reached Limerick the next day, others still 'not thinking themselves safe there' pressed on to County Clare 'being above 100 miles from the Boyne'. Nor were some of the foot beyond reproach:

> though the action was not till noon several foot soldiers made such haste that they were seen in Dublin before three of the clock, having in that short time run near twenty miles, which perhaps might have had some colour of excuse had the enemy been at their heels, but there was none to hurt and it was only their own fear pursued them.

There was chaos as both parts of James's army collided in their rush for the narrow crossing over the River Nanny and the Dublin road beyond. Stevens was marching in the Lord Grand Prior's Regiment 'in Duleek lane, enclosed with high banks' when the Jacobite horse smashed into them:

> The horse came on so unexpected and with such speed, some firing their pistols, that we had no time to receive or shun them, but all supposing them to be the enemy (as indeed they were no better to us) took to their heels, no officer being able to stop the men even after they were broken.

Without effective leadership, the Jacobite retreat degenerated into a panic-stricken stampede. Stevens recounted:

> it was certainly an unparalleled fright that caused our own horse to ride over the greatest part of our first line of foot and break ten or twelve of our battalions, firing upon them as enemies, and yet I must confess some of these were the men that with great bravery had sustained the shock of the enemy's horse, and were outdone by numbers not by valour.

In the confusion, the Duke of Berwick was about to order Jacobite musketeers to fire on a party of their own horse, but realized his error in the nick of time. Arms, ammunition, even coats, hats and shoes, were abandoned by the Jacobites as they fled. 'Our cavalry pursued the enemy as far as possible,' commented a Danish account, 'and finally his baggage and guns became the booty of our men.' It was an ignominious episode.

Some measure of discipline was ruthlessly restored to the Jacobites at Duleek when Zurlauben ordered his Blue Regiment of German troops to fire on any troops who would not fall into line before the river crossing. With some semblance of order returning to the Jacobite retreat, Stevens reported that Louis XIV's regiments at last came into their own: 'Only the French can be said to have rallied, for only they made head against the enemy, and a most honourable retreat, bringing off their cannon, and marching in very good order after sustaining the shock of the enemy, who thereupon made a halt.'

The French General, la Hoguette, was later dismissive of the Irish troops, writing to Louvois, his Minister of War, that 'les ennemies ont chassé devant eux les troupes irlandaises comme les moutons.' Leaving aside the lack of any action by the French at the Boyne, it would seem that la Hoguette and Lauzun were among 'les moutons', Stevens noting that none of the 'glory' of the French stand before Duleek was 'to be attributed to the Count of Lauzun, or La Hoguette, who at first left their men'.

None the less, the determined resistance by the French enabled the great majority of the Jacobite army to retreat safely,

> For the enemy finding the French stand and some of our horse to make head never pursued their victory or improved their advantage, which if they had done a small party might have cut us off, so that none had been left to make head again and but few of those present to lament the misfortune of the day.

Having negotiated the narrow river crossing and evaded their pursuers, most of the Jacobite army withdrew westwards to Limerick. Lauzun advised James to withdraw to Dublin, 'for fear the Enemie, who were So strong in hors and Dragoons, should make detathments [sic] and get thither before him'.

In his despatches to London, Southwell erroneously commended Lauzun for an 'admirable' retreat, adding that 'Our King was in the head of all this action, pursuing them from hill to hill for seven mile about, and came not in hither till about ten at night, where he slept in the Prince's [George of Denmark] coach . . .'

The pursuit of the Jacobites, 'more hunted than defeated', was called off as darkness fell. Returning to camp at Oldbridge, Bellingham 'was almost fainte for want of drink and meat'. It had been a 'dismal day' for Jacobites, a shattering experience, as Stevens recorded:

> Grief (though the greatest) was not my only burden, marching from three in the morning afoot till dark night, the excessive heat of the sun, and a burning thirst proceeding from the aforesaid causes, which was so vehement I could not quench it though drinking at every ditch and puddle.

The Williamites were also anxious not to stretch their supply lines, since the 'baggage was not come up'. There was also the need to consolidate their position before heading for the capital. After all, they were unaware of James's plans, and Drogheda was still held by the Jacobite detachment which had been sent there to hold the crossing against any attempt to outflank James on his right.

The day after the battle, Wednesday 2 July, the Williamites began their mopping-up operations. In Württemberg's account, 'we halted to bring up the baggage, knapsacks and greatcoats which had remained in the camp,' while 'Five battalions under Brigadier Mellonière were detailed to summon Drogheda which surrendered. The garrison marched out without arms leaving all their baggage behind. There were three regiments of foot and 300 unattached troops in the town.' The need to consolidate was stressed in the report by the Rev. Davies:

> In the morning as soon as it was light we returned to Duleek, where our foot was, and sent a detachment to bring up our baggage from the last camp. In the afternoon six troops of horse and three regiments of foot that came from Munster to join King James appeared on the flank and alarmed us, and, sending two spies to discover who we were, we took and hanged them, the rest marching back without any engagement . . .

It was time for stocktaking. By Southwell's calculation, which can be taken as the official Williamite estimate,

> We have taken Lieutenant Generall Hamilton, and do beleive that the Earle of Carlingford and Lord Dungan are killed. We have also taken eight or nine of the enemy's great guns, 5 or 6,000 of their armes, 70 or 80 waggons, besides great store of tents and baggage, some plate, money and fine things.

As the Williamite army resumed its march south, its soldiers found more arms ('for 4,000 men'), ammunition and copper money abandoned by the Jacobites.

As to the numbers killed, Bellingham reckoned that 'We kill'd about 2000 of theyr men . . . We lost not above 200 in ye whole action, many of which were kill'd by our own men through mistake.' Story estimated between 1000 and 1500 Jacobite losses and around 400 Williamites killed, while Parker said Jacobites 'not quite 800 killed', Williamites 'not above 500 killed'. Plunkett, the Jacobite commentator, put the losses at 500 Jacobites and 1000 Williamites. Tradition has it that fourteen cousins of the Talbot family sat down to breakfast at Malahide Castle on the morning of the battle, and by nightfall they were all dead. Among those killed were the Jacobites O'Neill, Carlingford and Dungan, and the Williamites Caillemotte, the Rev. George Walker and the Duke of Schomberg.

Although the Irish army had survived to fight another day, principally because of the bravery of Sheldon's Horse, the Boyne had a crucial psychological impact. Its effect on the Jacobites was devastating, while the Williamite victory provided an urgently needed boost to morale in England. The notion advanced by Hilaire Belloc, in his biography of James, that the Boyne was merely a 'delaying action' and that 'A retreat was intended from the first, and was successfully carried out,' does not accord with the facts. James's 'one blow' for Ireland had ended in ignominious failure.

The French contingent indulged in mutual recriminations in their letters home, while the Irish Jacobite leadership was disheartened and divided. Some, like Tyrconnel, were willing to submit to William if the terms were right; others, like Sarsfield, were determined to fight on. Whereas William had been in the thick of the fray, James had taken no active part in the battle and had fled the field. The contrast between the two kings at such a critical moment in Ireland's history explains why the memory of one was to be accorded cult-status, while the other earned nothing but obloquy.

Would the Boyne prove to be the key battle of the Irish war, and decide the country's future? Unless the French were willing to exploit their advantage at sea and step up their support, the battle would prove decisive. The Irish simply lacked the resources to mount an effective offensive. The question would no longer be whether the Williamites would win, but when, at what cost and on what terms.

The final equation would be of no small consequence to the Irish. Although they could only delay the inevitable, they might yet be able to influence the terms of the new settlement. William was desperate to conclude matters as quickly and as cheaply as possible, so that he could concentrate his efforts and resources on the Continental campaign. The longer, therefore, that the Irish were able to resist, the stronger their hand in any peace negotiations. The Irish would be fighting for an honourable settlement.

CHAPTER ELEVEN

'A FOOLISH VERDICT'

I

The question of James II's future role in Ireland was settled within hours of his retreat from the Boyne. According to James's own memoirs, Lauzun had advised him to withdraw from the battlefield and head straight for Dublin, where he 'might with the troops he had with him, and the garison he found there' prevent the Williamites seizing the capital. Lauzun's advice, however, did not stop there. James later claimed that his commander-in-chief:

> advised him not to remain at Dublin neither, but go with all expedition for France, to prevent his falling into the Enemies hands, which would be not only his, but the Prince his Son's utter ruin; that as long as there was life there was hope, and that if once he was in France again, his cause was not so desperate, they being in all probability Masters at Sea.

Tyrconnel reportedly endorsed Lauzun's assessment. It seemed, however, that James needed little encouragement to leave Ireland.

News of the Jacobite defeat preceded James's return to the capital by a couple of hours, a Protestant Dubliner reporting that 'at about six or seven at night people began to come to town, by whom it was said the King's army was defeated and was retreating hither, which proved true.' On James's arrival in the city at 'about nine', he reportedly met Lady Tyrconnel at the Castle. A Williamite version of their encounter suggests that, when she asked what he wanted for his supper, he 'gave her an Account of what a Breakfast he had got, which made him have but little Stomach for his Supper'. An oft-cited anecdote has James saying, 'Your countrymen, madam, can run well,' and Lady Tyrconnel replying, 'Not quite so well as your majesty, for I see you have won the race.' Exquisite though it is, there is no contemporary reference to this exchange.[21]

What does seem clear is that James proceeded to turn on his Irish subjects, 'detesting the base cowardice of the Irish, with whom he resolved never to oppose more the English, and to end his reign here for ever ...' The only debate is whether his criticisms were delivered later that night at a meeting with his Privy Council, or early the following morning when he saw the Lord Mayor of Dublin 'and some others'. Whenever James's bitter speech was made, its contents were recorded by a Dublin Protestant. The King claimed that although he had:

> often been cautioned that when it came to the touch they [the Irish] would never bear the brunt of a battle, I could never credit the same till this day, when having a good army and all preparations fit to engage any foreign invader, I found the fatal truth of what I had been so often precautioned.

James's assessment of the Irish army ignored the lack of basic equipment or training. He acknowledged that 'the army did not desert me here, as they did in England,' but found this small consolation:

> yet when it came to a trial they basely fled the field and left the spoil to the enemies, nor could they be prevailed upon to rally, though the loss in the whole defeat was but inconsiderable; so that henceforward, I never more determine to head an Irish army, and do now resolve to shift for myself, and so gentlemen must you.

James was resolved to play no further part in the Irish war. Before leaving Dublin for the last time, however, he did at least urge that the capital ought not to be 'fired':

> I do therefore now charge you on your allegiance that you neither rifle the city by plunder, nor destroy it by fire, which in all kingdoms will be judged very barbarous, and must be believed to be done by my orders, and if done there will be but little mercy expected from an enemy thus enraged.

Early in the morning of Wednesday 2 July, 'about four or five', he left Dublin for the last time, riding south 'towards Bray', where he left his cavalry escort to hold the bridge till noon. But he need not have worried about being pursued. The Danish Ambassador reported that Schomberg's son, leading the Williamite detachment, had no orders to intercept the Jacobite retreat. William seemed disinclined to pursue the enemy, which suggests that William wanted to avoid having an embarrassing prisoner on his hands.

Heading further south, James and his escort rested their horses that evening at Shelton House, near Arklow. Their visit was recalled in 1791 by Hugh Howard, brother of the first Viscount Wicklow:

> An old man, one Richard Johnson, who was son to the gardener at Shelton told me that just after the battle of the Boyne, being then a young boy, as he was standing one evening in company with a labouring man of the name of Coghlan in Shelton avenue ... he saw two tall gentlemen, grandly mounted and all covered with dust.

The two strangers rode to the house,

> alighted, and sat down in the porch, where they had some cold meat and a jug of strong beer. While they continued there, which was only for a few minutes, one

of them was seized with a violent bleeding at the nose, which stained that side of the porch where the gentleman sat.

After the bleeding had stopped, the two men rode away. The young Johnson 'afterwards knew for certain' that the person whose nose had bled was King James II. As to the blood-stained post, this was later taken down, and 'long carefully preserved'. Hugh Howard claimed to have seen it, but by 1791 it had been destroyed by a servant who had allegedly used it to light a fire.

When James reached Duncannon Fort, on Waterford harbour, he boarded a French ship, but was subsequently driven into Kinsale. There he found a party of French frigates under the command of Forant, who had escorted three grain-ships into the harbour. Four of Forant's frigates provided James's escort back to France. He left Kinsale on Friday 4 July, just under sixteen months after he had first stepped ashore. Before his departure, he received a letter from Louis XIV, reporting the French victory at Fleurus, and offering to land James in England at the head of an army of 30,000 men. But by the time that James reached Versailles he discovered that Louvois and Seignelay had put a block on the project. The Williamites were later relieved that James's flight had diverted a small part of the French fleet. As Clarke, the Williamite War Secretary, noted, the French frigates which provided James's escort 'by that means were prevented from scouring St George's Channel, intercepting provisions and cutting off all correspondence with England'.

James had never seen his expedition to Ireland as anything other than the first step to recovering the English throne. When he left the island, he went unlamented by his ill-used and ill-fated Irish subjects, entering Irish folklore as Séamus a' Chaca, James the Shit. The Williamite commentator, the Rev. Story, reported that a letter intercepted from an Irish officer at Athlone writing to his father in the country referred to James's flight to France, with the comment that 'it was no great matter (he said) where he [James] was, for they were better without him.' It was also reported that following some banter with Williamite officers, Patrick Sarsfield retorted: 'Change kings, and we'll fight you again.'

The bitterness and disillusion felt among the Irish nobility in July 1690 is symbolized in the story told by Sir William Wilde, Oscar Wilde's father, of the burning of Athlumney Castle, in the Boyne valley, by its last lord, Sir Launcelot Dowdall:

Sir Launcelot, hearing of the issue of the Battle of the Boyne and the fate of the monarch to whose religion and politics his family had long been so attached, and fearing the approach of the victorious English army, declared, on the news reaching him, that the Prince of Orange should never rest under his ancestral roof. The threat was carried into execution. Dowdall set fire to his castle at nightfall, and, crossing the Boyne, sat down upon its opposite bank, from whence, as tradition reports, he beheld the last timber in his noble mansion blazing and flickering in the calm summer's night, then crash amidst the smouldering ruins, and when its final eructation of smoke and flame was given forth, and the pale light of morning was stealing over that scene of desolation, with an aching and a despairing heart, he turned from the once happy scene of his youth and manhood, and, flying to the Continent, shortly after his royal master, never returned to this country.

II

The first Jacobite troops entered Dublin around the same time as James. Ormonde reported that at 'about ten at night a regiment of Dragoons came into Stephen's Green, and lay there all night on their arms'. But Sheldon's cavalry sustained their impressive display throughout the day. A Williamite supporter heard the noise of music outside, and rushed to greet, as he imagined, the arrival of the triumphant Williamites. 'We were greatly surprised', he recalled, 'when . . . we heard the whole of the Irish horse coming in, in very good order, with kettle-drums, haut-boys, and trumpets.'

By the time Lauzun and Tyrconnel arrived the next morning, 2 July, both James and the city Governor, Simon Luttrell, had fled. 'Such a Wednesday as this I never did see the like to,' commented one Protestant eye-witness:

> About six or seven last night they began to come thick to town, and were coming all night, but the gross of the army came this morning, both horse and foot passed over our bridges, but in great disorder and distraction, and their regiments scattered and broken.

Dublin was in chaos. 'Many families left the town; great removing of goods, etc . . .'

Stevens recounted a forlorn spectacle. Some Jacobite officers were ashamed at the depleted strength of their regiments, and paused on the outskirts of the city for 'three hours' displaying their colours in the hope of attracting a few more stragglers. Though only 100-strong, yet by that stage 'one of the most considerable' regiments, the Grand Prior's:

> marched through the skirts of the city, passing over the river at the Bloody Bridge, which is the farthest off in the suburbs, the others being now only the remains of four regiments, the others being quite dispersed or gone other ways, we halted again in a field at Kilmainham, a hamlet adjoining to the city.

James had left orders that his army should head for either Kinsale or Limerick. Before the day was out, the bedraggled remnants of the Jacobite force, including Stevens, were heading westwards. As O'Kelly observed, Irish officers and soldiers seemed to find their way 'as if they had been all guided to Limerick by some secret instinct of nature'.

The sudden departure of the Jacobites seemed like a new dawn for Protestant Dublin. As one of their number commented the following day, Thursday the 3rd, 'There was very great joy, and sorrow and sadness was gone away,

when we crept out of our houses and found ourselves as it were in a new
world.' The capital remained in a state of near-anarchy, as the Protestant mob
raided and looted Catholic homes. As the Duke of Württemberg noted on the
Thursday, 'while the army was in the march, a deputation came from Dublin
and sought the King's protection; apparently most of the Catholics have withdrawn.' The following day, 'two battalions of the Dutch Guards were detailed
to take possession of Dublin.'

On Friday 4 July, the Williamite army 'observed a day of rest', a welcome
relief for many of its soldiers. Bonnivert had camped 'neare a fine house
belonging to a papist' the day before, but had fallen 'sick of a violent feavor and
an extream fitt of ye gout in ye same time'. 'Very hott', noted the inimitable
Colonel Bellingham, who must surely rate as the Williamite weather-man.
Undeterred, or possibly by now accustomed to the heat, Bellingham dutifully
provided William 'with an account of ye stores and provisions yt were in
Dublin and 20 miles around', and presented his King 'with a baskett of cher-
ryes, ye first he eat since he came to ye kingdom. He tooke them with his own
hand very kindly.'

William's approach to the outskirts of Dublin on Saturday the 5th was
heralded by the city's Protestants in eulogistic terms:

> the never to be forgotten sight of the glorious King William . . . Here ended the
> tyranny, oppression, arbitrary power, will and pleasure, against all law, all charity
> and Christianity, all promises and assurances made by a Popish Prince to a most
> dutiful people, the Protestants of Dublin.

In Story's words, Dublin had been 'a Nursery of Protestants' ever since the
days of Queen Elizabeth. And who better than Bellingham to describe what
sort of a day it was on Sunday the 6th, when William rode in triumph through
the city: 'A hott but gloomy day. Ye King with all ye nobility came to town, and
heard Dr. King preach at St. Pattricks. There was great joy at ye King's
arrivall, by bonefires, etc.' As Württemberg reported, the 'Te Deum' was sung
at the Cathedral.

The triumphalism pervading Dublin was the worst kind of atmosphere in
which to reach decisions about the future conduct of the Irish war. This was
borne out by the Declaration, issued on Monday the 7th under the names of
William and Mary, at Finglas. 'We are now in so happy a prospect of our
Affairs', the joint monarchs self-righteously proclaimed, 'that We hold it
reasonable to think of Mercy, and to have Compassion upon those whom we
judge to have been seduced.'

Drafted by the Williamite Secretary of State for Ireland, Sir Robert Southwell, the Declaration was designed to divide the bulk of Irish Catholics from
their landed and aristocratic leadership. With a turn of phrase which now
appears strikingly, even shockingly, transparent, Southwell's plan was 'to invite
in all of the meaner sort . . . but not to be meddling with the landed men till it

appears into what posture they throw themselves or into what corners they retire'. He envisaged that this would 'bring in the bulk of the nation and that the rest will afterwards look the more abject'. Royal pardon would be granted only as follows:

We shall take into Our Royal Protection, all poor Labourers, Common Souldiers, Country Farmers, Plowmen, and Cottiers whatsoever: As also Citizens, Trades-men, Towns men, and Artificers, who either remain'd at home, or having fled from their dwellings, shall by the first of *August* next repair to their usual places of abode, surrendering up what *Arms* they have to such Justices of the Peace as are or shall be appointed by Us . . .

On the other hand,

For the desperate Leaders of this Rebellion, who have violated those Laws, by which this Kingdom is united and inseparably annexed to the Imperial Crown of *England*; who have called in the *French*, who have Authorized all Violences, and depredations against the Protestants, and who rejected the Gracious Pardon . . . So are We resolved to leave them to the Event of War, unless by Great and Manifest demonstrations, We shall be convinced that they deserve Our Mercy, which we shall never refuse, to those that are truly penitent.

The tone of the Declaration left little doubt that it would take a great deal of persuasion to convince William and Mary that any Jacobite landowner who chose to throw himself on their mercy was 'truly penitent'. And, even if any of James's officers were prepared to take that risk, where was the guarantee that their property would be respected? There was none. In addition, tenants of landowners 'who have been concern'd in the Rebellion against Us' were to keep hold of their rents 'until they have notice from the Commissioners of Our Revenue'.

The Williamite commentator, Story, observed that 'A great many of the *Irish* Officers complained, That this Declaration was too narrow in excluding them from any Advantage by it; and that they were obliged afterwards to stick together, as being their only safety.' Plunkett, the Jacobite observer, noted that the Declaration made most Irish officers more determined than ever to fight on, and possibly die, rather than accept such conditions. Story argued that the Declaration 'was narrower than his Majesty's Royal intentions, on purpose to comply with the *English* Proprietors of that Countrey'. In Plunkett's words, it 'was a foolish verdict' to exclude 'the estated gentlemen' from the Prince's mercy.

The Declaration failed to divide the Irish. Besides providing no guarantee for landowners, it held out no promise of religious toleration. Its vindictiveness and narrow concern to promote the interests of the new English landowners was an ominous portent. A further declaration by William, issued on 1 August, also failed to offer adequate guarantees. The Williamites' attempt to drive home their victory at the Boyne was to prove counter-productive.

III

'How to begin this letter I don't know, or how ever to render God thanks enough for his mercys,' Queen Mary wrote to William on Monday 7 July, adding that the day before she had been 'out of my senses with trouble'. 'King William having vanquished K James in Ireland,' noted Evelyn, 'there was much publique rejoicing . . . K. J. is reported gon back to France: Drogheda and Dublin surrendered: and if K. W. be returning, one may say of him as of Caesar, Veni, vidi, vici, for never was such a kingdome won in so short an Expedition.' But the celebrations were overshadowed by the threat of a French invasion. As Evelyn added, 'to alay much of this the French fleete having exceedingly beaten the Dutche fleete, & ours not daring to interpose, ride at present in our Chanell, threatning to Land, which causes an extraordinary alarme &c'.

The mood of Williamite triumphalism in Dublin received a nasty jolt when the news of Beachy Head finally reached the city on Tuesday 8 July, exactly a week after the Boyne. Württemberg reported that William 'got news of the naval battle, which greatly displeased him, as the English showed little spirit and left the Dutch in the lurch. It is to be hoped that when they get the news from Ireland they will show more vigour.'

'Here are great feares of some French shipping coming on our coasts to burn our ships,' Bellingham noted as the rumours of a naval defeat first began to circulate in Dublin. The Marquis of Carmarthen, formerly Earl of Danby, who had been appointed Lord President of the Council, wrote to William warning him of intelligence reports that the French were planning to send twenty-eight frigates to Irish waters. If de Tourville's fleet followed, they would easily outnumber Cloudesley Shovell's squadron and would become masters of the Irish Sea. William and his army would be cut off in Ireland, and the whole outlook transformed.

By the end of the week, the Williamites were again on the march, but the news from London of the defeats at Beachy Head and Fleurus caused William to change his plans and divide his army into two contingents as Story noted:

> For though His Majestie was sensible, that going with his whole Army towards Athlone, and so into Connaght, was the readiest way to reduce the *Irish*; yet having some Reasons to apprehend the *French*, after the Battel of *Flerus*, might send off Detachments from their Army; and so disturb *England*; or at least send part of their Fleet, and burn his Transport-Ships, he made haste to secure *Waterford* Haven for them, since the Bay of *Dublin* is no Place of Safety.

William himself would lead the contingent heading for the southern coast, while Lieutenant-General Douglas led the other detachment west. On 9 July, before setting out for Waterford, William appointed commissioners, including the Bishop of Meath and the Earl of Longford, to enforce the terms of his Finglas Declaration. They were empowered, as Story put it, 'to enquire into, seize, and secure all Forfeitures, to the Crown by the Generall Rebellion of the *Irish* Nation'. The victors at the Boyne were claiming the prize of legal legitimacy. They would seize the property of the vanquished and label them as rebels.

At Castledermot on Wednesday 16 July, William received a letter of nine days earlier from his ministers in London. News of the Boyne had just reached them when they wrote, but they were still deeply concerned at the danger of a French invasion. De Tourville's fleet controlled the English Channel, and they urged William to return from Ireland with at least some of his troops. He replied that he would have to stay with his army for a further week or so, but would then return to Dublin, and sail for England. He promised that he would be back in England by the end of July.

William proceeded as far south as Carrick. The Jacobite garrison at Waterford surrendered peacefully to Major-General Kirk, and was allowed to march from the town, although William steadfastly refused to concede any guarantees of estates or religious rights. The fort at Duncannon, at the entrance of the harbour – James's original point of departure for France earlier that month – also gave in without a fight. William had thus secured valuable port facilities, which would greatly assist his campaign in Munster where the Jacobites still held the ports of Cork and Kinsale.

Returning as planned to Dublin, William heard from London that Torrington had been arrested following the débâcle at Beachy Head and that several Jacobite 'Designs were discovered and prevented'. He was encouraged to learn that 'the loss at Sea was not so great as was first reported; and that the *French* had only burnt a small Village in the *West of England*, and gone off again'. The brief sortie to which Story referred was an attack by 2800 French troops on Teignmouth.

The French fleet was still moored off the Devon coast during the remainder of July and into early August. The 'danger' for William was, therefore, only 'partly over'. At the end of July, Shovell's squadron escorted 3000 infantry and 1200 cavalry back across the Irish Sea to England as reinforcements against any invasion. William's priority, however, remained a speedy conclusion to the Irish war and he 'resolved to return to the Army'. His main objective was the reduction of the main Jacobite base at Limerick by the end of the 1690 campaigning season.

De Tourville had failed to follow up his victory at Beachy Head, his attack on Teignmouth proving an utterly futile gesture. Louis XIV and Seignelay, his Minister of Marine, were furious with their Admiral. When the fleet returned to Brest in early August, de Tourville was relieved of his command. The French objective in defeating the Anglo-Dutch fleet had been to secure

Ireland for James as a base for his subsequent invasion of England and Scotland. Yet after Beachy Head, de Tourville had sent only a small detachment of
ships under d'Amfreville to Irish waters, and no attempt was made to gain
control of the Irish Sea and sever William's communications. It is unlikely that
the French would have wasted such an opportunity had ill-health not prevented Seignelay from accompanying the French fleet, as had been his intention.

PART FOUR
IRELAND BESIEGED

CHAPTER TWELVE

'STILL HAUNTING OUR ROADS'

I

On 16 July 1690, while William was at Castledermot considering his Cabinet's panicky letter about the danger of a French invasion of England, the Jacobite leaders were holding a council of war at Limerick. Tyrconnel 'was of opinion all was lost, and therefore thought convenient to make the best conditions with the enemy and surrender before it was too late'.

John Stevens, the officer in the Grand Prior's Regiment, provides a graphic first-hand account of the demoralized and depleted state of the Jacobite army which was assembling at Limerick. Most of Sunday 13 July 'was spent in building huts . . . all our tents lost the unfortunate day at the Boyne'. The officers' baggage, sent to Dublin for safe-keeping before the Boyne, had been 'much plundered by those who were appointed to preserve it, and most of what they left ransacked by our own dragoons, and even by some of our officers . . .' As a result, 'very many of us were left almost naked, not having as much as a shirt to change.'

At a review of troops on Monday the 14th by Brigadier Wauchope, the Grand Prior's Regiment was

> found to consist of 150 men with arms fixed, 50 unfixed, and almost 100 without arms. A dismal and most shameful sight, the king a fortnight before giving pay and bread to 800 men in this regiment all well armed and clothed, and now reduced to this without firing one shot at or scarce seeing the enemy.

Yet the baleful scene depicted by Stevens was merely one ingredient in the catalogue of woe recited by Tyrconnel to the Jacobite council of war. According to Plunkett, who sympathized with the Lord Deputy, Tyrconnel argued that after the Boyne,

> the king returned to France: that the French brigade was going away: that the brass money . . . was brought to no value: that there was no stores of provisions: that the province of Connaught . . . was not able to maintain the army and the vast multitudes of people entering thither from Munster, Leinster and Ulster: that Limerick was a very weak town, yet was their chief defence against the

enemy: that, if the Prince of Orange should be beaten in a pitched battle, England with the assistance of Holland, would send another army, and another after that, rather than be at the mercy of the king [James], if he should not be restored by the Irish: that the most Christian king [Louis XIV] was not in a state to send competent aids, by reason that he had so many enemies, as kept all his armies at work.

From this gloomy analysis, Tyrconnel concluded that 'while the Catholic army was entire, it was the proper time to get advantageous conditions from the Prince of Orange, who would readily grant them to secure his crown.'

William was anxious for a speedy peace, and it made sense to start talks while there was still a sizeable Irish army. Yet William's Declaration at Finglas, issued nine days earlier, scarcely suggested that he was in any mood to compromise. Rather, it smacked of a man intoxicated by recent victory and confident of a total conquest of the country.

William's hard-line stance undermined Tyrconnel's peace party. The Lord Deputy's approach was vehemently opposed by the die-hards, notably Patrick Sarsfield, the 'darling of the army'. The Irish army still held the line of the Shannon and the key ports of Cork and Kinsale in the south, and Galway in the west; they had not suffered particularly heavy losses at the Boyne; and their allies, the French, were masters of the seas. The Jacobites, however, were irrevocably split. The internal divisions, which had characterized the Jacobite campaign before the Boyne, became uncontainable in defeat. 'These animosities indeed amongst themselves', as James himself later argued, 'were come to so great a pitch, that now when the enemy gave them some respite, their whole attention was to make war upon one another.'

Tyrconnel's power quickly waned. Although nominally remaining Lord Deputy, 'yet there was not the due subordination to him, and many private cabals were held not only without his knowledge, but to oppose his authority.' Effective control rested with a group of die-hard army officers, including the Luttrells, the O'Neills and Connel, a lieutenant-colonel to Lord Slane.

Lauzun shared Tyrconnel's assessment of the Jacobite plight, but the French would not be averse to seeing the war continue, although Lauzun and his fellow officers seconded to Ireland were anxious that it should do so without their continued participation. When the die-hards in the Irish army heard that the French were planning to leave Limerick, they plotted to oust them prematurely from their quarters in the city and steal their weapons before their departure. Tyrconnel got wind of the plot and it was foiled. Meanwhile, Lauzun urged that extra ships be sent from France so that the best Irish regiments could also be transported to the Continent, as 'he would be sorry to see them go to the Prince of Orange, particularly three cavalry regiments which are excellent.'

Before the end of July, however, the Jacobites achieved a significant triumph. On Thursday 17 July, the Williamite army under Lieutenant-

General Douglas laid siege to Athlone, on the River Shannon. They met with stout resistance from the Governor, Colonel Grace, who broke the bridge across the river and withdrew to the Connaught side of the town. Jacobite reinforcements were despatched from Limerick on Wednesday the 23rd, and the same day news reached Douglas that Sarsfield was leading a force of 15,000 to relieve the town. Story reported that finally, on the evening of Thursday the 24th, Douglas

> called all the Collonels to a Council of War, where he told them the necessity of removing from the Town; for we had very little Bread all the while, and there was some reason to believe the *Irish* Army would cut off our Communication from *Dublin*.

Douglas and his troops withdrew at break of day on Friday the 25th. The Jacobites had successfully held the line of the Shannon.

Rumours swept through both armies about the state of affairs in England following Beachy Head. During the Williamite march from Athlone, Story recounted that 'we had an Account of a Conspiracy in *England* against the Queen, and that some French were landed there, having burnt some Towns on the Coast; and it was reported also that the late King [James] was landed in that Kindgom.' Yet despite the setback at Athlone, and their continued anxiety about the position in England, the Williamite commanders remained confident, arrogant even, that they would soon reduce Ireland. Thus, Württemberg wrote to the King of Denmark from Carlow on 27 July: 'There is great surprise at the obstinacy of the Irish; they are not prepared to accept amnesty and wish to try their last chance at Limerick. But the best that can be said of them is that they show more fidelity than courage.'

II

On Saturday 2 August, the French left Limerick, as Stevens reported, 'to the great satisfaction not only of the inhabitants, but of all the garrison that remained in town'. They had been dismissive of the prospects for the Jacobites, which was not the most tactful stance to adopt after their own performance at the Boyne. The French headed for Galway, 'thinking it impossible Limerick should hold out a siege, offering to lay wagers it would be taken in three days. William was a shade more generous to the Irish, reckoning their resistance would be broken within fourteen days.

William arrived at his army's camp, situated 5 miles south-east of Limerick, by the end of the first week of August. The city itself lay in a loop of the Shannon, with the Castle and old English part of Limerick situated on an island (King's Island) in the river. The old English town was linked to Irish town, lying to the south, by Ballsbridge, which crossed a branch of the Shannon. The long, stone Thomond bridge stretched across the main river, from alongside the old Castle in English town to the bank opposite, which lay to the

west in County Clare. The French regarded the old town walls as next to
useless, Lauzun allegedly claiming that 'the King of France ... would have
taken it with baked apples'. The Irish, however, no doubt recalling their
experience at Derry, seemed to regard any walled city as impregnable.

Some Jacobites were ready to accede to William's demand to surrender, but
Berwick and Sarsfield argued for resisting the attack. According to Story, the
waverers were won over by Sarsfield, who opposed the idea of surrendering
'with a great deal of Heat, telling them, that there were great Divisions and
Insurrections in *England*; that the *Dauphin* was landed there with Fifty
Thousand Men, and that the Prince of Orange would be obliged soon to draw
home his Army into *England*.' Curiously, the Williamite occupation of Sing-
land hill, to the south of Limerick, gave solace to some Irish soldiers. According to Sir Robert Southwell, the Gaelic leader Hugh Balldearg O'Donnell had
recently arrived in Limerick from Spain, and told the Jacobites that 'the
English should conquer, till they came to the well neer that hill, but from
thence forward they should be defeated, and driven out of the land.' Some of
the Irish were willing to listen to O'Donnell's claims, on account of a prophecy
that an O'Donnell with a red spot would liberate Ireland from the English
(Balldearg is Irish for 'red spot'). As Southwell added, ''Tis hard to believe,
how this dreame had obteind among the common sort.'

William had finally recovered from the injury caused by the cannon-ball,
over five weeks earlier at the Boyne. As Southwell wrote on Sunday 10 August,

> His Majestie may to-morrow leave off the plaster from his shoulder, where the
> bullet toucht him, for the skin is just now growing over. While he rode in his
> coach, it often incommoded him; but since he is returned to the Army he is
> always on horseback, and as vigerous as ever I saw him.

But, if the siege of Limerick was to succeed, William was dependent on the
arrival of a siege-train bearing eight pieces of great artillery coming from
Dublin, with powder, tools, and small bridge boats, and comprising in all about
a hundred waggons and carts.

Yet Sarsfield was set on a daring exploit to upset William's plans. He had
received details of the Williamite dispositions and the siege-train from a
French gunner who had deserted from William's camp. By Monday 11
August, the siege-train was approaching Limerick, and stopped for the night at
Ballyneety, about 8 miles to the south-east. Manus O'Brien, a local landowner,
brought word to the Williamite camp that Sarsfield, with a party of cavalry and
dragoons, had crossed the Shannon at Killaloe and was on his way to intercept
the train. At first O'Brien's warning went unheeded, but eventually word of it
reached William. It was not until midnight, however, that a Williamite detachment set out to reinforce the siege-train's guard, since its 'Guard under Captain Poultney were but 80 troopers, and 12 fusileers'.

Before the reinforcements had gone very far, they saw 'a great Light in the

Air and heard a strange rumbling Noise'. Sarsfield had achieved a spectacular coup. The siege-train was within 10 miles of William's camp, and its escort had thought themselves safe. Earlier that night, they 'turned out their horses into the fields, and went to rest, thinking all secure'. But, as Southwell explained, they were a sitting target: 'Colonel Sarsfield's comeing at the head of 500 chosen Horse and 60 Dragoons, on Tuesday 12th at two in the morning fell suddenly on our convoy, and being presently masters of all, he burn't and destroy'd whatever the time would lett him.' Tradition has it that Sarsfield had been guided by the legendary Galloping Hogan, a guerrilla-style Irish resistance fighter who knew the terrain intimately. The Jacobites killed about sixty people, including guards, waggoners and some locals, and wrought havoc with the train.

The sensational news quickly reached the Williamite camp, as the Rev. Davies recounted:

> About three in the morning we were all awakened by the firing of two great cannon near us, which made our house shake and all within startle, and about an hour after were alarmed by a man that fled to us almost naked, who assured us that the enemy had fallen upon us, taken all our cannon, ammunition, and money, and cut off the guard, being a squadron of horse and a few foot . . .

Sarsfield told a Williamite officer held captive during the raid that 'if he had not succeeded in that Enterprise, he had then gone to *France*.' The enterprise was devastating. Sarsfield's party had 'cut holes' in the boats rather than blow them up, 'but all the powder was blown up, the match and instruments of the guns, and waggons of corn, were all burned, and great pieces of each blown over the fields round about . . .' It was an Irish success which has entered the island's literature. In Ó Bruadair's words:

> He left not a bomb or a copper pontoon
> In Baile an Fhaoitigh that he did not disperse
> Like the smoke of a candle up into the sky.

III

As the siege of Limerick dragged on, William displayed his customary disregard for his personal safety. His camp was so close to the Jacobite guns 'that the bullets fall into it, and do much mischief, even close to the King's tent'. When William chose a new site, it was still 'not out of reach of the bullets'. When he went to inspect a weak point in the city walls, Southwell worried that 'onely Count Schomberg and an other [were] with him, yett by a musket bullet, Count Schomberg's horse was shott in the thigh.' A few days later, William had another 'narrow escape' when he was riding 'towards Cromwell fort' and would have been hit by a shot from a twenty-four pounder, but at the crucial moment someone stopped him for a word. According to Story, the cannon-ball

'would have struck His Majesty and Horse too, all to pieces, if his usual good
Angel had not defended him'.

'We hear now at night that Sarsfield is still haunting our roads,' Southwell
reported, 'soe that out bread carts being in danger, we are sending out a fresh
party to find him out.' Sarsfield's guerrilla tactics were paying handsome
dividends for the Irish. By Thursday 14 August, William was seeking further
assistance from the Cabinet in London, mindful that the French were still at
Galway and might yet return to Limerick: 'There is nothing we should more
approve then to see a good squadron of our shipps in the Shanon, under Sir
Cloudsly Shovell, or any other fit commander . . .' Lack of pay was also causing ill-discipline among the Williamite troops, as Southwell lamented: 'Our
Army for want of pay, make strange destruction round us, there being no
distinction between Protestant and Papist, as to plunder and ill usage.'

When the weather changed towards the end of the month, it proved to be
the last straw for William. Southwell had observed in the middle of August that
'The rivers in this country have not been soe low in the memory of man.'
Referring to 'the unaccustomed good weather we have had', Southwell added,
'We heartily pray it may not leave us, till we have done this work.' The Irish
Secretary was to be bitterly disappointed. A week later, the long heat-wave of
the summer of 1690 finally ended. On the morning of Monday 25 August, 'it
began to pour down at such a furious rate that some of the trenches have been
two foot deep.' Southwell hoped that the weather might soon improve again,
for he fully realized the significance of Limerick, and the implications if the
siege should fail: 'Tis this success must crown all we have hitherto done, and
we should have a very long after game to play without it.'

Morale among the Williamites became as downcast as the weather, Southwell finding: 'this one days fierce raine a strange damp as to our successe
among many of the chiefe officers, and that our army must draw off or be
ruined if the raine should hold; nay that it would be a great taske in these
deepe wayes to gett off our cannon.' Even William himself was affected.
Southwell found him considering the best route for his return to England:

> Being this evening alone with his Majesty he asked me in his darke and reserved
> way what men of warr were now at Waterford. I told him none was there now
> but the *Jersey* that had newly brought in the money. He then asked me the
> difference of the portage from Dublin to Chester, and from Waterford to
> Bristoll. And after a while, he sayd he therefore asked, as thinking to returne to
> England by this way.

Two days later, on Wednesday the 27th, the Williamites made a desperate
last bid to storm the city. They had demolished 'one of the towers, and made a
breach in the wall close by it'. Story related from the Williamite side that the
raiding party had 'entred the Breach pell-mell . . . and above half the Earl of
Drogheda's Granadeers and some others were actually in the Town.' Within

the city, Stevens at first 'thought they had been our guards retiring . . . they being in all red coats, till we discovered the green boughs in their hats which was the mark of distinction worn by the rebels, whereas ours was white paper'.

According to Colonel Munchgaar, commander of the Williamite Prince Frederick's Regiment, 'the Irish ran from the counterscarp, and something good could have been accomplished had the proper dispositions been made beforehand.' The Irish, however, soon fought back, 'and did us great damage from the walls with grenades, stones and muskets as well as their cannon which flanked on both sides.' Story reported that the Williamites were assailed by 'Bullets, Stones, (broken Bottles, from the very Women, who boldly stood in the Breach, and were nearer our Men than their own)'. After three hours, during which 'The action continued hot and dubious,' the Williamites were eventually forced to withdraw, with heavy losses, estimated by the Jacobite Stevens as high as 3000, and by the Williamite Story as 500 killed 'on the spot' and a further 1000 injured.

On Friday the 29th, the Williamites finally raised the siege, bequeathing an heroic legend to Irish history and subsequently securing a curious place in mid-eighteenth-century English literature. Laurence Sterne's *Tristram Shandy*, in which the character Uncle Toby habitually whistles 'Lillibthe', includes a description of the siege by Corporal Trim, which appears to have been taken from a Williamite veteran:

> We were scarce able to crawl out of our tents at the time the siege of Limerick was raised . . . and had it not been for the quantity of brandy we set fire to every night, and the claret and cinnamon and geneva with which we plied ourselves, we had both left our lives in the trenches . . .[22]

The weather was cited by Bellingham as the reason for ending the siege: 'the raines falling so heavily these 2 dayes past and the trenches so full of water, it was thought fitter to raise ye seige.' In the grisly claim and counter-claim which followed, Stevens wrote of the 'Williamite dead lying everywhere unburied'. Crows and ravens, 'which seemed to have resorted from all parts of the country', grew 'excessively fat' from feeding on the corpses. Story, the Williamite, alleged that the Jacobites dug up 'most of our dead Officers and Soldiers, only to get their Shirts and Shrouds'.

'The ill-success at Limerick', conceded the Williamite War Secretary in Ireland, Dr George Clarke,

> is well known to be owing to the want of ammunition, occasioned by Sarsfield's falling upon the artillery, etc., at Cullen, as it was coming up to the siege, so that after a fruitless attack of the breach, which we had not powder or shot to make larger, the King left the army and embarked at Duncannon for England.

William had attacked Limerick rather than Cork and Kinsale, which would have been easier targets, because he wanted to force the settlement by the end of the summer. But he had failed, and now felt that he could no longer delay his return to London.

The French troops in Ireland sailed from Galway exactly a week after William had left Duncannon. Also aboard d'Amfreville's fleet of around thirty ships was Tyrconnel, anxious to explain his position to James, accompanied by the Earl of Abercorn and Wauchope. D'Amfreville was later joined by other French squadrons, and a fleet of forty large ships entered Brest at the end of September.

It struck many as odd, in Ireland, Britain and France, that Lauzun and the French troops left immediately after the Jacobites had scored a signal success at Limerick. Story, who had withdrawn eastwards to Tipperary with other Williamites, was puzzled:

> that the *French* shou'd absolutely quit *Ireland*, at a time when we had raised our Siege, which might have given them hopes of re-gaining the next Year what they lost this; at least, to defend the Province of *Connaught* against us, and so protract the War beyond what they cou'd have hoped for.

Story later heard that James had appeared 'very unexpectedly' in France as the great victories of Fleurus and Beachy Head were being celebrated, and 'to palliate matters as to himself, he laid all the blame on the *Irish*, that they would not fight.' This allegedly led Louis to conclude that 'all was lost in that Kingdom', and ordered Lauzun 'to make the best of bad Market, and to come off for *France* as well as he could, with all his Men'. Lauzun initially delayed his departure from Galway so as not to discourage the Irish defending Limerick, but no countermand was received from Louis, and Lauzun was determined not to stay in Ireland any longer.

The Duke of Berwick assumed command of the Jacobites in Tyrconnel's absence. Sarsfield was promoted to the military council, allegedly being given the last seat to placate the Irish army. Limerick had revived Jacobite spirits and forced the peace party to eat their words, but the Irish war remained a battle over the terms of a settlement. Writing from the Williamite camp at Tipperary on 9 September, Württemberg reported to the King of Denmark:

> The state of Ireland is such that if an amnesty could be given to the leading people the war would soon come to an end. But the amnesty is limited to the poor common soldiers, as the English were very eager for the confiscation of the Catholics' estates. For the Irish say openly 'we are fighting not for King James, nor for the Popish religion, but for our estates'.

CHAPTER THIRTEEN

THE WINTER WAR

I

In Dublin, on Monday 15 September 1690, Viscount Sydney and Thomas Coningsby were sworn in as the new Lords Justices of Ireland, taking 'the usual Oaths of Chief Governors of the Kingdom, before the Comissioners of the Great Seal, with the accustomed Formalities'. The ceremony was the cause for celebration, Story describing 'the People by their Bonefires, and other signs of Joy, expressing their Satisfaction afor the restoring of Civil Government'. Later that autumn began a tradition which was to remain an annual feature of life in the Irish capital for more than a century:

> The Fourth of November, being His Majesties Birth-day, was observed with all the Splendour that the Place could afford, all the Town Militia were drawn out, being 2500 Foot, two Troops of Horse, and two of Dragoons, all well Cloathed and Armed; and at night the Lord Justices made an Entertainment for the most Considerable Persons in and about the Town.

Yet the country was still divided by war. Although the French had sailed from Galway, the Jacobites still held the line of the Shannon, and controlled not only the whole of Connaught but also parts of Munster, including Limerick, the strategic ports of Cork and Kinsale, and Kerry, regarded as the 'granary of Limerick'. The Williamites held Leinster and Ulster, but after raising the siege at Limerick they retreated from the Shannon, leaving a desolate no-man's land between the two front lines.

William had returned to London by early September, but his failure to take Limerick threatened to tie his troops down in Ireland for a further campaigning season. This setback was the direct consequence of a mistaken strategy after his victory at the Boyne. The insistence on attempting to humiliate the Irish ensured that the views of the die-hard Jacobites prevailed. Their determination was vindicated at Limerick, and greatly improved their prospects of securing better terms.

William still hoped to force an end to the Irish war before the 1691 campaigning season, so that he would be free to concentrate his energies and

English resources on the Continent. Although the weather had deteriorated and the nights were drawing in, he was determined to tighten his grip on the rest of the island outside Limerick and Connaught. At the same time, the Williamites would put out feelers to the Jacobites and signal their readiness to bargain. Whether the gap between the two sides was yet bridgeable was another matter.

The military pressure was soon intensified. In August, shortly after Tourville's French fleet had left the Devon coast, William approved a daring plan by the Earl of Marlborough, commander-in-chief of the English army, to seize Cork and Kinsale.[23] These key ports provided the Jacobite life-lines to France. After delays caused by bad weather, Marlborough sailed from Portsmouth with a fleet of over eighty ships and 5000 troops in mid-September, two days after the swearing in of the new Williamite Lords Justices in Dublin.

General Solms was appointed overall commander of the army in William's place, with instructions to support Marlborough's campaign and keep the Jacobites away from the south Munster coast. But before Marlborough reached Irish waters Solms had also left the country and was replaced by another Dutchman, General Ginkel. Danish troops under Major-General Tettau and Danish, Dutch and Huguenot cavalry under Major-General Scravemoer were sent to the Blackwater and the town of Mallow, north of Cork. Württemberg also joined in the exercise to support the assault on the Jacobite ports.

Jacobite strategy in the autumn of 1690 made little sense. No effective measures were taken to counter the build-up of Williamite troops in Munster. Although their lines of communication from Limerick to the southern ports were vital, the Williamites were allowed to seize Kilmallock, to the south of Limerick. Sarsfield, meanwhile, had busied himself besieging Birr Castle in the distant midlands, but was eventually forced to retreat.

Marlborough's assault-force landed at Passage West, on the Lee estuary, 7 miles downstream from Cork, on Tuesday 23 September. The next day, his troops marched on the city. Württemberg's presence as a commander of the support troops was a potential problem, as he held senior rank to Marlborough but was not commissioned in the English army. Any problems of *amour propre* were overcome when Marlborough and Württemberg agreed to share the command of the operation by alternating the days on which each officer took overall charge.

At Cork, the Jacobite garrison of 4500 men was under the command of Colonel Roger MacElligott. He had a chequered past, having led one of the English regiments in the service of William of Orange, and later serving in the garrison at Portsmouth for James in 1688. After being interned by William on the Isle of Wight, he had fled to France, returning to Ireland with James in March 1689. Berwick urged MacElligott to withdraw and burn Cork, rather than risk losing both the port and so many soldiers. MacElligott, however, was determined to resist the Williamite onslaught at virtually any cost.

As a walled city built on an island in the Lee, Cork would have been a formidable fortress, but it was dominated by hills on both the north and south. On Thursday the 25th, MacElligott's guards abandoned their outposts over-looking the city on Cat Hill, high above the southern banks of the Lee, and near Shandon Castle to the north. The Williamites were in a commanding position and began bombarding the city on Friday the 26th.

Negotiations began the following day, but proved inconclusive. Mortar bombs and heavy gunfire from batteries of 18-24- and 36-pounders brought from Waterford continued to rain down on the city and 'made a considerable Breach'. In the ensuing battle, the Duke of Grafton, a captain in Marlborough's fleet, was mortally wounded, dying a few days later. An illegiti-mate son of Charles II, Grafton was deeply mourned by Williamites.

MacElligott realized that he could not hold out and sought terms. He sur-rendered on condition that his troops in the garrison would be treated as prisoners of war, that there should be 'no prejudice done to the officers, soldiers or inhabitants', and that Marlborough agreed to seek clemency for them from William. Plunkett was disparaging about MacElligott's being 'forced to yield the town, and the garrison, to be prisoners of war, for want of powder, which the enemy knew the day before – a strange neglect in the business of highest consequence.'

Five days after landing at Passage West, the Williamites entered the city. They were again unable to control their troops, the Rev. Davies reporting that,

> Many seamen and other loose persons entered the city through the breach and other places and plundered many houses, especially of papists. As soon as the bridges could be mended, the Earl of Marlborough and Major-General Scravemoer entered and took much pains to preserve the city from further damage ... In the afternoon all the papists were ordered by proclamation on pain of death to repair to the East Marsh, where all that had been under arms were secured and after that put under guard, the officers in the County Court House and the rest in the churches and other places.

Cork was denied the military courtesy shown by the Williamites at Drogheda and Waterford, where the Jacobite garrisons were allowed to march away. The prisoners suffered a terrible fate. Shortages of supplies and malad-ministration caused many deaths from starvation and sickness. MacElligott and the Earls of Clancarty and Tyrone were transported to the Tower of London. Tyrone soon died. Clancarty escaped and made for France, but his 135,000-acre Irish estate was confiscated. MacElligott languished in the Tower till 1697, when he was eventually set free and entered the French service.

The Jacobites suffered a double calamity by losing Cork. Not only was it the largest port on the south coast and the country's second city, its garrison was now unable to reinforce Kinsale. The commander at Kinsale, Sir Edward

Scott, who like MacElligott had also served in the Portsmouth garrison, had sent two regiments to Cork. As a result, he was left with fewer than 2000 troops to hold the two forts guarding the entrance to Kinsale harbour. The Jacobites would have been better served concentrating their defence at Kinsale, as it was easier to defend and had more ammunition.

Later on the afternoon of Monday 29 September, as Story reported:

> a Party of about Five hundred Horse were sent under Brigadier *Villars* to inspect *Kingsale*; he sent a Trumpeter at his Approach to summon the Town, but the Governor threatened to hang him up for bringing such a Message, and then set fire to the Town, and retreated to the Old fort.

The fire defiantly started by Scott was put out by the Williamite horse, and the town subsequently provided Marlborough's assault-force with shelter against the weather.

Just three days after the capture of Cork, the main Williamite force encamped beyond the impressive walls of the recently built Charles fort near Kinsale. Standing high above the eastern shore of the harbour, it would remain unassailable until the Williamites could bring their heavy guns to bear on its walls. Stormy autumn weather meant that these had to be transported laboriously by land, instead of being brought round the coast. In the meantime, Major-General Tettau launched an assault across the harbour, capturing the smaller and older James fort on the opposite, western shore.

It was not until Sunday 12 October, ten days after the Williamites' arrival, that their first gun battery started firing. After a further three days of increasingly heavy bombardment, with the fort's outer wall breached and the Williamites ready to invade, Scott finally sought terms. His wife, a MacCarthy, left the fort in some style, being driven in her coach through the breach in the wall.

When the Williamites took possession of Charles fort, they:

> received a very considerable Magazine, and great plenty of all sorts of Provisions, sufficient to have supported a thousand Men for a Year; there were 1000 Barrels of Wheat, 1000 Barrels of Beef, Forty Tuns of Claret, a great quantity of Sack, Brandy, and strong Beer.

During the siege of Kinsale, Marlborough and Württemberg had been in perpetual fear that Sarsfield would attack from the north. The Williamites were exposed to such a challenge, and would almost certainly have been forced to raise the siege. Yet no Jacobite relief force appeared, Berwick later claiming that he had set out from Limerick with 8000 troops but turned back when confronted by a stronger Williamite contingent near Kilmallock.

The Jacobites had paid a high price for neglecting their southern ports. They had scored a signal success by forcing back the Williamites from Limerick and thus maintaining their hold on the line of the Shannon. Yet within six weeks they had lost their most direct supply-lines to France and seriously undermined their ability to withstand any further siege of Limerick.

Their allies were also culpable, as Story acknowledged:

> this some have look'd upon as one of the greatest blemishes in the *French* Politicks, that they should neglect the Fortifying of *Kinsale*, one of the best and securest Harbours in the World; and by keeping of which, they might have ruined our Western Trade especially, and yet endeavour to Fortifie *Limerick*, an Inland Town, of no use to them.

II

The war had become one of attrition. Conditions were appalling. The wretched scene in western Ireland was surveyed in a letter written by the Marquis d'Albeville to James in late October, but intercepted by the Williamites:

> The whole contrey that remaynes yett to us is lay'd wast, without village or house, no victuals to be had in the contrey anywhere, and but very little in the cities, where all the houses, especially here at Lymerick, are pull'd down by the souldiers, burning and selling the timber, so as that they want now themselves house roome, and this hitherto don in the face of the Governor and government. All plowing is abandoned; the officers and souldiers haveing seiz'd upon the poor people's garrons [horses], robbing and takeing away the very roots they have for their liveliehood, souldiers rob one another, and the very shoes of one another's horses; whole houses pulled down to gett a little iron . . . The desolation is great and general; our conduct as bad as can be; no discipline, no obedience in officers or souldiers; no vigorous resolution in military or civil affairs.

The Marquis had sought to assure James that despite the chaos, 'his [d'Albeville's] endeavours were not useless' in preventing people from submitting to William, or as he put it, preserving them 'from the thoughts of protections from the Usurper'. It was hardly a ringing declaration of confidence.

Prominent among the Jacobites prepared to countenance the thought 'of protections from the Usurper' were the so-called 'new interest' Irish. In many cases they were merchants and professional men, who had bought land since the 1660s under the terms of the Cromwellian land settlement, as modified by Charles II. Some Catholics had also recovered at least part of their land under Charles II's modest reforms. In Galway, Catholics still owned over 50 per cent of the land and significant number of 'new interest' Irish were among the county's landowners.

The 'new interest' Irish were typified by men like the judge Denis Daly, a Galway man who had been among James's strongest supporters against repeal of the land settlement in the 1689 Jacobite Irish Parliament. Now, they supported a settlement with William. O'Kelly, the hard-line Jacobite commentator, was scathing of the 'new interest', 'so called because they had purchased from usurpers the inheritance of their own countrymen . . .', and who were prepared to submit to William because they put 'their private gain before the general interest of religion and country'.

On the Williamite side, the failure to conclude the war by the autumn of 1690 increased the pressures to offer more favourable terms. After the setback at Limerick, morale in the army was low. As the Danish Williamite, Colonel Munchgaar, wrote in mid-September,

> We went into the field without money, and we go into quarters now just the same way. Recently we got 14 days pay and we owed nearly three months. Sometimes the common soldiers have been three or four days without bread, and the men now know the difference between Denmark and other countries; most of them wish they were on the way home.

The European perspective was an important ingredient in the Williamite peace party. It was not simply a matter of demoralized soldiers wanting to return home. There was alarm at French successes during the 1690 campaign on the Continent. Württemberg, the German commander of the Danish force, observed that 'a stroke of the pen could end the war in Ireland, and if the king [William] wishes to help his allies he will give it.' Among the Williamite high command, the Dutch contingent, Ginkel in Ireland and Bentinck in England, were keen to see an early end to the Irish war and favoured offering concessions to the Jacobite Irish landowners.

In late September 1690, Württemberg reported that feelers had been put out to assess Jacobite opinion through an intermediary, a Catholic barrister named John O'Grady:

> The Catholic gentleman who Lt. Gen. Ginkel had sent to Galway has returned and has produced a power of attorney from the government that King James left behind . . . [who] have declared that if aid from France (with which they are being cajoled) does not arrive soon they intend to lay down their arms . . . on condition that they retain their estates and the exercise of their religion as in King Charles's time.

The soundings appeared to suggest a readiness to consider surprisingly modest terms.

Despite the limited Catholic demands and notwithstanding William's desire to see an end to the Irish war, there were countervailing pressures which militated against an early settlement. The major obstacle was land. The Williamites expected to appropriate substantial acreages from the defeated Jacobites. William himself wanted to confiscate sufficient property to meet his own demands and distribute land to his supporters. He would also face demands from the Irish Protestants for land as compensation for the hardships they claimed to have suffered under Tyrconnel's rule.

During the winter of 1690–1, the presumed spoils of the Irish war were already being fought over by the English Crown and Parliament. William claimed that he had the right to distribute the confiscated lands as he saw fit. Parliament disagreed, arguing that the land should be sold and the revenue used to cut the taxes being levied to finance the Continental campaign. English

MPs were arguing that they had the right to determine the disposal of state assets, which, in this case, had recently been expropriated from the Catholic Irish. The highest, Protestant bidders would inevitably be the main beneficiaries.

But there was still a long way to go before any peace settlement could be agreed. As Württemberg's contact with a Jacobite officer well illustrated, Irish mistrust of the English remained a formidable barrier between the two sides. The German Duke knew Colonel Thomas Butler of Kilcash from the latter's days in Hungary, and wrote to him about the issues of religion and employment. Butler responded that he and his fellow officers did not doubt William's good intentions, but 'were unable to endure the yoke of the English, who after his death will not fail to break their word, so hostile are they to the nation'.

In a further attempt to gauge Jacobite Irish interest in a settlement, Ginkel, the Williamite commander-in-chief, was authorized to issue a further Declaration on 4 February 1691. According to Württemberg, this pledged that 'all who still adhere to King James and who submit will enjoy their estates again, and that the officers will get half pay until they are actually employed'. But it cut no ice. It lacked authority because it was issued under Ginkel's name, not William's.

The gap between the two sides was unbridgeable. While the Williamites were arguing how to apportion the confiscated acres, the majority of Jacobites still sought restoration of the lands they had lost forty years earlier. The Irish wanted the repeal of the Cromwellian land settlement, not its extension.

At Sarsfield's instigation, Berwick ordered the arrest of three leading members of the peace party, Alexander MacDonnell, the Governor of Galway, Lord Riverston (formerly Thomas Nugent), the Jacobite Secretary of State, the Judge Daly. Any hopes that the Jacobites might be willing to discuss terms were dashed. It seemed that an end to war would have to come through military means, not by negotiation.

III

One of the myths of the war is that the fighting died down during the autumn and winter of 1690–1.[24] In reality, there was little let-up. Marlborough had returned to England by the end of October, but the Williamites were keen to add to their strategic victories at Cork and Kinsale. In Munster, they moved on Kerry, and in the midlands attempted crossings of the Shannon at Jamestown and Lanesborough.

On the Jacobite side, Sarsfield, mounted a vigorous defence of the Shannon and succeeded in making incursions into the midlands. The rapparees, guerrilla-like bands of Irish resistance fighters operating throughout the countryside and successors to the earlier 'tories', constantly harried the Williamites. Writing to Mountcashel in France, in February 1691, Sarsfield claimed that Tettau's invasion of County Kerry was frustrated because 'Colonel Sheldon burnt the houses and the forage for twenty miles around, so

that the enemy was obliged to retreat without having accomplished anything.'
Yet this seemed to have been a pyrrhic victory, since Sarsfield was obliged to
concede in a further letter that shortage of forage was a serious worry for the
summer campaign.

In the midlands, the Williamite attack on the Shannon crossings at
Jamestown and Lanesborough were repulsed. The Jacobite positions to the
east of the river were not only maintained, but extended. As Sarsfield reported,

> we have preserved our quarters on the side of the Shannon in the county West-
> meath, the King's county and around Nenagh, for not having succeeded in their
> attempt on the passages of the Shannon, they hoped at least to oblige all the
> troops we had on the other side of the river to cross to this side, in order to
> starve us, but we had secured all the passages so well that their plans have been
> without effect, and, on the contrary, we have extended our boundaries.

The Williamite commanders were criticized for their failures and were subsequently recalled from service in Ireland, Lieutenant-General Douglas and
Major-General Kirk were transferred to Flanders, and Sir John Lanier
returned to England. In their place, Hugh Mackay, who had crushed the
Jacobite revolt in Scotland, and Thomas Talmash were sent to Ireland.

Persistent attacks by the rapparees were an additional burden for the Williamites, even in those provinces under their control. Story described how the
rapparees concealed themselves so effectively in the countryside that 'you may
as soon find a hare as one of them.' In January, following an attempt by a party
of rapparees to steal fifty horses, Colonel Munchgaar at Waterford wrote that
'They give no quarter to English Protestants, but they spare the Danes, Dutch
and French,' and cited an incident where the rapparees had spurned a Protestant Lord Constable's offer of £100 to be spared, but set free a Danish trooper
taken at the same time. The *Dublin Intelligence* carried a sickening account of
the mutilation inflicted on a Williamite soldier, and reported the frequent
killings of rapparees by the Williamite troops. Sarsfield attested to the rapparees' contribution to the Jacobite cause when he again wrote to Mountcashel
in March:

> Our mountaineers [rapparees] take horses from them [the Williamites] every
> day, and if we had a little money to reward them, our cavalry would be very well
> mounted at the enemy's expense . . . We have already had more than a thousand
> this winter, and they brought me thirty seven from Lanier's quarters, of which
> twenty two were out of his stable.

Throughout the winter, however, the feuding factions in the Jacobite
leadership were still at loggerheads. A delegation of Sarsfield's supporters,
consisting of Henry and Simon Luttrell, Nicholas Purcell and Peter Creagh,
Catholic Bishop of Cork, followed Tyrconnel to France and lobbied James
against allowing him to resume overall command in Ireland. The King gave
them a hearing, but they had been delayed by bad weather, and by the time

they arrived Tyrconnel was already on his way back to Ireland, having been promoted to the rank of Lord Lieutenant of Ireland by James and awarded the Knighthood of the Garter, it being reported that he had the late Duke of Grafton's blue garter.

Tyrconnel had turned the reports of the Williamite peace overtures to his advantage, winning assurances of further French help, 'lest the despair induced [the Jacobites] to accept the offers of the prince of Orange'. In response to lobbying by the hard-liners, James also accepted that a French general should be sent to Ireland for the 1691 campaign season. On Tyrconnel's return to Ireland, Berwick left for France. As a result, Tyrconnel assumed overall command of both civil and military policy. But he was still unable to placate the majority of die-hards, despite having returned from France with an earldom for their leader – James had elevated Sarsfield to the peerage as the Earl of Lucan.

In early 1691, the French fleet delivered personnel and supplies to the west coast of Ireland in two stages. Tyrconnel had arrived at the Shannon on 10 January, aboard a frigate escorted by four French warships, and accompanied by Sir Richard Nagle and Sir Stephen Rice, and the French officers, Fumeron and Noblesse. On 25 January, more French officers and engineers arrived at Galway aboard the second complement of ships. The combined convoy delivered arms, grain, flour, iron, steel, rope, harness, tools, back-baskets, straps, sacks, shirts, powder, match and flint.

The French engineers were soon employed strengthening the Jacobite positions, notably Limerick, where the work continued 'daily, not excepting Sundays from the middle of February till the 20th of April'. According to Stevens,

> The soldiers were promised three pence, ensigns fifteen pence, lieutenants twenty pence, captains half a crown a day in silver for their work, that is the soldiers to work and officers to inspect them, which made all willing to undertake the task, having no other pay and being in such want.

After the first three weeks, however, these wages were deferred. When they were eventually paid six weeks later, there were wage cuts, Stevens recording 'that the officer's pay falling so short I refused to follow the work any longer'.

Invaluable though the new-year supplies were, the Jacobites would soon need further assistance. As Sarsfield wrote to Mountcashel in March 1691, the Jacobites 'shall have this summer a more numerous army and better soldiers than those who were at the river Boyne', including as many cavalry and dragoons,

> provided they send us from France enough oats to keep them before the end of spring, for by then our forage will be consumed. We have not much in truth, this country we hold producing hardly any grain. That is the greatest difficulty we shall have to surmount.

The safe arrival of French supplies in Ireland angered William. It was a further setback to his hopes of bringing an early end to the war. His frustration was expressed by the Earl of Nottingham, who was accompanying William in the Netherlands:

> his Majesty observ'd with some resentment that those shipps might easiely have been intercepted, had his orders bin pursued for some men of warre to cruise off of the coast of Ireland, which his Majesty thinks proper to be done still, because possibly some other succours may be sent thither from France.

The same day, the Marquis of Carmarthen was writing from Whitehall to the Hague 'in great anxiety for the businesse of Ireland, upon which (whatever may bee thought to the contrary) all other things as to England will depend'. Carmarthen stressed the importance of Ireland: 'if the affaires of Ireland should go backwards (or indeed but stand still) I appeale to your lordship how much an English Parliament will valeur a towne or 2 taken or a battle gained elswhere.' Nottingham, replying from the Hague, endorsed these sentiments: 'I do entirely agree with your lordship that scarce any advantage against the enemy abroad will be of much use to the K[ing] as the reduction of Ireland . . .'

CHAPTER FOURTEEN

BATTLING ACROSS THE SHANNON

I

During the first half of 1691, the Williamites continued to find it a great deal easier to wish the ends in Ireland than will the means. Delays in the preparations for the coming campaign created a chorus of complaint in England. Political pressure for an early end to the Irish war increased with the news of the French capture of Mons in the southern Netherlands. This gave the Irish at Limerick cause to celebrate, as Stevens noted: 'on the 19th [April] Te Deum was sung in the church of St. Mary being the cathedral. The cannon was also three times discharged, and as many volleys of small shot, and there were bonfires and other demonstrations of joy.'

English disquiet was further stirred by the renewed failure to blockade Ireland, since the fleet was busily engaged at the eastern end of the English Channel securing William's crossings to and from the Continent and guarding the London trade. At Limerick, on 9 May, Stevens reported that there was 'arrived in the river Shannon a French squadron of men-of-war, having sent some ships to Galway, and about noon landed the French general M. St. Ruth, who was received with real demonstrations of joy'. As St Ruth landed on the Limerick quay, 'he was saluted by a discharge of the artillery from the Castle.' Plunkett added that 'In his [St Ruth's] proceeding he found the soldiery of the town ranged on each side of the street. The Viceroy [Tyrconnel] came to meet him a hundred paces from his palace and gave him the *bien-venu* into Ireland and then brought him to dinner.' The people of Limerick again found reason to sing the 'Te Deum', for 'it was like the gaining of a victory to people in so great distress'.

Williamite propaganda reported that St Ruth's arrival 'was lookt upon like the pouring of brandy down the throat of a dying man'. Parker, the Williamite Captain, observed caustically that St Ruth 'brought with him a small matter of money, and a great many fine promises; but no men, which yet their King had faithfully promised them'. In fact, there had been no promise that the French army would return, but the cargo aboard Nesmond's fleet of twenty-five warships, five frigates, two fireships and fifty-one transports demonstrated that the

French were still committed to prolonging the Irish war. Landing with St Ruth were:

146 officers, 150 cadets, 300 English and Scots, 24 surgeons, 180 masons, 2 bombardiers, 18 cannoniers, 800 horses, 19 pieces of cannon, 12,000 horse shoes, 6,000 bridles and saddles, 16,000 muskets; uniforms, stocking and shoes for 16,000 men, some lead and balls, and a large supply of biscuit.

Charles Chalmont, Marquis de St Ruth, 'being an old experienced Officer', had been posted to Ireland 'by the approbation of King James'. St Ruth had recently formed a favourable opinion of Irish soldiers, a contemporary commentator noting the previous September, 'St.-Ruth reports that in the late battle in Savoy the Irish troops had done wonders.' The respect was reciprocated, Mountcashel's Brigade thinking highly of St Ruth. He also brought with him a ruthless reputation, and the nickname *le missionaire botté* (the missionary in top boots) for his part in the persecution of the Huguenots five years earlier.

St Ruth, however, was hindered by not speaking English. Berwick, who by that stage had returned to France, regarded him as 'by nature very vain'. Nor were matters helped by Tyrconnel's attempt to combine civil and military command. St Ruth was unimpressed with what he found in Ireland. The defences at the town of Athlone, the main Jacobite stronghold on the Shannon and the key to Connaught, were poorly prepared, and he was unable to assemble the Irish army until the latter part of June.

Before the summer's campaign began, the Williamites had planned a further attempt to achieve a negotiated settlement. Ginkel consulted Lords Justices Porter and Coningsby in Dublin, and a draft statement was sent to England for approval.[25] The draft restricted the terms to those Jacobites still in arms, who were to be offered the restoration of their estates, notwithstanding any attainders, and permission to exercise their religion as in a particular year of Charles II's reign (the precise year was left blank). It was realized within the Williamite leadership in Ireland that Protestant opinion would regard the terms as too lenient to the Catholics. Porter wrote to Nottingham, the Secretary of State in London: 'The English here [in Ireland] will be offended that the Irish are not quite beggared, and what the house of Commons will say when they see those lands gone which they designed for the payment of the army you can better judge than I.' Despite his own desire to see peace in Ireland, William was unhappy with the leniency of the terms. He insisted on a modified and less generous offer, which was eventually published during the summer.

By May 1691, delays in the Williamite preparations for the new campaigning season were finally at an end. According to Captain Parker, 'General Ginkle assembled the army near Mullingar, which was computed to be about 23000. The Irish army was assembling at the same time on the other side the Shannon, near Athlone, and was esteemed to be much about our number.'

The Williamite artillery train was at last on its way to Mullingar from Dublin, 'being such an one as never had been seen before in that Kingdom'.

On Saturday 6 June, the Williamites marched from their camp at Mullingar, heading for Ballymore, lying about halfway towards Athlone. Sarsfield had established the fort at Ballymore as an advance position to guard against renewed attacks on the Shannon crossing at Athlone and provide a base for Jacobite operations on the eastern shore of the Shannon. The old fort of Ballymore was positioned on a piece of land jutting out into a lough, Sarsfield regarding it as virtually impregnable. According to the Williamite Parker, 'This place the enemy had fortified, and had posted about 1000 men in it.' Much to Sarsfield's chagrin, however, Ulick Bourke, the officer in command at Ballymore, surrendered within a couple of days. Story, the Williamite commentator, thought 'it seemed very inaccountable to most People, that the Enemy neither endeavoured to relive or quit this place, since they lost in it above a Regiment of their best Men.' The garrison spent the rest of the war imprisoned on Lambay Island, off the County Dublin coast, to the north of Howth Head.

Ginkel, however, failed to exploit the element of surprise in his easy victory at Ballymore. Instead of pressing on to Athlone and arriving there well before St Ruth could muster the Irish army, he delayed for a further ten days. He was waiting for pontoons which were being transported from Dublin, and which he mistakenly thought essential for crossing the Shannon. Eventually, on the 19th, the Williamites moved towards Athlone, and were joined by Württemberg and his Danish force. The troops had been assembled by him at Cashel, County Tipperary, from their winter quarters in south-east Ireland.

As the combined force of around 20,000 Williamites converged on Athlone, they found that the eastern banks of the Shannon bore the 'miserable effect of war . . . in a very melancholy manner'. Parker related that the Jacobites,

> to prevent a famine among themselves, had drove all useless mouths from among them the last winter, to our side of the Shannon: And we, for the same reason, would not suffer them to come within our frontiers; so between both, they lay in a miserable starving condition. These wretches came flocking in great numbers about our camp, devouring all the filth they could meet with. Our dead horses crawling with vermin, as the sun had parched them, were delicious food to them; while their infants sucked those carcases, with as much eagerness as if they were at their mothers breasts.

Ginkel's bombardment of Athlone began on Saturday 20 June. Stevens, approaching with the Irish army from the west, 'heard the cannon at Athlone firing hotly all the day'. The next day, St Ruth's forces were encamped on the western side of the Shannon, 2 miles beyond Athlone, with 16,000 foot, 3000 horse and 2000 dragoons, a force roughly equal in overall size to the combined Williamite army.

The Jacobite garrison at Athlone had abandoned the English town on the Williamite (Leinster) side of the Shannon, and had withdrawn across the bridge, which they again broke, defending the old Irish town on their own (Connaught) side. The Jacobites held an immensely strong position, as the river was deep and fast flowing, and could only be forded with great difficulty at the best of times, let alone under fire. St Ruth believed that it would be impossible to ford the Shannon, reportedly commenting of Ginkel that 'His master should hang him for trying to take Athlone, and mine ought to hang me if I lose it.'

In the early hours of Sunday the 28th, a small party of Williamites braved the fire from the Connaught bank and daringly laid planks across the gap in the bridge. But as Stevens reported, 'no sooner was it done than five or six of our men . . . notwithstanding the enemy's continual fire, took up the planks, and throwing them into the river, returned in safety.' Later that day, as 'the great and small shot never ceased firing,' Williamite grenadiers set fire to the Jacobite side of the bridge. The blaze raged so fiercely that the houses nearby caught fire. Stevens was one of the officers fighting the blaze:

> The enemy in the meanwhile bent thirty pieces of cannon and all their mortars that way, so that what with the fire and what with the balls and bombs flying so thick that spot was a mere hell upon earth . . . And this I think was the hottest place that ever I saw in my time of service.

The riverside part of Connaught Athlone was steadily reduced to rubble by the heavy pounding from the Williamite batteries; moreover, 'besides the bombs, the enemy threw out of their mortars a vast quantity of stones.' Falling masonry was an additional hazard for the garrison inside the town, Stevens being 'knocked down with a stone that flew from the castle wall, which only stunned me, a good beaver I had on saving my head'.

Further fierce exchanges across the bridge between the grenadiers of the two sides persuaded the Williamite commanders to defer any further attempts 'till new Measures were Consulted on'. Time was beginning to run out for Ginkel. At their council of war, 'the difficulties of staying there any longer were represented, all the Forrage being consumed for several Miles round, so that they must resolve to do something with Expedition.' As Story reported, if Ginkel failed at Athlone it would greatly encourage the Jacobites and dishearten the Williamites at the start of the summer's campaign.

The Williamites experimented with a different approach. As Parker recounted, three Danish soldiers under sentence of death were offered a pardon:

> if they would undertake fording the river. The men readily agreed to it, and putting on armour, they entered the river at noon-day, at three several places, some distance from each other. Our men in the trenches were ordered to fire, seemingly at them, but yet over their heads; from whence the enemy concluded them deserters, and did not fire at them until they saw them returning.

The Danes' success in crossing the river and returning to the Leinster side should have alerted the Jacobite garrison. Yet St Ruth had insisted on regular changes in guard. His laudable intention was to give all his raw recruits first-hand experience of action, so that they would be better prepared for the summer's campaign. It was to prove his undoing. According to Story, treachery also played a part. He reported that two Jacobite officers had crossed the river to inform Ginkel that the Jacobites believed that no more efforts would be made to cross the bridge, and that inexperienced troops were entrusted with guarding the town.

On Tuesday 30 June, as the changing of the guard was due to begin, the Williamites were ready poised:

> So, at six o'clock in the morning, captain Sandys and two lieutenants led through the ford, up to the armpits, sixty grenadiers in armour, twenty abreast, followed by a great body. The garrison fired at them, and the English army fired in amongst the garrison with great and small shot. But amidst this furious storm, the adventurers gained the bank through a small breach that had been made in a small work of earth and speedily pierced into the place, casting before them their grenades, which, bursting, made frightful effects amongst the raw soldiers of the garrison, who had not been used to such squibs.

The Jacobite guards fled the onslaught 'so that there was no time for any relief to enter the place'. The Williamites 'past over so fast that in less than half an hour we were Masters of the Town'. St Ruth's failure to demolish the ramparts at the rear of the town gave the Williamites a strong position to defend once they had stormed the garrison.

The fall of Athlone was a catastrophe for the Jacobites. Within a matter of weeks, Sarsfield's hard-won winter gains had been wiped out. Their line of defence had been broken with sickening ease. Irish morale slumped. They retreated:

> with great confusion and disorder, such a panic fear having seized our men that the very noise of ten horsemen would have dispersed as many of our battalions, above half the soldiers scattering without any other thing but their own apprehensions to fright them.[26]

Their enemy had achieved a major coup at the outset of the summer's campaign, crossing the Shannon and moving into Connaught.

II

A speedy conclusion to the Irish war remained the Williamite priority. On 7 July, the Earl of Nottingham, who had returned to Whitehall from the Hague, wrote to Admiral Russell, commander-in-chief of the English fleet, instructing him that:

> whatever you can do that may contribute to the speediest reduction of that kingdom [Ireland], that our troops may be elsewhere employ'd, is of so great importance that you will not neglect any opportunity that may be safely laid hold of for promoting that service.

The Williamites sought to capitalize on the enormous psychological shock suffered by their enemy at the loss of Athlone. On 9 July the Lords Justices, Thomas Coningsby and Charles Porter, offered fresh peace terms. Ginkel wanted to offer very lenient terms, believing that making concessions would be far cheaper than the cost of prolonging the war, but he failed to persuade William to go so far. The new peace proclamation failed to persuade the Jacobites to give up their fight, despite their setback at Athlone. At the same time, however, it antagonized Protestants in both England and Ireland, who regarded the offer as far too generous.

With the Williamite army poised to press ahead into Connaught, what should be the Irish army's best response? St Ruth favoured a pitched battle. Sarsfield argued for withdrawing further west and establishing a base from which to launch counter-attacks well behind enemy lines, thrusting deep into Leinster. The Williamites again allowed the Irish a valuable breathing space. Ginkel delayed an advance from Athlone for more than a week, as he had at Ballymore, on this occasion waiting for further supplies of ammunition and spending the time clearing up some of the colossal damage his gunners had inflicted on the old Irish town. But he had no idea how close at hand were St Ruth and the Jacobite army.

St Ruth had withdrawn across the River Suck at Ballinasloe, but then selected an extremely strong position to stand and fight, on Kilcommodon Hill, 5 miles south-west of Ballinasloe, near the ruins of the old castle of Aughrim. The Irish had regrouped quickly after the débâcle of Athlone. By 8 July an army totalling around 20,000 was mustered ready for battle.

Ginkel, however, assumed that the Jacobites had retreated towards Galway. He left Athlone on Friday 10 July and headed west. The following day, St Ruth and the Irish army were suddenly discovered only a few miles beyond the Suck. According to Captain Parker, 'Our first day's march was to Ballinasloe; here the General had an account that St. Ruth had taken up the strong camp of Aghrim, within three miles of us, where he seemed resolved to stand a battle.' The next morning, 'the General ordered all the tents and baggage to go back to Athlone.' The map provided by the Trench (or Le Tranche) family, local Huguenots, helped Ginkel assess the Jacobite position. The two armies were of roughly equal size, with the territorial advantage clearly lying with the Irish. Although Ginkel concluded that 'it would be no easy matter to attack' St Ruth's army, he 'resolved however to march towards them next day'.

St Ruth's advantage, holding a strong defensive position, was well described by Parker:

> The right flank was covered by a large morass, which extended along their front till it passed their center. From thence to the castle of Aghrim (which covered their left flank) were a parcel of old garden ditches, within which was posted their left wing of Foot; and they had a body of Horse drawn up on a plain behind these ditches.

The morass made any frontal assault extremely hazardous, and the options for attack on either flank were limited. Plunkett wrote of St Ruth's position:

> Before his front he had a morass, over which there was a passage, through which the enemy's horse could come to his right and left flank. That on the right was a little ford caused by a stream issuing from the morass. That on the left was an old broken causeway, only large enough for two horses to pass it at a time, and was sixty yards long. Beyond this causeway was the castle of Aughrim, on a line, and on the left within forty yards, into which St Ruth put on that day colonel Walter Bourk and two hundred men.

It was a foggy morning, and it being a Sunday the Irish army took mass. The battle became a crusade. The effect was immediately apparent to their opponents. Parker noted that when Ginkel 'marched the army in four columns up to the enemy, and found them drawn up in two lines to very great advantage . . . [the Jacobites] looked as if they were resolved to win the day or lose all'. According to a report by a Catholic bishop, as many as eighty priests were killed during the battle, as they carried crucifixes and urged on the Irish soldiers.

The eye-witness accounts of the Battle of Aughrim often contradict one another and are confused, notably, the precise location of Sarsfield and his role in the fighting. According to O'Kelly, Sarsfied commanded the cavalry on the left, while Plunkett places Sarsfield on the right, and the Williamite version by Captain Parker has Sarsfield at the rear of the Irish army with instructions not to move without orders.

What does seem clear is that following preliminary skirmishes during Sunday, the battle began between four and five o'clock in the afternoon. The Williamites adopted the plan advocated by General Mackay with an attack on the Jacobite right flank. This led the Jacobites to transfer more of their troops from their left flank near Aughrim Castle in order to meet the challenge. The Williamites then launched an assault on the weakened Jacobite left. Four regiments of English foot crossed the boggy ground, at times 'up to their Middles in Mudd and Water'. The Irish, however, 'maintained their ground on the right and in the centre with great obstinacy and resolution, and repulsed our men in those places several times with considerable loss'. The English regiments were forced back across the bog by the Irish foot and horse to Ginkel's gun battery. Württemberg reported that 'Some of the Irish officers were so full of valour that they leaped over our *chevaux de frise*.' St Ruth was encouraged when he saw the Williamite foot driven back across the bog and, 'in a great Ecstasy, [he] told those next him, *that he wou'd now beat our Army back to the Gates of Dublin*'. The performance of the Irish was said to have impressed him so strongly that he reportedly called out, 'le jour est à nous, mes enfants.'

Ginkel next ordered Ruvigny's Horse to attack the narrow pass by Aughrim

Castle, on the Jacobite left. St Ruth saw that his left flank was now hard-pressed and ordered reinforcements to counter the Williamite challenge. But disaster struck him as he began to ride to his left across Kilcommodon Hill, towards the action near Aughrim Castle. The incident, and its effect on the Jacobites, was described by Plunkett:

> But as he was riding along down a little hill, a cannon-ball from the other side, directed by the cannoneer amongst the troops that were going to defend the pass, missing all others, struck the marquis of St Ruth in the head, at which he fell, and at the same time it laid the nation prostrate at his feet. A cursed ball, that carried such a measure of woe!

From the other side, Parker corroborated the catastrophic effect of St Ruth's death on the Jacobite forces, occurring at such 'a very critical juncture, when his orders were much wanted; for their centre and right wing still maintained their ground; but seeing their left put to flight, and not having orders from their General, they soon ran into confusion, and were put to a total rout.' De Tessé's attempts to rally the infantry in the Jacobite centre were in vain. O'Kelly believed that if St Ruth 'had lived but an hour longer, the Irish would be victorious that day', and that with him 'died all the hope and good fortune of Ireland'.

The incident generated its myths. It was said that an Irish farmer, Kelly, and his shepherd, Mullen, had pointed out St Ruth to a Williamite gunner. It was also claimed that the gunner was unable to raise the cannon's elevation suffi-ciently to aim his shot at St Ruth, until Trench – of the local Huguenot family – put the heel of his boot under its muzzle. Trench's reward for his war service was the deanery of Raphoe. Hence the eighteenth-century Protestant toast 'to the heel of the Dean of Raphoe'.

Added to the tragedy was a suggestion of treachery. The Irish cavalry defending the narrow pass at Aughrim Castle failed to stand their ground. Ever since, it has been known as 'Luttrell's Pass' after Henry Luttrell, the Jacobite cavalry officer in command at the time. Luttrell had been a die-hard and was one of the delegation who had lobbied James against Tyrconnel dur-ing the winter. By the time of Aughrim, however, he had come to the view that it was pointless fighting any longer. In common with other cavalry officers, his first concern was to retain his land. Plunkett, a supporter of Tyrconnel's, was particularly scathing about Luttrell's action. The suggestion of treachery seemed to gain credence when it was later discovered that Luttrell had been in correspondence with Ginkel about possible peace terms.

Once the Williamites had broken through on the Jacobite left and centre, the retreat became general and quickly degenerated into wanton killing. Many Irish soldiers were trapped and slaughtered. As Parker recorded, 'Our horse made a great slaughter of the Foot in the pursuit, which we continued till night came on. The enemy had near 4000 killed, and above 2000 taken, and we have above 3000 killed & wounded.' By Story's reckoning, nearer 7000 Jacobites were killed and 450 taken prisoner. All their guns and baggage were seized, along with eleven horse standards and thirty-two regimental colours. Williamite losses were calculated at about 700 dead and over 1000 wounded.

Yet the outcome at Aughrim might so nearly have been very different. As Parker observed, 'Never did the Irish fight so well in their own country, as they did this day, (the Foot only excepted, which were posted within their ditches) and had it not been that St. Ruth fell, it were hard to say how matters would have ended . . .'

Although Aughrim sounded the death-knell for Irish resistance, the decisive turning-point in the war had occurred at the Boyne twelve months earlier. If the Irish had won at Aughrim, they could only have prolonged the war into another summer. Immediately after the battle, Tyrconnel wrote to James informing him that help must be sent from France, or the Irish must be allowed to settle. The Irish simply lacked the resources to launch a major offensive and drive the Williamites from the country. To do that would have required much stronger support from the French than was ever likely to be forthcoming.

Aughrim soon assumed great symbolic significance for both sides. A month later, the Earl of Nottingham wrote from Whitehall, 'The Irish colours taken in the late battle are brought over and I think the Queen will order them to be hung up in Westminster Hall.' Today, the battle's symbolism derives from its place as the last defeat on Irish soil of the old Irish army and Catholic nobility. The battle was the subject of a section in a Jacobite poem on the war, written in Latin. In the eighteenth century a verse drama by Robert Ashton, *The battle of Aughrim, or the fall of Monsieur St Ruth*, won popular acclaim from Protestants, and went through twenty-two editions between 1740 and 1764.

In Thomas Flanagan's *Year of the French*, the character Dennis Browne comments, 'After Aughrim we all had to find our way in a new world.' Richard Murphy's four-part poem, 'The Battle of Aughrim', inspired by the battle, opens with reference to land ownership and religion, the issues at stake at Aughrim:

> Who owns the land where musket-balls are buried
> In blackthorn roots on the eskar, the drained bogs
> Where sheep browse, and credal war miscarried?
> Names in the rival churches are written on plaques.

Land and religion dominated the calculations on both sides as the war entered its closing stages.

III

A week after Aughrim, the main Williamite army approached Galway. Story had reason to hope that its surrender might not be long delayed:

There lived a great many rich Merchants in it of late by reason of conveniency of its situation for Trade with *Spain* or *France*, but most of them are *Irish*, which might be one great reason to expect the having it delivered upon reasonable Terms, rather than by resistance to have it ruined.

Galway was the weak link in Jacobite Connaught, the home of leading members of the 'new interest' Irish and a centre for the peace party. Although Daly, MacDonnell and Riverston had been arrested following the discovery of their contacts with the Williamites, their influence survived. D'Usson, despatched to organize Galway's defences, discovered a local mood of defeatism.

A stronger garrison at Galway might have encouraged more determined resistance, which would have delayed the Williamite drive on Limerick. But though Galway harboured defeatist elements, its citizens were able to drive a hard bargain over their terms of surrender. Ginkel's readiness to make concessions reflected the pressure on the Williamites to end the war. During July, Viscount Sydney, accompanying William at Gerpines in the Netherlands, wrote to the Earl of Nottingham telling him of the King's frustration that the Irish war was preventing a bold initiative on the Continent: 'he [William] would be glad if a descent could be made in France with some of the troupes that are in Ireland, but that businesse being not yet done, and there being no preparations yet made for it, he is affraid it will be impossible this yeare.'

Ginkel inevitably found himself criticized by English and Irish Protestants, who regarded the terms agreed at Galway as far too lenient. Some measure of the concern which the terms aroused in Whitehall can be gained from Nottingham's reply to Sydney on 28 July. Nottingham admitted that the terms amounted to 'very large concessions', which were 'censured here as such, especially by the [Protestant] gentlemen of Ireland', but added a breathless apologia, concluding that, 'it was the most likely method to bring this warr to a speedy conclusion that his Majesty may employ his troops elsewhere.'

The Williamites proceeded to mop up other pockets of Jacobite resistance. Their move on Sligo, still held by Teague O'Regan, was initially thwarted by Balldearg O'Donnell. He had not fought at Aughrim but was blocking the Williamite advance with his Gaelic force. Having made his point, however, O'Donnell accepted favourable terms. In mid-September, O'Regan finally surrendered.

Jacobite resistance was limited to Clare, Kerry and Limerick. They had a large army still, but few arms, and the cavalry officers stationed in Clare were concerned at the shortage of forage. Morale was low after the shattering defeat at Aughrim. Tyrconnel sent urgent word to James in France that unless the French provided help at once the Irish must be allowed to seek terms. But the Irish found the prospect of slogging on even longer, principally to please the French, an unattractive proposition. As Fumeron, the French supply officer in Ireland, wrote to the French Ministry of War, 'If they hold out till October, as we are urging them to do, it is only on account of the hope that some have of getting help from France . . .' The letter also included the first reference to the possibility of Irish soldiers leaving for France following a peace settlement. The French were ready to commit further resources to the Irish war, in the hope of forcing the Williamite army to remain in Ireland over the winter of 1691–2. Despite these promises, there were serious delays in delivering and loading the supplies.

On Friday 14 August, Tyrconnel died at Limerick after suffering a stroke. As Sir Richard Nagle wrote, 'his loss at this time was extream pernicious to the welfare of this poor Nation.' He had revolutionized the position of Catholics in Ireland, paving the way for James's campaign and was immensely experienced in the problems of governing Ireland. Above all, he had been determined at the time of his death to continue the fight, and his loss eroded the Irish resistance. Rumours that he had been poisoned while drinking 'Rattafeau', a drink of 'Apricock-stones bruised and infused in brandy', reflected the factionalism within the Jacobite camp. Tyrconnel was buried in Limerick Cathedral, but no stone marks his unknown grave.

Within days of Tyrconnel's death came the damning revelation that Henry Luttrell, the officer who had conceded the vital pass at Aughrim, was corresponding with Ginkel. Luttrell was arrested by d'Usson, the French commander of Limerick, and condemned to death. Ginkel's threat of revenge against the Jacobites being held prisoner secured Luttrell's reprieve. Porter, the Williamite Lord Chancellor of Ireland, reckoned that Jacobite morale was low, and some were already deserting or 'coming in', and that Luttrell's contacts with Ginkel would cause more of them to desert:

> They have gotten a great number of men together but very fiew well armed or disciplined. The generall calls them Rapparees and every day many of their best men desert. The Lord Kynsale as Mr Justice Cox writes and his followers are come in, and some others in the county of Cork. I cannot think otherwise then that this business of Lutterell's and the approach of our army will strangely divide them, his interest was very great with the Irish and they will believe he had good grounds for what he was doeing.

Yet the Williamites were in a quandary about the terms of the peace. Following Galway's surrender, Nottingham had written to Sydney in the Netherlands that 'his Majesties pleasure is to be known what method shall be taken with Sarsfield and those that adhere to him.' The Jacobite commander still had 'a great body of horse', and the question was whether they should 'be treated as an enemy and his standing out shall be looked upon as a continuance of the warr', or should 'be proceeded against the rebells and used accordingly when any of them are taken and not as prisoners of warr'.

Not for the first time, and by no means the last, the military commander in the field was a dove, while the administrators behind their desks in the capital were hawks. Ginkel favoured more liberal terms, but the Lords Justices sensed that any concessions would be deeply unpopular with Irish Protestants. Ginkel also advocated a blockade of Limerick, but the Lords Justices wanted him to execute a full-blooded siege.

Ginkel's advance on Limerick was prolonged by his own caution and the difficult conditions, as Nottingham reported to Sydney:

> Monsr. Ginkell was on the 20th five miles from Limerick and had not got his great cannon, the draught horses being much spoiled and many wanting. The raines began to fall very violently and the men began to grow sick, but he hoped to take the town or to bombard it and so block it up as that the enemy should not be able to subsist.

Ginkel finally approached Limerick on Tuesday 25 August. He was supported by a squadron of English ships in the Shannon. It was not, however, till a fortnight later that his battery of heavy artillery was ready for action. In Whitehall, impatience at the lack of news from Limerick mounted by the day. On Tuesday 15 September, Nottingham drafted a courtly reminder to Ginkel, observing that Queen Mary was pleased with his resolution to do the utmost to reduce Limerick, 'for it is of the greatest importance imaginable to her Majesties affairs both at home and abroad'.

The following night, Wednesday the 16th, a detachment of Williamites managed to cross the Shannon upstream from the city and establish themselves on the County Clare side of the river. Clifford, the Jacobite officer defending the crossing, put up little resistance, and treachery was again suspected. Ginkel issued a further peace declaration, extending the previous terms by offering pardon and a guarantee of their property to the Irish army and the citizens of Limerick if they surrendered in eight days. This had a profound impact on Irish opinion. There was still no sign of the further assistance promised by the French.

On Saturday 22 September, the Williamites launched a determined assault on the Clare side of the bank, forcing the Jacobites back to Thomond bridge, which spans the river to the old English town and the Castle on King's Island. In the confusion, the drawbridge to the Castle was raised by a French officer. The Jacobites' retreat to safety was cut and they were massacred. The Williamite version of events records that 'Before the killing was over they were laid in heaps on the bridge, higher than the ledges of it.' The Irish in Limerick Castle were cut off from their cavalry regiments in County Clare. This was not disastrous militarily, as the garrison had no need of the cavalry's support to survive, but the slaughter in sight of the Castle dealt a further blow to Irish morale.

Although the Jacobites had been out-manoeuvred by military cunning and diplomatic skill, they were not yet finished. They held a city which had been reinforced since the previous year's siege, they were not in the desperate conditions endured by the people of Derry two years earlier, and there was the prospect of fresh supplies from the French. And, had they but known, their opponents were wondering whether to retire to winter quarters.

Psychologically, however, the Jacobites were beaten. Holding out at Limerick would only postpone the war's end. It had been obvious for more than a year what the result would be, but it was becoming impossible to see how prolonging resistance would improve the peace terms. The Jacobite council of war on Sunday the 23rd degenerated into mutual recriminations between the French and the Irish. Defeatism coloured every judgement. Clifford was blamed for the Williamite crossing into Clare, provisions were said to be in short supply, there was still no news of the French fleet and there were fears that if the French ever did appear the English ships stationed in the Shannon would prevent their landing.

That night the Jacobites 'beat a Parly on both sides of the town . . . and a Cessation was concluded for that Night'. As Story reported,

> The 24th in the Morning, Lieutenant General *Sarsfield* and Major General *Waughup* came out to the General [Ginkel], and desired it [the cessation of hostilities] might be continued for three Days longer, till they could send to their Horse, who then were encamp'd towards *Clare*, in order to their being included in the general Capitulation which they then proposed, and the Request was granted.

After such a bitter war, and the long-drawn-out final stages, there was surprise on both sides that the Jacobite surrender occurred as suddenly as it did. Clarke considered the surrender from a Williamite perspective:

> It may appear very strange that a numerous garrison, not pressed by any want, should give up a town which nobody was in a condition to take from them at a time when those who lay before it had actually drawn off their cannon and were preparing to march away, and when that garrison did every day expect a squadron of ships to come to their relief if they had needed any.

Clarke attributed the sudden laying down of Irish arms to Sarsfield's personal ambitions abroad. It was a very English interpretation. Some of the Irish thought Sarsfield had been wrong to surrender. Plunkett remained loyal to Tyrconnel to the end:

> If the duke of Tyrconnell were then alive (I utter it with certainty), he would not hearken to any offer of a surrender, because he expected to retrieve the country by spinning out the war. He grounded his expectation upon the courage of the army made evident unto him by the battle of Aughrim, and upon the reinforcement he was to receive out of France in the following spring.

In the end, the role of the French had proved decisive, although not in the way that the Irish had hoped. As George Clarke concluded,

> the Irish did not find themselves so assisted by France as they expected, and the French officers who were in the town were very weary of service, so that *they first*

proposed capitulating, as Sarsfield [later] averred openly in the presence of the French Intendent.

It was ironic that the war should end little more than a fortnight before the long-overdue French convoy sailed into the Shannon. 'It was very happy that the treaty was concluded as it was,' wrote Clarke, 'for a very little time after Mons. Châteaurenaud came into the Shannon with his squadron.' Clarke added that if Châteaurenault:

> had not shown great regard for what had been agreed ashore, [he] would undoubtedly have destroyed or taken all our ships with ammunition and provisions that lay there, as well as seven men-of-war, English and Dutch, that were with them, and could not get out of the river.

Plunkett summed up Irish frustration with the French, arguing that by not giving more help to the Irish they had been their own worst enemies:

> Here we cannot omit to tell our opinion, that the king of France made a false step in the politics by letting the Irish war fall, because that war was the best medium in the world for destroying soon the confederacy abroad, by reason that the confederate princes could not prolong the foreign war without the army and money of England . . .

Irish bitterness towards the French persisted. A century later, Wolfe Tone bemoaned Louis XIV's error in 'feeding the war little by little till the opportunity was lost'. At the end of the day, the French interest in Ireland was subordinate to their interest on the Continent. Ireland mattered more to the English than it did to the French.

The Irish gentry had been badly let down by their European allies. In his poem, 'The Shipwreck', Ó Bruadair laments the demise of his country's Catholic elite (translated from the Irish):

> I had hoped to live in comfort when our gentry would be free,
> As steward or as petty provost happily with one of them;
> But, since I am reduced to old shoes as the net result of all,
> Finis be unto my writing of the men of Fódla's land.

PART FIVE

LEGACIES AND LEGENDS

CHAPTER FIFTEEN

IRELAND BETRAYED

I

War had cost Ireland dear. Deaths in the conflict amounted to 25,000, though many more soldiers and civilians died from disease and as a result of the food shortages and the disruption visited on local communities. The country was devastated.

Yet the peace talks were conducted in a civilized fashion. It was not at Limerick that Ireland was betrayed, but in the subsequent unravelling of the Treaty in the English and Irish Parliaments. The end result would ultimately rob Ireland of its Catholic nobility as a major political force; cast tens of thousands of Irishmen into permanent exile where they would fight, and many die, on foreign soil; and subject the majority of Irish people to economic and political discrimination.

On Friday 25 September 1691, the officers of the Irish Horse came in from the Clare countryside. The commander of the Irish Horse, Sheldon, and the Lords Galmoy, Westmeath, Dillon and Trimblestowne joined Sarsfield and Wauchope, the Catholic Primate Dominic Maguire and the Catholic Archbishop of Cashel John Brenan at the dinner hosted by the Williamite commander Ginkel. Afterwards the Irish were rowed back across the river by French seamen. The following day, Sarsfield and Wauchope re-emerged from the old English town and again dined with Ginkel. Throughout the talks, the Williamites paid Sarsfield the courtesy of recognizing him as the Earl of Lucan, although the title had been granted by James II at his court-in-exile.

From the outset of the talks, Ginkel accepted Sarsfield's demand that those who wanted to leave for France should be allowed to do so. In return, they would forfeit their estates in Ireland. Ginkel saw no need to refer the agreement on military matters to the civil authorities, Lords Justices Porter and Coningsby. The military terms were included as distinct articles in the final Treaty. In all, around 12,000 Irish soldiers left for France (their story, and that of their descendants, is told in the following chapter).

The hard bargaining came over the civil terms. Land and religion had been Ireland's unresolved issues at the outset of the war, and were the hardest to resolve at the peace. The instructions issued by Queen Mary on 28 August empowered the Lords Justices to conclude a treaty with the Jacobites, granting 'to persons now in Limerick or in the army thereabouts any such terms which you think fit and necessary and which are in your power to give'. But there was to be no general pardon, and the terms had to be consistent 'with the laws of Ireland as they stood in the reign of our late dear uncle King Charles II'.

The Irish had not surrendered unconditionally, and on Sunday 27 September they signalled their intention to obtain the best possible settlement. They demanded a pardon of all 'past Crimes and Offences whatsoever'; the restoration of estates owned by Catholics at the time of James II's flight from England in 1688; freedom of worship and a priest for each parish; no discrimination against Catholics in civil or military employment; the right of Catholics to be members of corporations and to enjoy trading rights in towns and cities; the maintenance of the Irish army in William's service; and the ratification of these terms by Act of Parliament. This last demand showed that the Irish were concerned that the assurances from Ginkel might subsequently be swept aside, and thought that ratification would provide their best guarantee.

Had the Irish demands been accepted, Catholics would have enjoyed a better position than at the time of Charles II. Ginkel rejected the proposals out of hand, the Dutch commander replying that 'Though he was in a manner a Stranger to the Laws of *England*, yet he understood that those things they insisted upon were so far contradictory to them, and dishonourable to himself, that he would not grant any such Terms.' The Irish then asked Ginkel what he would agree to, and he sent a draft of his proposed terms.

On the morning of Monday the 28th, Sarsfield and other Irish negotiators, including the Jacobite Solicitor-General, Sir Toby Butler, came to the Williamite camp to discuss Ginkel's terms. Butler immediately queried Ginkel's preamble, which stated:

> Articles granted by Lieutenant Ginkel, commander-in-chief of their Majesties' forces, to all persons now in the City of Limerick and in the Irish army, that is in the counties of Clare, Kerry, Cork and Mayo and other garrisons that are in their possession, this – day of October 1691 in the third year of their Majesties' reign.[27]

On this wording, the terms would have excluded the civilian population living in areas still controlled by the Irish army, and they would therefore have been liable to lose their property. Sarsfield objected that he would fight on at Limerick and 'lay his bones in these old walls rather than not take care of those who stuck by them all along'. As a result, the second article was designed to extend the terms of the Treaty to everyone under Irish protection.

The final terms were agreed later that day, but Ginkel could not complete the details until the arrival of the Lords Justices, Porter and Coningsby, three days later. The Treaty of Limerick was signed on Saturday 3 October 1691.

Porter, Coningsby and Ginkel signed for the Williamites, Sarsfield, Galmoy, Sir Toby Butler and Colonels Purcel, Cusack, Dillon and Brown for the Irish.

Of the thirteen civil articles, it was the second which caused immediate controversy. The words 'and all such as are under their protection in the said counties' had been included to meet Sarsfield's concern, but, when the articles were read out in Limerick the day after signing, it was discovered that the key words were missing from the signed version. As a consequence, the inhabitants of Limerick, Clare, Kerry, Cork and Mayo were liable to have their property confiscated. When the omission was pointed out, Ginkel and the Lords Justices immediately assured the Irish that the 'missing clause' would be reinserted. But the error could not be put right straight away, as Ginkel's son had already left for England with the signed articles. Ginkel later gave evidence that the clause was omitted by mistake, and William accepted that human error was to blame. Notwithstanding the efforts of the English Privy Council to persuade him otherwise, the King inserted the missing clause as a matter of honour when the Treaty was presented to the Irish Parliament for ratification in February 1692.

This immediate row over the 'missing clause' was a precursor to a further dispute over the wording of the Treaty. The first article granted Catholics in Ireland such freedoms in practising their religion as were consistent with the laws of Ireland, or as they had enjoyed during Charles II's reign. The word 'or' was an addition to the draft of the original terms, and later became the issue of considerable debate. Other articles made it clear that only those who had held out till the end, and who were now prepared to give allegiance to William, were entitled to be pardoned and to have their property restored. Such gentlemen would also be allowed to ride with a sword and a case of pistols, keep a gun in their houses, and follow a trade as freely as they had in Charles II's time. In the interests of peace, individuals on either side were banned from bringing private lawsuits for acts committed during the recent 'great violences'. This infuriated Protestants, because they felt they were being treated no better than Catholics, who would thus be allowed to keep any gains from crimes commit-ted under cover of war.

The Treaty was a compromise, born of William's European preoccupations, which was bound to leave both Catholics and Protestants feeling dissatisfied. The Irish had secured better terms than they could have dared hope after the Boyne. Those Irish who had fought on, or who were under the Jacobites' protection, had won the prospect that they would be able to retain their estates. The real losers were those Irish who had surrendered after the Boyne, or who lived in the areas under Williamite control by 1691.

The Irish had sought parliamentary ratification as a safeguard. In the final Treaty, the Lords Justices and Ginkel gave an undertaking that William and Mary would use their 'utmost endeavours' to have the terms ratified by the Irish Parliament, and procure such further security for Catholics 'as might

preserve them from any disturbance'. Yet it was in the parliamentary cockpits
at Dublin and Westminster that the Treaty of Limerick would come under
strongest pressure.

II

Although the war in Ireland was over, and the peace signed, both the English
and the Anglican Protestants in Ireland continued to feel insecure. Their insecurity was to have a major impact on the fate of the Treaty of Limerick, and
would fashion Ireland's distinctive eighteenth-century political culture.

Apart from a brief four-year interlude, England and France were locked in
Continental war for more than twenty years after Limerick. In England, the
four-fold increase in Government spending, occasioned by the wars, increased
the burden of taxation. Landowners who had applauded the 'Glorious Revolution' deplored its sequel, the 'National Debt'. William was not the most
popular of monarchs, and never fully overcame the doubts about the legitimacy
of his, and Mary's, reign. The Jacobite threat was ever-present, with invasion
scares, notably in 1692 and 1708, and the discovery of an assassination plot
against William in early 1696, in which Berwick was implicated. There were
continued fears that the Irish in England were a potential fifth column.
Limerick also signalled a distinct hardening of attitude by William's Government towards the Jacobite Highlanders in Scotland. Anxious to demonstrate to
his European allies that the civil war in the British Isles was at an end, William's efforts to achieve a settlement in the Highlands culminated in the massacre of the MacDonalds at Glencoe in early 1692.

In Dublin, the Anglican Protestant landed gentry felt that they were not fully
entrenched in power. Many argued that the Treaty of Limerick fell far short of
a lasting settlement. 'Had the Irish been totally reduced by the loss of all their
estates,' wrote the Accountant-General for Ireland, James Bonnell, to Robert
Harley, 'this country would have been looked on by the English as a secure
place and many would have flocked here.' Some of the dispossessed Catholics
stayed near their old homes in the hope that they might recover their estates,
not that the Anglican Protestant landed gentry needed any reminding of how
they had acquired their land, and how it might be taken back. The anxiety
induced by Louis XIV's inclination to play the Jacobite card was exacerbated
by the valiant performance of the thousands of Irishmen who were fighting for
the French, and who would constitute a formidable army if they were ever
brought across the seas to fight again in their own country.

From the outset, Ireland's Anglican Protestant community were divided
over the Treaty. On 4 November 1691, the Lord Chancellor of Ireland, Sir
Charles Porter, reported that Lieutenant-General Ginkel 'came hither last
night, and was received with all the reall demonstrations of joy that this citty
could show'. Porter wrote to the English Secretary of State, Nottingham, that
'wee celebrated the commemoration of his Majestyes birth with the universall

content and pleasure of the whole town. I doe assure your lordshipp in my life I never observed so universall a satisfaction in the behaviour of all sorts, both Papist and Protestant.' Yet the ink was barely dry on the Treaty before other Anglican Protestants were attacking what they regarded as an unacceptable compromise. The Church of Ireland Bishop of Meath, Anthony Dopping, unleashed a fierce attack, claiming that Catholics would be able to 'play their pranks over again on the first opportunity'. Reporting this episcopalian outburst to Nottingham, the Lords Justices felt that they had:

> particular reason to complaine of the behaviour of the Bishop of Meath, who though another was to preach the thanksgiving sermon, pressed that he might doe it, and upon that occasion did make the most bitter invections against the whole body of the Irish that could be invented, stirring up the people, too prone of themselves to it, to continue their animosities against them, and useing them with all reproachfull tearmes of anger, contempt and despight.

The pressures of Continental war had created the need for the Williamites to compromise at Limerick, yet ironically those same pressures soon gave the Treaty's critics greater political leverage. Ireland rapidly slipped down William's list of priorities. His absence on the Continent for months at a time from early 1691 and his need for funds to sustain the war effort had given English MPs a taste of greater power. Before 1691 was out, the newly assertive English Parliament intervened in Irish affairs, and flagrantly violated the Treaty. Westminster replaced the Oaths of Allegiance and Supremacy in Ireland with a new oath and declaration against transubstantiation, which had been introduced in England in 1689, and to which no Catholic could possibly subscribe. At Limerick, the Irish had negotiated successfully to avoid any such requirement, the second article of the Treaty making it clear that all the Irish in Limerick, Clare, Cork, Kerry and Mayo were to be allowed to practise their professions with the proviso that they took the Oath of Allegiance. The English Parliament's Act was a marked erosion of the position enjoyed by Irish Catholics since the Restoration more than thirty years earlier. An important effect was to exclude all Catholics from the Irish Parliament. None of the signatories at Limerick had foreseen that the Treaty would thus be ratified by an entirely Protestant Parliament.

Westminster's violation of the Treaty prompted fresh European intervention in Ireland, although this time it was diplomatic pressure from William's ally and not military invasion by his enemy. In January 1692, the Pope's concern led Leopold I, the Austrian Emperor, to seek an assurance from William that Irish Catholics would be treated fairly. The Catholic Emperor, however, did not believe in setting an example, since the Protestants in Hungary suffered persecution at the hands of their Austrian ruler. But William did not wish to alienate his Austrian ally or the Pope, and reassured the Emperor that he would give the Irish no cause for resentment, provided they behaved as loyal subjects. None the less, Westminster's violation of the Treaty stood.

On 11 January 1692, William issued a proclamation calling on those who had lost land to submit their claims for the recovery of their former estates. A total of 491 claims were heard up to the end of 1694. This process appears to have been remarkably fair, since 483 claims were upheld, and the successful claimants recovered their land. No new anti-Catholic laws were passed. Catholic barristers, including Sir Toby Butler, the former Jacobite Solicitor-General, and Tyrconnel's adviser, Sir Stephen Rice, were able to practise, and a number of Catholics were able to carry arms as laid down in the Treaty. William also sent a copy of the Treaty to Dublin intending that it should be ratified, although it did not proceed through the Irish Parliament.

Mindful of the overriding need to sustain his European coalition against Louis, William initially had sought to abide by the terms of the Treaty. But he was less mindful of political considerations in England and Ireland, where the pressures against the articles of Limerick continued to mount.

III

William's maladroit handling of the lands confiscated during the Irish war caused deep resentment. His insistence that he alone had the right to dispose of the forfeited lands had provoked an angry clash between Crown and Parliament before the Irish war ended. Many Anglican Protestants had expected to acquire more land than turned out to be the case, while a growing number of English MPs came to argue that the sale of forfeited Catholic lands would yield substantial proceeds for the state.[28] They believed that these revenues should go towards meeting the cost of William's wars, and thereby ease the massive burden imposed on English taxpayers.

Even when every allowance is made for the convention that monarchs rewarded their supporters after a successful campaign, William's land grants in Ireland displayed gross insensitivity. His close associates were massively favoured. About 60 per cent of the land granted from Irish forfeitures was awarded to seven foreigners, including the Dutchmen, the Earl of Athlone (Ginkel) and the Duke of Portland (Bentinck). The remaining 40 per cent of the forfeitures was shared out among thirty-seven people. These included Williamites who had distinguished themselves in the Irish war, Anglican Protestant relatives of dispossessed Catholics, and Williamite supporters, like Henry Sydney, who was also appointed Lord Lieutenant in March 1692 in succession to the Lords Justices, Porter and Coningsby. Most notorious of all, however, was the grant of the 'private estate', the extensive property which had been awarded to James, Duke of York, later James II, by the Act of Settlement of 1662, to Elizabeth Villiers, William's mistress. Thus was insult added to injury.

Discontent with lack of progress in the European war, its mismanagement and colossal cost were the backdrop to the political intrigues of 1693 and 1694.

The Tories in the Government became the scapegoats, leaving William little choice but to turn to the Whigs, who generally took a tougher, anti-Catholic line. Their dominance was to last until 1700. In June 1693, the hapless Sydney was succeeded in Ireland by three new Lords Justices, Sir Henry Capel, Cyril Wyche and William Duncombe. Of the three, Capel was the strongest Whig, and soon emerged as leader of the critics of the articles of Limerick in the Irish Parliament.

The Irish Lord Chancellor, Porter, became the principal target of attack for Capel. Porter had incurred the wrath of hard-line Anglican Protestants by signing the Treaty of Limerick and stopping lawsuits for actions committed during the war, which prevented Anglican Protestants taking legal action against their Catholic opponents. For his pains, Porter was denounced as a 'Jacobite'. In late 1693 he was hauled before the English House of Commons, along with Coningsby, his fellow signatory of the Treaty, to face impeachment. Although they cleared their names, Capel was in the ascendant.

An early casualty of Capel's rise to power was the Privy Council's hearing of land claims. From early 1694, no further claims were heard for five years. With the Whigs dominating William's Ministry in London, Capel was appointed Lord Deputy and Sole Governor of Ireland in the spring of 1695. Porter, however, remained Lord Chancellor. As a member of the established Church of Ireland, Porter was able to rely on the support of many Anglican Protestants who were suspicious of appointees of a Whig government. Whigs were inclined to favour Protestant dissenters, and Anglican Protestants were wary of the strong Presbyterian presence in the north, an anxiety exacerbated during the 1690s by renewed large-scale immigration of Presbyterians from Scotland to Ulster.

When the 1695 session of the Irish Parliament opened in August, Porter was able to count 166 MPs as 'friends', against 112 'enemies', with a dozen neutrals.[29] In August, Porter won William's approval to proceed with ratifying the Treaty in the Irish Parliament. Capel, however, was able to persuade the Irish Privy Council against preparing any such legislation, and wrote to William arguing that the Irish Parliament would not ratify the Treaty while Porter remained Lord Chancellor. William retreated and a further attempt at ratification was stalled.

Capel died in the spring of 1696 and Porter before the end of the year, but the conflict persisted between critics and supporters of the Treaty. William, however, was unconcerned about devising a clear Irish policy.

IV

The breaking of the deadlock which blocked ratification of the Treaty of Limerick in 1697 owed more to events in Europe and a wish to end the continual rows in Dublin than to any new commitment by William to Ireland.

The Treaty was still unpopular among many of the Anglican Protestants.

Yet it was equally clear that amendments to the Treaty made to meet their objections would cause angry protests from Catholics. But Irish Catholics, although they were co-signatories of the Treaty, were unrepresented in the Irish Parliament, and the reactions of European Catholics were less of a worry to William as the Nine Years' War against Louis XIV drew to a close.

The bill to ratify the Treaty of Limerick was a travesty of the original articles. Under the procedure laid down by Poynings's Law, Irish MPs and peers had either to accept wholesale the legislation approved by the English Privy Council or to reject it completely. There was no scope for amendment. In order to be certain of the bill's being passed, the main criticisms of the Treaty thus had to be met before the bill was presented to the Irish House of Commons. The draft which the English Privy Council received from Dublin Castle omitted from the second article the crucial words 'and all such as are under their protection in the said counties'. This was the so-called 'missing clause', which had caused such controversy immediately after the Treaty had been signed. The English Privy Council referred the matter to William in Holland. Despite William's earlier insistence that the 'missing clause' should be re-instated as a matter of personal honour, he approved the draft as it stood. The commitment on which Sarsfield had insisted at Limerick was discarded.

There were other major differences between the bill presented to the Irish Parliament on 6 September 1697 and the Treaty which had been signed at Limerick. No reference was made to the first article, which had promised Catholics throughout Ireland the same freedoms they had enjoyed in the reign of Charles II. A time limit of just two years was imposed on the hearing of future claims for the recovery of estates. No mention was made of the ninth article, which stated that Catholics under the protection of the Treaty would be required to take only the Oath of Allegiance. Although the sixth article banning lawsuits for actions committed during the war was confirmed, the war was said to have started not with the revolution in November 1688 but on 10 April 1689, the deadline originally set for people in Ireland to acknowledge William as their lawful monarch. Anglican Protestants were thus given at least some opportunity, which they had to take up within a year, to seek redress for grievances suffered during Jacobite rule.

Opposition to the bill in the Irish Parliament came from two groups, the hard-line critics who still regarded the articles as too lenient, and MPs who feared that Anglican Protestants would suffer financially from the omission of the 'missing clause'. In the six years since the Treaty had been signed, Anglican Protestants had been buying land and taking out leases from Catholics in the five counties specified in the second article. If the 'missing clause' was omitted, and Catholics were required to forfeit their estates, a substantial number of Protestants would suffer financially. The hard-liners, however, wanted the 'missing clause' omitted and the sixth article amended to allow them greater opportunity to bring lawsuits against Catholics.

The Lords Justices reassured MPs that Protestants would not suffer financially through the omission of the 'missing clause'. The Lord Chancellor or Ireland, John Methuen, lobbied 'personally above a hundred members' to win sufficient support for ratification, and had 'to represent to them the necessity of passing the bill, because the King did believe it absolutely necessary for his own honour, the quiet of the Kingdom and to prevent complaints of his Allies'. The Irish House of Commons passed the bill on 14 September.

The Lords presented a stiffer challenge, but the main opposition came from supporters of the Treaty, who objected that the bill was in breach of the original terms. As Bishop King argued, 'We could not reconcile it to the King's honour or the public faith if under pretence of confirming articles granted on valuable considerations, we should have consented to an act that broke them.' The Lord Chancellor was again engaged in intensive lobbying. 'Nothing is more surprising', an English minister observed, 'than to see a House of parliament in Ireland making difficulties on a Bill because it is not favourable enough to Papists, and that bishops should appear in the head of the opposition is wonderful to the last degree.' On 23 September, after eight hours' debate on the third reading in the Lords, the bill was finally passed by a majority of only three votes, 23 to 20. Excluding proxy votes, the majority was one, 17 to 16. Fourteen of the bill's opponents entered a strong protest against the bill, but their efforts to reinstate the original Treaty were in vain.

Criticism from William's Continental allies, who were also concerned about other anti-Catholic legislation, was brushed aside. The Duke of Bavaria, a member of the anti-French coalition, raised the issue of Irish Catholics during his visit to London, a month after the vote in the Irish House of Lords. William's reply was less than convincing: 'I have to fall in with the wishes of the Irish Parliament which is well aware of the turbulent spirit of the regular [Catholic] clergy and has to take measures for the preservation of the peace.'

The hearing of land claims under the terms of the Treaty, as ratified by the Irish Parliament, was resumed before a panel of nine judges. As with the earlier hearings, the process was fair. Within the two-year time limit set for this second round, 791 claims were heard and only 8 were not allowed. In total, almost 1200 claims were approved between 1692 and 1699. Successful applicants included members of nearly all the leading Jacobite families – Antrim, Clanricarde, Dillon, Iveagh, Mountgarret from the peerage; Fitzgeralds and Nugents from the Pale; and Kellys, O'Briens, O'Reillys and MacNamaras from the Gaelic Irish.

In the event, omitting the 'missing clause' had less effect than was expected. The lengthy dispute between William and the English Parliament over the forfeited lands meant that no legislation had been passed to confiscate estates of Irish Jacobites. Instead, legal proceedings were taken in the High Court, but no prosecutions had been brought in Clare and Mayo, which were most affected by the 'missing clause'. William continued this policy of restraint from prosecution and, as a result, Catholics continued to hold land in those counties.

With the Treaty ratified and revenues buoyant, no meeting of the Irish Parliament was summoned between 1698 and 1703. During those years, however, the English Parliament moved to settle the controversy over the substantial lands confiscated from Irish Catholics who were not covered by the terms agreed at Galway and Limerick. William's grants of their forfeited Catholic estates had caused a furore. English MPs believed that considerable sums could be raised for the public purse from the sale of forfeited lands, and refused to let the matter rest. In 1699, commissioners were appointed to inquire into the forfeitures, but they received a hostile reception in Ireland. With the passage of time, Anglican Protestants had bought or leased land from the beneficiaries of William's grants. About one hundred purchasers had paid almost £60,000 for land from Albemarle (Bentinck), Athlone (Ginkel), Romney (Sydney) and others. The largest purchaser was William Conolly, later Speaker of the Irish House of Commons. They stood to suffer considerable financial loss if William's grants were overturned.

In 1700, the English Parliament passed the Resumption Act, which declared null and void all William's land grants. The forfeited estates were vested in trustees appointed by Parliament, not the Crown. It was a humiliating, personal defeat for William. On 11 May 1700, he wrote to a beneficiary of his grants, the Earl of Galway, formerly Ruvigny, the Huguenot commander:

> you may judge what vexation all their extraordinary proceedings gave me, and I assure you, your being deprived of what I gave you with such pleasure was not the least of my grief. . . . There have been so many intrigues this last session that without having been on the spot and well-informed of everything it cannot be conceived.

Jacobites enjoyed only limited success in recovering their estates under the provisions of the Resumption Act. Compensation was paid, however, to those who had bought or taken out leases from the beneficiaries of William's grants, and private bills were passed to protect their interests. In 1702 a bill was introduced to allow those who had purchased land from William's beneficiaries to buy in their purchases at a reduced price. About 80,000 acres were thus allotted to fifty 'Protestant purchasers' on special terms. Eventually, 568,000 profitable acres, previously owned by 179 Jacobites, were sold to 360 purchasers. The 'private estate', formerly owned by James II and granted to Elizabeth Villiers, was distributed among 170 new owners. Most of the purchasers were families established in Ireland before 1688, the overall result being to break up old, large Catholic estates and redistribute them among a greater number of Protestant owners.

By 1703, Catholics owned 14 per cent of the land in Ireland, compared with 22 per cent in 1688. Among the survivors of the Williamite war, the main losers were those who surrendered immediately after the Boyne, and those who opted to fight in France rather than remain in Ireland. Ironically, the citizens' army of Derry also suffered great financial loss. Despite well-founded claims, the British House of Commons repeatedly refused to grant any back-payment to the soldiers, let alone meet their costs of equipment.

By the time of William's death in 1702, England was again embroiled in Continental war. The renewed external threat and the continued fear of Jacobite insurrection were powerful influences motivating Dublin and London to deprive Irish Catholics of the means to defend the modest position they had rescued from the débâcle of the Williamite war.

V

Anti-Catholic legislation had long been an adjunct of English rule in Ireland. The penal laws, in one form or another, dated back to Elizabethan times. They were generally passed during the periodic fits of insecurity to which the English and the Anglican Protestants in Ireland were prone, and their implementation often served as a barometer of the febrile political atmosphere in London and Dublin. Although they were not a systematic code and were not always rigorously enforced, their existence on the statute book humiliated Catholics and the threat of enforcement was pernicious.

English national security and the Anglican Protestant interest were seen as being dependent on one another. Security and religion were also bound together. The strength of the Anglican Protestant interest in Ireland was indivisible from the strength of the established Church, the Church of Ireland. The concern which Anglicans in England felt about their Irish sister Church was demonstrated in Mary's letter to William of 7 July 1690, written immediately after she heard of his victory at the Boyne. The Church was the first issue she raised, one which she was not prepared to leave for a later letter, despite the bearer being 'impatient to return' to Ireland. 'I must put you in mind of one thing', she wrote, after expressing her excitement at William's news,

> that you wou'd take care of the church in Ireland. Every body agrees that it is the worst in Christendom . . . You will forgive me that I trouble you with this now, but I hope you will take care of those things which are of so great consequence as to religion.

Anglicans wanted to see their Church prosper in Ireland, because it would help secure their interest and because they believed it to be the 'true religion'. This 'missionary' aspect had been an important motivation in English colonization of Ireland since the Reformation.

Story, himself an Anglican chaplain, argued against relying on penal laws to bolster the Church of Ireland: 'True Religion is not to be planted by Penal Laws, or the Terrour of Punishment, which may fill a Church with Temporiz-

ing Hypocrites, but never with Sincere Professors.' Story's proposed solution
was to strengthen the Church of Ireland,

> by finding out some means to allow each Minister a Competency, and then
> oblige him to reside upon it, whether his Parishioners be *Papists* or *Protestants*;
> since the Living among those People, and the frequent Conversation with them,
> wou'd be of more force than all the Penal Laws in *Christendom*.

But this approach would take time, and the political will was lacking. With
security fears uppermost in English and Anglican Protestant minds, penal laws
appeared to offer a speedy solution to an immediate problem.

In February 1693, the Whigs engineered a debate in the English House of
Commons on Irish affairs and summoned hard-line Irish Anglican Protestant
MPs as witnesses. In an Address to the King on the State of Ireland 'in the
safety and preservation whereof, this your majesty's kingdom is so much concerned', the Commons recited Anglican Protestant grievances over the terms
agreed at Limerick, and repeated allegations that the army was recruiting 'Irish
papists and such persons who were in open rebellion against you, to the great
endangering and discouraging of your majesty's good and loyal protestant subjects in that kingdom'. In 1694, a Commons committee called on the Irish
Parliament to pass 'such laws as shall be necessary for the security of
Protestants'.

From Dublin Castle, Capel, the Lord Deputy, proposed legislation which
would disarm Irish Catholics, prevent their recruitment by the army and
curtail their foreign education. His aim was to deny Catholics the means to
escape English rule, and to isolate them from their Continental sympathizers.
These proposals were, in fact, revivals of the previous penal measures.
Catholics had many times been ordered to hand in their weapons, they were
already effectively banned from military service by the requirement to take
oaths, and the sending of Catholic children overseas had been forbidden in
1611. Nonetheless, Capel's bills were passed by the Irish Parliament in
September 1695. The English Privy Council, however, had insisted that the
Treaty of Limerick be taken into account, so that those Catholics covered by
the terms were still allowed to carry the specified quantity of arms.

Capel's bill for disarming Catholics included a significant addition. It
required Catholics to give up all horses above the value of £5. This would
prevent them breeding good horses, which was a back-handed compliment to
Sheldon's Irish Horse, who had delayed the Williamite victory at the Boyne
and thereby prolonged the war. The measure would also deprive the Catholic
aristocracy of horses strong enough for their coaches. Moreover, since no
reference had been made to horses in the articles of Limerick, the ban applied
to Catholics throughout Ireland, including those who had been under Jacobite
protection at the time of the peace.

In October 1695, the Irish Lords and Commons each prepared further anti-

PLATE XVI

Nineteenth-century representation of the flight of the Wild Geese after the Treaty of Limerick, October 1691.

PLATE XVII

Irish soldiers fighting for the French, 1750.

PLATE XVIII

Tapestry of the Battle of the Boyne in the old House of Lords, Dublin.

PLATE XIX

(Left)
the obelisk
commemorating
William's victory at the
Boyne, which stood in
the valley from the
1730s until the 1920s.

(Below left)
detail from the
eighteenth-century
painting by West,
showing King William
at the Boyne on a white
charger.

(Below right)
the huge Williamite
goblet of Charles
Cobbe, an eighteenth-
century Protestant
Archbishop of Dublin.

PLATE XX

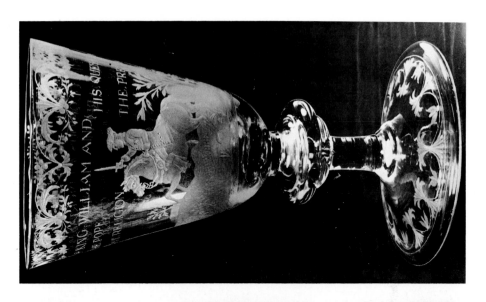

PLATE XXI

The Volunteers on College Green, Dublin, 4 November 1779. Trinity College can be seen behind William III's statue.

PLATE XXII

Loyalist poster opposing Home Rule meeting, 1883.　　Ulster Division, the Somme, July 1916 (detail).

PLATE XXIII

The cult of King Billy: left, a loyalist wall-painting, and right, a banner held aloft during an Orange Day parade.

Catholic legislation. Their proposals for the suppression of monasteries and the banishment of all regular Catholic clergy were duly submitted by Capel to the English Privy Council, in keeping with Poynings's law. Irish Catholics, however, appealed to William's Catholic ally, the Austrian Emperor, and as a result of his intervention with William the planned legislation was dropped. The Catholics' reprieve did not last long. In 1697, the Irish Parliament again considered the bill suppressing the monasteries and banishing Catholic clergy, which now also included Catholic bishops and other regular clergy. Any who returned would face the death penalty. The impact of its enactment on the Catholic Church was severe. Five bishops were already on the Continent, and a further four had followed by 1701. The position of the four bishops who remained in Ireland was precarious, to say the least.

The brief interlude of peace in Europe revealed the divergence of interests between London and Dublin, which had been largely submerged by the war and the Jacobite threat. The tensions were exacerbated as rapid economic growth in Ireland gave way to rising prices. The attempts in the English Parliament from 1697 to restrict Irish wool exports, in response to demands from the west-country lobby, generated an impassioned constitutional controversy. The issue centred on the role of the Irish Parliament – did it possess some degree of independence, or was it entirely subordinate to Westminster? The debate was a precursor to later disputes about representation in English colonies. The wool bill passed by the English Parliament finally received royal assent in May 1699.

Ireland's subordinate position had been emphasized in October 1698, when Westminster voted to station 12,000 troops of the English army in the country. William wanted to maintain a sizeable land army after the end of the Continental war, but had run foul of English fears of a standing army. The ingenious solution was to limit the size of the standing army stationed in England to 7000, while transferring the bulk of the troops to Ireland and making the Irish foot the bill. Yet the troops remained firmly under English control, and were readily available to be sent to fight in Europe and the colonies. The Irish Parliament, fortuitously, had already sanctioned a major programme for building barracks, partly to counter the continued problem of rapparees, partly to meet the pressing need for accommodation in the garrison towns.

VI

In 1701, the outbreak of the War of the Spanish Succession saw the English army's Continental reserve despatched from its quarters in Ireland to fight a new campaign against Louis XIV. The old English and Anglican Protestant insecurities were revived. Despite James II's death in the same year, the Jacobite flame had not been snuffed out. Concern at the very real prospect of a Catholic succession had prompted the English Parliament, also in 1701, to pass the Act of Settlement, which established the Hanoverians' right of succession, on condition that they remained Protestant.[30] William's death in 1702 and Anne's accession coincided with economic recession, which endured for the first five years of the new reign. It was in this climate of continued insecurity that further penal measures were introduced.

In blatant contradiction of the articles of Limerick, which required only an Oath of Allegiance from Catholics, an additional oath was introduced. The Oath of Abjuration, which renounced James II's claim to the throne, had been introduced in 1696 in England following the scare over the plot to assassinate William, and was now extended to Ireland. In 1703, it was demanded of Irish barristers and was required of voters the following year. By 1709 virtually anyone was liable to be called on to take it.

The Williamite land settlement remained the most convincing proof, as far as Anglican Protestants were concerned, of the undue leniency of the 1691 Treaty. At its completion in 1703, Catholics still owned about one-seventh of the profitable land in Ireland. A new Irish Parliament was elected in the same year, and the Tory Lord Lieutenant, the second Duke of Ormonde, was desperate that MPs should vote sizeable revenues. In order to win parliamentary support for increased taxes, Ormonde offered to extend the Williamite land settlement. A precedent had been provided in England, where three years earlier Jack Howe's bill had banned Catholics from buying any land whatever. Ormonde proposed an 'anti-Popery' bill, curtailing Catholic rights of inheritance and preventing their buying any land from Protestants, or taking out a lease for longer than thirty-one years. Before the bill was sent to England for approval by the Privy Council, the Irish Commons added a provision requiring Catholic landowners to abandon primogeniture and divide their land equally between their sons. Only if the eldest son converted to Protestantism would he be allowed to inherit and retain the family estate intact.

Despite lobbying by Irish Catholics and England's Catholic European allies, the English Privy Council contrived to toughen up this draconian bill. In line with Howe's recent Act, no Catholic would be allowed to purchase or take a long lease on any land. The bill also further restricted the practice of the Catholic religion. Parallel measures required Catholic parish clergy to register and banned the entry of foreign-educated secular clergy.

In eloquent attacks on the bill from the bar of the Irish House of Commons, the Catholic law officers of Tyrconnel's Catholic Government of fifteen years earlier, Sir Toby Butler and Sir Stephen Rice, argued that the proposals grossly violated the articles of Limerick. The bill's provisions would remove from Catholics the rights they had possessed by law in Charles II's reign. Butler claimed that the bill amounted to:

> the destroying of the said articles granted upon the most valuable consideration of surrendering the said garrisons at a time when they had the sword in their hands and for anything that then appeared to the contrary might have been in a condition to hold out much longer.

Rice protested that the bill would be 'an apparent breach of those articles and the public faith' and was moved to proclaim that it would 'highly justify the French King's breaking the edict of Nantes'. Defending the proposals with a series of disingenuous and semantic arguments, the Irish Parliament passed the bill.

It was not only Catholics, however, who were victimized by the 'anti-Popery' bill. Presbyterians had been William's most fervent supporters in Ireland, but the Anglican Protestants felt threatened by their strength in the north and their identification with the anti-episcopalian Scottish Church. The Toleration Act of 1689 in England had extended religious toleration to dissenters, but the Anglican Protestants had thwarted attempts to extend the Act to Ireland, rejecting the Presbyterian argument that closer co-operation between the Church of Ireland and their own was essential in face of the alleged Catholic threat. But Anglican Protestants knew that, if the Protestant interest in Ireland again came under threat, the Presbyterians would rally to its defence, whether or not they enjoyed greater equality. In consequence, the Presbyterians existed only on suffrance. They were bitter at their experience of local and occasional persecution, and the interference of the episcopal courts, which bastardized the children of their marriages. In 1703, the English Privy Council, reflecting Tory prejudices against dissenters, inserted a discriminatory measure into the 'anti-Popery' bill. Only those willing to take a 'sacramental test'[31] would be eligible in Ireland for public office, military commission and membership of local corporations. Irish Presbyterians were thus barred from serving the state which their determined efforts had done so much to create.

In 1709, as a result of the vicissitudes of English politics, the extreme Whig, the Earl of Wharton, was appointed Lord Lieutenant. Wharton, who had written the satirical anti-Irish lyrics of 'Lilliburlero' at the time of Tyrconnel's appointment as Lord Deputy, twenty-two years earlier, was characterized by Swift as 'a presbyterian in politics and an atheist in religion'. Wharton marked his tenancy at Dublin Castle by vigorously championing a further wave of anti-Catholic measures. As handmaiden to his efforts, he could call upon the French attempt to launch a sizeable Jacobite invasion of Scotland the previous year, when Anglican Protestants had observed 'the satisfaction which too visibly appeared in the faces' of Irish Catholics before news came through that the invasion had failed.

Wharton closed loopholes in the existing penal laws. 'Priest-catchers' and informers against Catholic landowners or purchasers were offered lucrative rewards. Voters would be required to take the Oath of Abjuration. Similarly, priests registering under the 1704 Act were required to abjure the would-be James III, although this was to all intents and purposes unenforceable. Wharton also proposed extending the English Toleration Act to Irish dissenters, but the harassment of their worship had practically ended and they feared that it would delay the removal of the discriminatory 'test'. After

Wharton's resignation in 1711, the position of Presbyterians failed to improve significantly. The *regium donum*, the grant to Presbyterian ministers, was cancelled in the Tory Government economies of 1714, but was soon restored and a Toleration Act was passed in 1719. None the less, the 'test' remained, despite the efforts of English Whig governments to persuade the Irish Parliament that it should be repealed.

Throughout the first half of the eighteenth century, the pattern of crackdowns and draconian anti-Catholic measures coincided with the periodic scares of foreign invasion and Jacobite insurrection. Bills were introduced proposing the most severe punishments for unregistered clergy, of castration (1719) and hanging (1723), but they failed to become law, and were not revived. The apogee of the penal laws was reached in 1727 when the Electoral Reform Act imposed on all Catholics an outright ban on voting. The Anglican Protestant gentry, however, were already beginning to turn a blind eye to infringements of some of the more extreme penal laws, and became increasingly embarrassed at some of the *causes célèbres*, which revealed the harshness of the measures on the statute book. None the less, Anglican Protestants would remain wedded to the preservation of the penal laws for many decades.

VII

The penal laws, and the society which they created in Ireland, completed a process which the victorious Williamites had sought to impose after the Boyne, but which the Jacobite rearguard action had thwarted. During the first half of the eighteenth century, the Anglican Protestants entrenched themselves in power and completed a land settlement entirely in their favour. Whereas Catholics still owned 14 per cent of the land in 1703, on Arthur Young's estimate in 1776 their share had fallen to just 5 per cent.

In many cases, however, estates remained in the same families which had owned them in the seventeenth century. Cynical conversions to Protestantism became commonplace as a response to the penal laws, not only to retain land but also to gain access to Parliament, public office and military commissions. The administrative, political and social elite in mid-eighteenth-century Ireland was thus defined by its Anglicanism. Incorporated within it were descendants from the 'new English', 'old English' and even Gaelic identities, and among its number were a high proportion of professionals and a strong element of the self-made. William Conolly, Speaker of the Irish House of Commons and one of Ireland's largest landowners when he died in 1729, was from poor origins in Donegal.

By the 1720s, there was emerging in Ireland a distinctive political culture, which has since become known as the 'Protestant Ascendancy', although the term was not coined until the late 1780s, long past its heyday.[32] The Anglican Irish elite no longer regarded themselves as the embodiment of the 'English interest' in Ireland. Instead, they saw themselves as Irish, and are probably best characterized as 'Anglo-Irish'. The Declaratory Act in 1719, in which the English Parliament unequivocally announced its right to legislate for Ireland, helped to fuel the furore in Dublin over the English Government's grant of a minting patent to William Wood of Wolverhampton to produce halfpennies for Ireland. 'By the laws of God, of nature, of nations and of your own country,' wrote Jonathan Swift to his fellow Anglo-Irish, 'you ought to be as free a people as your brethren in England.'

The corollary of Anglican Protestant domination was the exclusion of the vast majority of Ireland's people from any direct role in establishment politics or society. The few, remaining, Catholic landowners were isolated from the political privileges associated with property ownership in most societies of the period. But the notion that all Catholics were submerged in the so-called 'Hidden Ireland', whose values were expressed through the Gaelic poets of the period, implies an identity of interest which did not exist.[33] Experience varied between localities and regions. Extremes of poverty existed. Many were grindingly poor, and would remain so whoever was in power and whoever owned the land. In Dublin and the main ports and towns of Leinster and Munster, an active Catholic trading middle class flourished, and was to make an important contribution in later campaigns for Catholic emancipation.

None the less, Catholics had been dispossessed, and the penal laws were on the statute book:

> Being sunk in misery at all times is not the worst
> but the scorn that pursues us, now that the lions are gone.

Quoting these lines from a poem attributed to Eoghan Rua Ó Súilleabháin, Liam de Paor has written of the sense of 'a deep communal humiliation' which developed among Catholics.[34] This would later provide fertile soil for radical solutions.

A different strand of Irish radicalism was exported. For sixty years, until the late 1770s, tens of thousands of northern Presbyterians emigrated to the American colonies. The motivation for the exodus appears to have been primarily economic, though their lack of political and religious liberty contributed. Anglican Protestants were alarmed at the implications. 'The papists being already five or six to one', observed Bishop King in 1718, 'and being a breeding people, you may imagine in what condition we are like to be.' Yet they could not bring themselves to accord equality to Presbyterians.

Despite the fears of the English and of Ireland's Anglican Protestants that Irish Catholics would rally to the Jacobite cause at the slightest opportunity, and notwithstanding the many grievances which might have prompted them to do so, they showed remarkable restraint during the Jacobite invasion of Scotland in 1745. While Britain experienced eight months of insurrection, the only Irishmen actively assisting Bonnie Prince Charlie were the émigrés on the Continent and their descendants. One reason was the sane approach of the

Lord Lieutenant, Lord Chesterfield, who resisted the demands in Dublin for a repetition of the draconian anti-Catholic measures practised by his immediate predecessor in the wake of the British defeat at Fontenoy. Commenting in October 1745 on the lack of response of Irish Catholics during the British insurrection, Chesterfield wrote to the long-serving English Secretary of State, the Duke of Newcastle:

> The most considerable of 'em have been with me to assure me of their firm resolution not to disturb the Government and to thank me for not having disturbed them as usual at this time. I told 'em very fairly that the lenity [leniency] of the government would continue as long as their good behaviour deserved it.

It seemed that many of the more influential Catholic leaders were committed to the status quo. They included the landowners, tenant farmers and middle-class Catholics active in commerce, who benefited from a lax application of the penal laws, and risked losing more by backing the Jacobite cause than by acquiescing in the prevailing political system. Most Catholics, however, were still demoralized after the famine of 1739–41, and were therefore unlikely to raise support for the Jacobites.

Whatever the reasons, the lack of any involvement by Ireland's Catholics in the '45 marked a turning-point. English national security was no longer seen as being inextricably bound up with Anglo-Irish interests. This weakening of mutual dependence recast the nature of the relationship between London and Dublin. Catholic demands for emancipation from the penal laws, notably those organized in the 1750s by Charles O'Conor of Belanagare, a member of the Catholic gentry of County Roscommon, met a warmer response in London than Anglican-Protestant-Dublin.

The dismantling of the penal laws eventually began in the late 1770s. For many years the application of the legislation had been haphazard. But it was still there to be used against the opponents of Anglican Protestant domination. As a Catholic leader, Charles O'Conor became a target of informers and 'discoverers'. In 1756, his brother Hugh, a convert from Catholicism, seems to have been persuaded to seek his brother's estate. The legal battle lasted for twenty-seven years, consuming Charles's energies and finances, before Hugh finally abandoned his claim. But Charles's feelings as he endured a bitter legal struggle epitomize the human costs of the penal laws:

> After the storm of '88 my poor father was finally cast ashore on a broken plank, I have succeeded to him; this is the plank from which it is now hoped that I may be driven by penal law. I struggle to keep my hold, and if I am left nothing to inherit but the religion and misfortunes of a family long on the decline, the victim is prepared for the sacrifice, resignedly indeed though not willing.

CHAPTER SIXTEEN
'THE WILD GEESE'

I

'The Wild Geese come in their thousands with the October moon,' observed the writer Seán O'Faoláin, describing the origins of one of the most tragic, and romantic, legends in history.

> They blacken the sky and they cry the coming of autumn. Where there are low marshlands, or sloblands, they settle down, and then the cabins are cooking them with much butter or grease in the bastables all the Winter. About the estuary of the Shannon, and all up the river into Limerick, they must have whizzed and moaned, that Winter of 1691, when Ginkel offered the terms that ended the Jacobite War, and started bitter quarrels among the tired and tattered Irish. The flying Irish, down the Shannon or down the Lee with Sarsfield, looked up at the skies, and took the name, The Wild Geese. It was the end of a period. It was all but the end of a race.

The largest, single flight of 'Wild Geese' from Ireland followed the signing of the military articles at Limerick. The Jacobite commanders, Sarsfield and Wauchope, were concerned to keep the Irish army intact and ready for a fresh invasion at the earliest opportunity. They had to prevent the Irish regiments being either disbanded or enlisted into the Williamite ranks. The military articles represented a major triumph, since it was agreed that 'all Persons without any Exception, of what Quality or Condition soever, that are willing to leave the Kingdom or *Ireland*, shall have free Liberty to go to any Country beyond the Seas . . .' The continued Jacobite ambitions of their commanders and Williamite anxieties about Irish involvement in Jacobite plots in Britain meant that the Irish were specifically forbidden to resettle in England and Scotland. In return for the freedom to pursue a military career on the Continent, they were also required to sacrifice their estates, a provision which encouraged many landowning officers to remain in Ireland and seek the benefit of the civil articles. Otherwise, the Irish were to be allowed to go 'where they think fit, with their Families, Household-stuff, Plate and Jewels'.

Sarsfield's aim was to 'make another Ireland in the armies of the great king of France'. The Jacobite negotiators achieved this immediate objective. Not only was the Irish army preserved, but its right to serve in the French service was established even though England and France were at war. Moreover, the Jacobite troops would travel to France entirely at English expense: 'to Facilitate the Transporting the said Troops, the General [Ginkel] will Furnish fifty Ships . . . for which the Persons to be Transported shall not be obliged to pay, and twenty more, if there shall be occasion, without their paying for them.' It was a measure of William's desire to terminate the Irish war that Ginkel agreed to such terms. William simply could not tolerate the prospect of so many of his troops being detained in Ireland for another summer.

Much would depend on how many Irishmen were prepared to leave their native land. Both sides were soon accusing each other of breaking the terms of the military articles as they tussled for the future allegiance of the Jacobite troops.

Two days after signing the Treaty, Ginkel sent 'ten Field-pieces and six Canon into the Irish Town', and in the afternoon issued a Declaration:

> We cannot but let the officers and Soldiers of the *Irish* Army know how willing we are to indulge, and provide for them, that by remaining in this Kingdom, or serving Their Majesties abroad, and rather promote the *British* and *Irish* Interest, than the Designs of *France* against both: And do therefore promise and declare, that all Officers and Soldiers of the said Army that have a mind to return to their homes, shall have leave to do so with all their Goods and Effects, and there be permitted to live quietly and peaceably under the Protection and Encouragement of the Government.

The Irish were offered money for their horses and arms, and those willing to serve William were promised that they would have 'Quarters immediately assigned them, and receive Subsistence till Their Majesties further Pleasure'. Ginkel rebutted the allegations 'industriously spread about' that recruits from the Jacobite army would be 'sent into *Hungary*, and other remote parts', and gave a pledge that they would 'not be obliged to serve in any Place against their Wills'. This was an extraordinary promise, which would have delighted any soldier in the English army. By contrast, those who chose to go to France 'must not expect to return into this Kingdom again'.

On the afternoon of Monday 5 October, following Ginkel's Declaration, Sarsfield and Wauchope launched their own campaign to counter the Williamite inducements and retain, or recapture, the hearts and minds of the Irish army. They promised that the Irish could look forward to active service in France on an '*English* Establishment and receive *English* Pay', with the prospect that 'next Spring, or soon after, they would either by landed in *England*, or else in *Ireland*, with a powerful Army.'

The next day, Tuesday the 6th, brought the crucial moment of decision, when each Irish officer and soldier would have to decide whether his future lay in a Williamite Ireland or with Sarsfield's Irish army fighting on foreign soil. The morning began with an appeal to their souls: 'a Sermon was preached to each Irish Regiment by their Priests, declaring the Advantages to them and their Religion, by adhering to the French Interest, and the Inconveniences, nay, certain Damnation of joining with Hereticks.' As Story added, 'a good Quantity of Brandy [was] given them to wash it down,' invigorating even the most battle-hardened campaigner. Afterwards, the bishops gave the troops their blessing.

With the persuasive words of the clergy ringing in their ears and the brandy stirring their hearts, 14,000 Irish infantrymen were drawn up on the County Clare side of Thomond bridge, across the Shannon from Limerick Castle. The Williamites reiterated their appeal. The historic march past proceeded under the eagle eyes of Sarsfield and Wauchope on one side, and Ginkel and the Lords Justices on the other. Soldiers who wished to follow Sarsfield were required to march straight ahead, while those wishing to stay had to file off at a predetermined point. By the end of the exercise, Ginkel was greatly disappointed. Only 2000 of the Irish opted to remain at home, a little over 1000 chose to serve William, while around 11,000 committed themselves to follow Sarsfield.

Yet the final, agonizing decision whether to leave or stay would only come as the ships for France were about to be boarded. The soul-searching was prolonged by the logistical difficulties in arranging sufficient transports. Depressing reports began to circulate about the plight of the Irish in France. When the ships which had sailed from Limerick returned from France to Cork to collect the second Irish detachment, rumours spread that the Irish already there were being badly treated. As a result, some Irishmen who had been anxiously waiting to follow the first detachments of Wild Geese decided instead that they would stay in Ireland. But others who had planned to stay were disconcerted by their early experience of the new regime, and judged that they would be better off after all with Sarsfield in France. As the Lords Justices acknowledged in a letter in November, 'some thousands of those who had quitted the Irish army and gone home with a resolution not to go to France, were then come back again and pressed earnestly to go thither [to France], rather than stay in Ireland.'

The last shipment from Cork, on 8 December, produced harrowing scenes on the quayside. Wauchope, who was organizing the embarkation, ordered the soldiers aboard first, causing their wives to panic that they were about to be left behind. As Story reported,

> many of the Women, at the second return of the Boat for the Officers, catching hold to be carried on Board, were dragged off and through fearfulness, losing their hold, were drowned; but others who held faster, had their fingers cut off, and so perished in the sight of their Husbands or Relations.

In the event, the ships accommodated everyone who wanted to leave.

Around 12,000 Wild Geese finally headed down the Shannon and the Lee for France. They would be pawns in Louis XIV's Continental strategy, as James II had already become. They had little choice. If they were ever to dislodge William or his Protestant successors they would need the support of a major Continental power.

II

On their arrival in France, the commanders of the Wild Geese received reassuring words from James II at St Germain, his court-in-exile. 'We will not defer to let you know, and the rest of the Officers that came along with you', wrote the King, 'that we shall never forget this Act of Loyalty, nor fail, when in a Capacity, to give them, above others, Particular Marks of our Favour.' Yet James was not so overwhelmed with gratitude that he would honour the Irish by greeting them in person. His reluctance to meet his loyal Irish subjects was to prove a better guide to his treatment of them than his flattering words.

An embittered veteran of Sarsfield's Wild Geese later gave his son a written account of the early days on the Continent:

> No sooner had we arrived in France than King James made an arrangement with Louis XIV by which he had us put on a French footing, reserving for himself the difference in our pay for his own upkeep and that of his house. It was with pleasure that we agreed to this arrangement, although made at our expense. This help put him in the position of not contracting any other obligation with the King of France than the honour he had of being his ally.

James saw the Wild Geese in the same light as he viewed their country, as stepping-stones to the recovery of his English throne. By the time they had arrived, James's court was dominated by English and Scottish Jacobites. The Irish were shunned. Had Tyrconnel lived, he might have been able to press the Irish interest, but Sir Richard Nagle, James's Secretary of State in Ireland, found himself relegated to the background. As the Irish veteran later lamented, 'Men who not only contributed to the upkeep of the Prince [James II], but who risked their lives every day for his preservation and restoration hardly deserved such treatment.' The 6500 Irish troops who had sailed with Mountcashel in March 1690 had been incorporated into the French army as the Irish Brigade, but the new arrivals remained as a separate army. James II's 12,000 exile troops consisted of thirteen infantry regiments, three independent companies of foot, two cavalry regiments and two troops of horse guards. They were paid less than the Irish Brigade, and James showed scant regard for any commissions held in Ireland, demoting officers, and in some cases reducing them to the ranks. The exile army retained the red-coats, as did the Irish Brigade. They dyed the grey-coats which were issued to them scarlet, thus keeping the colour they had donned for the Stuarts. The Irish Brigade and other Irish regiments in the French service continued to wear the red-coats, usually associated with the English army, for almost a century.

It seemed, however, that at least one of the promises made to the Wild Geese before they left Ireland would be honoured. Following the death of Louvois, the French Minister of War, who had generally opposed any diversion of the French effort from the Continent, Louis sanctioned plans for the French navy to support an early invasion of England. By spring 1692, the exile army and the Irish Brigade were encamped on the Normandy coast as the French assembled a great fleet at Brest, consisting of 80 ships of the line and 300 transports. James and the Duke of Berwick were to embark with the troops, the King hoping, as a former admiral of the English fleet, that Admiral Russell and his charges would desert William and declare for the Stuarts.

The invasion force never left French waters. On 21 May 1692, the Anglo-Dutch fleet surprised the French, catching them off Cap La Hogue. In an engagement lasting several days, the French suffered a shattering defeat. As Evelyn observed when the news reached London, 'it pleased Almighty God, to give us such a Victory at Sea to the utter ruine of the French fleete, Admirall & all their best men of Warr, Transport shipps &c: as perhaps never was greater in this part of the World.' Russell had avenged Beachy Head, two summers earlier. As a result, there was no early prospect of the Wild Geese returning victorious to Ireland. After 1692, Ó Bruadair wrote his lament, 'My Heart Is Broken', in which he complained at the decline of Irish poetry, with the loss 'of the gentleminded folk' who had been the patrons of the bards.

Louis XIV forced James to release his exile army for service in the French forces, although most were allowed to remain under James's command. They fought William's Anglo-Dutch army in Flanders, where they confronted old adversaries from the Irish war. At Steenkirk, William launched a surprise attack on Louis' troops, under the command of Luxembourg. Both sides suffered severe losses. Among the Williamites killed were Douglas, Lanier, Mackay and Count Solms-Braunfels, all of whom had served in Ireland. Mountjoy, who had been exchanged for Richard Hamilton, was also among the dead, as was Hamilton himself, who had been captured at the Boyne but served under William after his release. Berwick was taken prisoner, but was exchanged for Ormonde. Sarsfield greatly distinguished himself in the battle gaining a mention in Luxembourg's despatches on 4 August 1692, for having shown 'that valour of which he has given such proofs in Ireland'. Sarsfield was raised to the rank of major-general in the French army before the next year's campaign.

In July 1693 at Neerwinden, Luxembourg out-manoeuvred William so successfully that 50,000 Anglo-Dutch were confronted by a French army 80,000-strong. But William's army dug themselves into strong positions and repelled numerous charges. In the final charge, as the cavalry drove the enemy down to the River Gheet, Sarsfield was struck in the chest by a musket-ball and fell to the ground. Popular legend has it that when he put his hand to his wound and saw it covered with blood, he exclaimed, 'Would to God this were shed for

Ireland!' Sarsfield died a few days later in the village of Huy, of a fever brought
on by his injury.

The Treaty of Ryswick in 1697, which brought an end to the Nine Years'
War, forced the French King to recognize William as King of England, Scotland and Ireland. Over 6000 of the combined total of 21,000 Irishmen in the
Irish Brigade and the exile army were dead or crippled. After the war, the Irish
Brigade was retained, but James's exile army was disbanded. Some were able
to join the Irish Brigade, but most were destitute, some becoming highway-
men, others reduced to begging. An exiled Irish poet spoke for many of his
compatriots, in his lament:

> When awake I am in France,
> When asleep I am in Ireland.
> Therefore it is little love that I have for wakefulness,
> My goal is ever to be asleep.

For most of the eighteenth century, it seemed that one part of Europe or
another was permanently at war. Soldiers were in high demand, and Ireland, a
poor country with relatively few opportunities for the sons of ambitious
parents, and caught in the repressive grip of the penal laws, provided more
than its share of recruits. Although the single, mass exodus of 1691 was never
repeated, Wild Geese continued to fly down the Shannon and the Lee for
many more years.

The death of the Spanish King, Carlos II, in 1700 led to the long-expected
conflict over the Spanish succession. When James II died in 1701, Louis XIV
turned to James's thirteen-year-old son James Stuart, the would-be James III,
to revive the Irish exile army, disbanded only four years earlier.[35] The young
James summoned the Irish exiles, and five regiments of foot were formed,
Galmoy, Bourke, Berwick, Dorrington and Albemarle. The Irish Brigade was
also brought up to full strength, comprising the Clare, Dillon and Lee (originally Mountcashel) Regiments. In addition, there was Sheldon's Horse.

Most of the Irish who fought with the French served in Italy, though others
were despatched to Flanders, Bavaria and Spain. The Dillon and Bourke
Regiments showed immense bravery at Cremona in northern Italy during the
winter of 1701–2. Only 350 of 600 Irish troops survived the Austrian army's
attack on the French quarters. Dillon's troops at Cremona were commanded
by Major Daniel O'Mahony, who later reported the events personally to Louis
XIV. In recognition of the courage of the Irish, the French King raised the pay
of all Irish exiles to the same level as the Irish Brigade. The Wild Geese fought
with distinction in the major battles of the war: Blenheim, Ramillies,
Oudenarde and Malplaquet. At the last of these, the Irish Foot three times
charged the British infantry, which included the 18th Royal Irish, with the cry,
'Long live James III and the King of France!'

In Spain, Berwick's efforts helped to ensure that Louis XIV's candidate,

Philip V, was restored to the throne. In 1702, Philip's ministers opened negotiations to form the first of the Irish regiments which were to serve in the
Spanish army under the Bourbon kings. They included Mahony's and Crof-
ton's Dragoons, and McAuliffe's, Comerford's and Vandoma's Infantry. Many
of their officers had been among the Wild Geese of 1691, and had fought in
the French service until their disbandment after the Treaty of Ryswick. The
'Hibernia', or Irish, Regiment, whose troops were commanded by Don
Reynaldo MacDonald, and the 'Ultonia', or Ulster, Regiment, led by Colonel
Demetrio MacAuliffe, were formed in 1709. The Ultonia was formed from
remnants of Galmoy's Regiment of Wild Geese in the French service, its link
with Ulster seemingly derived from the incorporation into Galmoy's Regiment
of the Charlemont Regiment, who in 1689 had defended Charlemont Fort,
County Armagh, under the command of Colonel Gordon O'Neill.

All told, the Wild Geese in the French service had suffered an estimated
20,000 casualties in the first great war of the eighteenth century. Their plight,
and that of the women who loved them, later provided the subject for Thomas
Davis's moving poem, 'The Flower of Finae', which tells the story of Eily
MacMahon and Fergus O'Farrell, her soldier sweetheart, whom she follows to
Flanders.

By 1715, only 3300 Irish soldiers remained in the French service. They
were reorganized into five one-battalion regiments, Dillon, Berwick, O'Brien,
Lee and Dorrington, and the cavalry, by then known as Nugent's Regiment,
remained in French pay. The French intended to disband Bourke's Regiment,
but Bourke persuaded James Stuart to release his troops from any duty to the
Stuarts, and contracted his men to fight as mercenaries in the Spanish service.
They became known as the 1st Irish Regiment, or Irlanda, and formed the
third of the regiments in Spain's Irish Brigade. Within a few years, the Spanish
Irish Brigade was fighting against the Austrians in Sicily and along the
Pyrenees against its former allies, the French.

The fate of the Wild Geese as pawns in the hands of Continental pay-
masters was never more poignantly demonstrated than during the Stuart
uprising of 1715. From Scotland, James Stuart called in January for the Irish
troops to be sent to join him, as 'it would end the dispute very soon.' Although
Lieutenant-General Dominick Sheldon and Brigadier Christopher Nugent
managed to make their way to Scotland, few others were able to follow. The
French Regent ensured that the Wild Geese were not an embarrassment to the
new Anglo-French alliance, which had followed the Treaty of Utrecht, ending
the last of Louis XIV's great wars. There was some justice in the comment
from one of the veterans of the Wild Geese that 'We were the victims of the
peace of Utrecht. We had already been the victims of that of Ryswick.'

After the failure of the '15, James Stuart and his court left France and
eventually resettled in Rome, where the Pretender received a pension from
Pope Clement XI. King Philip V of Spain remained the Jacobites' most loyal

ally, while Peter the Great of Russia also supported their cause. Both monarchs were patrons of the Wild Geese.

III

'I cannot but highly esteem those gentlemen of Ireland', wrote Jonathan Swift in July 1732, 'who with all the disadvantages of being exiles and strangers have been able to distinguish themselves by their valour and conduct in so many parts of Europe, I think above all other nations.' Swift was replying to Charles Wogan, an Irish exile soldier in Spain, who had written unannounced with an account of his own daring exploits and his thoughts on the plight of the Wild Geese. Wogan had emigrated to the Continent via England, where he had been captured at Preston and imprisoned in Newgate for his part in the 1715 Jacobite uprising, but had managed to escape. He was a native of County Kildare, from an 'old English' Catholic family, the son of Patrick Wogan, who had fought with Sarsfield against the Williamites. Charles Wogan is most remembered for his rescue of Princess Maria Clementina Sobieska in 1719 from Innsbruck, in the Tyrol.[36] He had selected her as the bride for James Stuart (James III, the 'Old Pretender'), but the Austrian Emperor, Charles VI, an ally of the new Hanoverian King in England, George I, prevented her leaving for the Jacobite Court in Rome. Wogan masterminded Clementina's escape and escorted her to Rome. For this display of gallantry, Wogan was created a Roman knight, and was subsequently known on the Continent as Sir Charles Wogan, or the Chevalier Wogan.

The Innsbruck incident was part of a much more ambitious plan in the spring of 1719, and one which greatly alarmed the authorities in London and Dublin at a time when the Hanoverian succession was only recently established. The Jacobites had prepared a major invasion of Britain, led by the Duke of Ormonde, to install James Stuart on the throne, with his new bride Clementina as Queen.[37] The Spanish Prime Minister, Cardinal Alberoni, ordered a fleet of five men-of-war and twenty transport ships, with 5000 soldiers, including 'many Irish', arms for 30,000 more and a suitable supply of horses, to be assembled at Cadiz, on the south-west coast. James Sarsfield, son of Patrick, and other Irish officers were selected to go to Ireland and organize an insurrection, to coincide with Ormonde's landing at Bristol.

In April, following a meeting of the Privy Council in Dublin Castle, which lasted until two o'clock in the morning, the Administration made public their 'certain intelligence' that James Sarsfield and other officers were in the country and 'had held conferences with diverse Papists of distinction, with design to foment a rebellion in favour of the Pretender'. A reward of £1000 was promised for securing Sarsfield or any other of his colleagues. As the official Proclamation made all too clear, the scare prompted the stock response of resorting to the draconian anti-Catholic penal laws:

inasmuch as there was reason to believe this traitorous design could not have been formed and fomented except by Papists, and other persons disaffected of the Government, excited by Popish Priests of the kingdom, all officials were required to apprehend all Popish Archbishops, Bishops, Jesuits, Monks, &c., in order that the laws against Papists, especially those of Limerick and Galway, might be put into execution; all seditious meetings, or assemblies of Papists and other ill-designing persons, were to be prevented, and all strangers, travellers, and others, were to be carefully examined, who should be suspected of disaffection to the person and government of King George.

James Sarsfield's planned insurrection was doomed. The Spanish fleet had sailed in March, but was severely damaged in a great storm off Cape Finisterre on the north-western tip of Spain, and the surviving ships were forced to seek the nearest ports. The small Jacobite force in Scotland was defeated in a skirmish. Sarsfield and his fellow officers were, however, able to escape from Ireland, despite the efforts of Dublin Castle. The following month, on 12 May, James Sarsfield died at St Omer in Flanders.

With the prospect of military careers on the Continent, young Irishmen continued to emigrate and perpetuate the tradition of the Wild Geese. Some were mere boys. Young Felix O'Neill of Creggan, County Armagh, left Ireland at the age of ten in 1730, to join the company of his uncle, Terence O'Neill, senior Captain of the second battalion, and later Lieutenant-Colonel, of the Hibernia Regiment in Spain. Another was Richard Hennessy, who left his home in Ballymoy, County Cork, in the 1740s to enlist in the French service. He would later establish the Cognac firm which still bears his name.

Both the young O'Neill and the young Hennessy fought in the War of the Austrian Succession, following the death of the Emperor in 1740. The War was to mark the peak of achievement by the Irish Brigades in both Spain and France. All three regiments in Spain's Irish Brigade took part in the Spanish invasion of Italy in 1741. They suffered terrible casualties over the next couple of years, and withdrew to Naples to recover. In August 1744, however, the Austrians launched a surprise attack on the town. Despite heavy losses, the Irish counter-attacked and drove the Austrians from the field. Money and honours were showered on the Irish Brigade. Each regiment received a motto for its flag, 'In Omnem Terram, ex hivit sonos eorum' (Their sound hath gone forth into all the earth)[38] and a nickname, the Irlanda becoming 'El Famoso', Hibernia 'La Columna Hibernia' (The Pillar of Ireland), the Ultonia 'El Immortal'. The Irish Brigade fought on in Italy until 1748, but suffered a series of defeats by the Austrians, commanded by Maximilian Browne, himself the son of Ulysses Browne, who had left Ireland with Mountcashel in 1690.

In Flanders, the French besieged the town of Tournai, but in spring 1745 were attacked by the allied army, consisting of British (including Irish), Dutch and Hanoverian troops. On 11 May, the two armies engaged at Fontenoy, the French, led by Maurice de Saxe, numbering around 50,000 and the allies, under the command of William Augustus, Duke of Cumberland, slightly fewer. The British broke through the French lines, and threatened to inflict a humiliating defeat on Louis XV, who was on the field that day. In a last, desperate effort to turn the battle, the French called on the Irish Brigade, who had been held in reserve, to launch an all-out assault on the British right flank. More than 3800 Wild Geese, under the overall command of Charles O'Brien, sixth Viscount Clare, and including the regiments of Dillon, Berwick, Bulkeley, Roth and Lally,[39] marched with bayonets at the level. Their bagpipes, fifes and drums played the Stuart hymn, 'The White Cockade', officers shouted 'Cuimhnigidh ar Luimnech agus feall na sassonach!' (Remember Limerick and Saxon perfidy). According to Voltaire's account, Thomas Lally, son of an Irish officer, added the cry, 'March against the enemies of France and your-selves without firing, until you have the points of your bayonets in their bellies!'

The gout-ridden de Saxe watched the slaughter from his coach as the British were hacked down and driven back. He is said to have commented, 'What finer reserve than six battalions of Wild Geese!' Louis XV was so impressed that he promoted Irish officers, including Hennessy, O'Neill, MacElligot and O'Connell. Characteristically, however, the Wild Geese paid heavily for their triumph, losing 656 men, one in six of their strength in the French service. The victory by the Irish Brigade over the British was the stuff of nationalist legend, and was eulogized by the nineteenth-century Irish poet Thomas Davis. In the campaigns of the 1730s and 1740s, the Irish lost an estimated 2000 killed or wounded during the war of the Polish Succession, and 5000 during the War of the Austrian Succession.

Fontenoy symbolizes the valour of the Wild Geese, yet the Irish Brigade's last-ditch defeat of the British had a deeper significance. This found expres-sion in the words of Henry Grattan, campaigner for Irish parliamentary independence, later in the eighteenth century: 'We met our own laws at Fon-tenoy. The victorious troops of England were stopped, in their career of triumph, by the Irish Brigade which the Penal Laws had shut out from the ranks of British history.' Yet at the time of Fontenoy the authorities in London and Dublin were not at all confident that they could continue to 'shut out' the Irish Brigade from 'the ranks of British history'. In 1727, the pamphleteer, Charles Forman had warned,

> As long as there is a body of Irish Roman Catholic troops abroad, the Chevalier [James Stuart] will always make some figure in Europe by the credit they give him, and be considered as a Prince that has a brave and well-disciplined army of veterans at his service, though he wants that opportunity to employ them at present which he expects time and fortune will favour him with.

By 1743, 'time and fortune' were turning James Stuart's way, as the French gave their support to plans for the Irish Brigade to invade both Scotland and southern England. The authorities in Britain and Ireland took alarm, but a combination of the English navy's vigilance and bad weather prevented the French invading in 1744, as they had planned.

Encouraged by Fontenoy, James Stuart's impatient son Charles took matters into his own hands. In July 1745, 'Bonnie Prince Charlie' crossed to Scotland, his finance, ships and armaments all provided by men of Irish descent. Four of Charles's closest advisers were Irish, including two professional soldiers, John O'Sullivan, Charles's Quartermaster and Adjutant-General, and Sir John MacDonnell, Colonel of Fitzjames's Horse. The Jacobites routed the British army at Prestonpans and marched south, reaching Derby by December. London lay less than a week's march away, and the British mainland force was adrift to the north.

Despite his remarkable progress, Charles Stuart urgently needed reinforcements. The French agreed to send detachments from the Irish Brigade. In November, six ships sailed from Dunkirk, carrying the Jacobite Lord Drummond's Regiment of Royal Scots, and around sixty men from each of the six Irish Foot Regiments and a small detachment from Fitzjames's Horse. Two of the ships, with a total of about 200 men on board, were intercepted. The remaining four ships landed safely, but the reinforcements cannot have amounted to many more than around 200 infantry and 40 or so cavalrymen. Two Spanish ships bearing Irish officers, and money and weapons, were also intercepted. Nothing came of the rumours that the entire Irish Brigade would soon embark for Britain.

From Derby, Charles Stuart withdrew northwards to join forces with the Jacobite Scottish and Irish troops who had landed in Scotland. During the early months of 1746, Irish officers in France, including Thomas Lally, and other Jacobite supporters, such as Antoine Walsh and Pierre André O'Heguerty, the Nantes ship-merchants, tried to persuade the French Government to provide effective support for the invasion. But Louis XV's ministers were unmoved, and most attempts by the Irish Regiments to provide further reinforcements were thwarted by the watchfulness of the English navy.

Jacobite hopes were dashed when Cumberland defeated the Stuart army at Culloden on 16 April 1746, and then proceeded to hunt down and massacre the Highland Jacobites. Charles Stuart escaped with the help not only of Flora MacDonald, but also of Richard Warren of Dillon's Regiment, Colonel O'Sullivan and Felix O'Neill, who had secured permission to leave the Hibernia Regiment in Spain and join the Jacobite invasion. O'Neill was captured and held in Edinburgh Castle. More than 300 Irish soldiers were taken prisoner, but were returned to France in 1747.

IV

The passage of time vindicated Swift's assessment of the many Irish 'exiles and strangers' on the Continent. Lord Macaulay, the English historian, later observed of eighteenth-century Europe:

there were indeed Roman Catholics of great ability, energy and ambition: but they were to be found everywhere except in Ireland: at Versailles and at Saint Ildefonso, in the armies of Frederic and in the armies of Maria Theresa ... Scattered all over Europe were to be found brave Irish generals, dexterous Irish diplomatists, Irish Counts, Irish Barons, Irish Knights of Saint Lewis and of Saint Leopold, of the White Eagle and of the Golden Fleece, who, if they had remained in the house of bondage, could not have been ensigns of marching regiments or freemen of petty corporations.

One of the most dramatic careers was that of Peter de Lacy from Killeedy, County Limerick, who left in 1691 as a thirteen-year-old ensign in the Jacobite infantry and served in the Athlone Regiment of James II's exile army during the Nine Years' War. He was recruited in his early twenties as an officer by Peter the Great, led victorious campaigns against the Turks and the Swedes, and progressed through the ranks to become field-marshal of the Russian army and, in the 1740s, military adviser to the Empress Elizabeth. At his death in 1751, de Lacy was Governor of Livonia.

In Spain, Lieutenant-General Ricardo Wall served as Minister of Foreign Affairs and Prime Minister under two successive kings from 1754 to 1763. 'If he had stayed in his native land', as Macaulay commented,

> he would have been regarded as an inferior by all the ignorant and worthless squireens who drank the glorious and immortal memory. In his palace at Madrid he had the pleasure of being assiduously courted by the ambassador of George the Second, and of bidding defiance in high terms to the ambassador of George the Third.

In Vienna, General Count Dermico O'Mahony was appointed Spanish Ambassador, and on St Patrick's Day 1766,

> gave a splendid reception ... All the well-known Irish in Vienna were invited. They and the Court were all of illustrious birth. Among them were Field Marshal Count Lacey, President of the War Council; the Generals O'Donnell, Maguire, O'Kelly, Browne, Plunkett and McEligot; four winners of the Grand Cross; two Governors; seven Theresian Knights; six Staff Officers; four State Counsellors. The highest nobility of Austria were also present to honour the Irish nation.

The achievements of the Austrian Wild Geese during the eighteenth century have been preserved for posterity. Of the thirty or so commemorative portraits at the Austrian Military Academy at Wiener Neustadt, at least nine are of Irish descent, and include Count Francis Maurice von Lacy, Count Maximilian Browne, Count Anton Wallis, Count Johann Macguire, Count William O'Kelly, Count Lavel Nugent, Count John O'Donnell and Count Johann von Purcell-Rorestown.

By 1762, fewer than half the soldiers in the Irish Regiments in France were of Irish origin. The officers, however, were of Irish descent. When France intervened in the American War of Independence in 1778, the officers of the

Dillon Regiment petitioned 'to be the first to strike a blow against England'. In spring 1779, Dillon's Regiment, light infantry from Walsh's Regiment, and several thousand French regulars embarked for the Americas aboard Admiral d'Estaing's fleet. In July, the detachment seized Grenada, and in September landed near Savannah, Georgia, where they launched a courageous but unsuccessful attack on the town. The Dillon and Walsh regiments later served as marines in the second French fleet sent to the West Indies and helped capture several British islands. Other Wild Geese helped take Senegal, in West Africa, from the British, and a few served with Lauzun's legion during the siege of Yorktown in 1781. The following year, the Hibernia Regiment in Spain's Irish Brigade captured the British Fort George at Pensacola. As a result, the British were unable to hold Florida, which could have served as a base for American Loyalists.

The American forces in the War of Independence counted many Irishmen and their descendants among their number. They included Major-General John Sullivan, whose grandfather had fought with Sarsfield and was one of the Wild Geese in 1691. The descendants of former Williamites also wore the American colours. 'Mad Anthony', or 'Dandy' Wayne, a major-general in the Continental army, was the grandson of a Williamite Captain of Dragoons at the Boyne, who had emigrated to Pennsylvania in 1722.

Within a few years of American independence, however, Revolution in France signalled the end of the Irish Brigade in the French service. Like most of the foreign troops, the majority of Wild Geese remained loyal to the monarchy. The last of the Irish Regiments were finally disbanded in 1792. A 'farewell banner' of white silk with a gold Irish harp surrounded by green shamrocks was conferred on the Irish by the future Louis XVIII. The legend '1692–1792 Semper et Ubique Fidelis' was inscribed upon it. The Dillon and Berwick Regiments became the 87th and 88th Regiments, and Dorrington's, which had become the Walsh Regiment in 1770, was formed into the 92nd.

Many thousands of Irishmen served on the Continent between the 1580s and the end of the Napoleonic Wars, some estimates putting the total as high as 500,000. The Wild Geese won distinction and honour denied them in their own land, but many Irish soldiers, including even high-ranking officers, were sadly neglected when it came to the regular payment of wages and salaries. According to a disillusioned Jacobite officer, writing during the 1692–1701 period, 'the women and children invited to go along with their husbands are now begging their bread from door to door, and cannot get it.' Even in the latter half of the eighteenth century, the descendants of the Wild Geese were still having to seek proof of their genealogies, as a means of access to royal courts and of gaining preferment and promotion. The hope that one day their lands in Ireland would be returned still lingered, but the widows of men killed in battle, often with large families, commonly found themselves destitute, their late husbands' service sheets their only inheritance.

The Wild Geese tradition survives down the centuries. Bernardo O'Higgins was the liberator and first President of Chile. Admiral William Brown was founder of the Argentine navy. In Europe, MacMahon, the French Marshal in the Franco-Prussia War, became President of the Third French Republic and was created Duke of Magenta by Napoleon III. Taafe was Austrian Prime Minister in the 1880s, at the time of the Mayerling tragedy. In the twentieth century, the last of the de Lacys in the Russian army maintained the tradition of supporting the monarch and fought in the White Russian army after the Bolshevik Revolution. During the 1930s, Bishop O'Rorke of Danzig won international status.

Today's descendants of the Wild Geese proudly preserve their family histories. The Gaelic clans of the O'Donnells and the O'Neills are among the most celebrated. The O'Neill, head of his clan, lives in Portugal. The O'Donel is a priest in Zimbabwe, and his heir, the Duke of Tetuan, lives in Spain. Count Gabriel O'Donell, whose ancestor saved the life of the Emperor Franz-Josef in an assassination attempt in 1848, resides in Austria. Nelly O'Brien de Lacy, a descendant of the family of the great Russian Field-Marshal, was born in Poland, formerly White Russia, and is now an artist living in Argentina. The present Duke of Magenta lives in Burgundy. There are Bartons and Hennessys in France, O'Callaghans and Kindelans in Spain, and many more.

CHAPTER SEVENTEEN
WHOSE HERO?

I

There is no question whose hero William is today. Depicted in flowing wig and Restoration dress, seated astride a white charger on the banks of the Boyne, he is a familiar adornment of Protestant wall-paintings of the north of Ireland. Every 12 July, his image emblazons the banners paraded through the streets to the sound of pipe and drum as Orangemen, their sombre suits bedecked with an orange sash, wearing bowler hats and carrying furled umbrellas, celebrate William's victory at the Boyne. An extraordinary anachronism to the rest of the world, this seventeenth-century king has become the potent icon of a tradition in Ireland, a symbol of fundamental rights and solidarity for one community, an image of sectarian aggression and triumphalism for the other.

How is it that someone who, three centuries ago, spent only two weeks in northern Ireland and three months in Ireland as a whole, and who is virtually forgotten in Britain, has become the focus of such deep divisions? The easy answer is that William symbolizes a decisive Protestant victory over the Catholic Irish. Yet the real story is much more intriguing. At different times, William has been hailed as a liberation hero, honoured as an establishment hero, proclaimed as a radical hero and revered as a conservative hero.

When William entered the capital after his defeat of James at the Boyne, he was greeted as the liberating hero by Dublin's Anglican Protestants. But by the autumn of 1690, at William's birthday celebrations, they had to content themselves with the memory rather than the man. To adapt a popular phrase, a cult was born. Although the rest of the country was devastated by war and the Jacobites still held Connaught, the capital rejoiced at its deliverance and the establishment of a new order. As the weekly newspaper, the *Dublin Intelligence*, reported:

> Soon after nightfall an extraordinary firework was begun before the lords justices' door on College Green representing the taking of a castle by storm, which was performed with great curiosity. At some small distance from the Castle, the cyphers of their majesties' names [William and Mary] interwoven and over them

an imperial crown were fixed, which for above two hours continued illuminated.

In Ireland, William's birthday, 4 November, continued to take pride of place for the official celebrations, but in England 5 November took precedence, combining the anniversary of William's landing at Torbay with deliverance from the Gunpowder Plot.

In England, some hailed William as Whig hero, but others were unimpressed by his legacy of Continental war and heavy taxation. Although his image improved during the eighteenth century, comparatively few memorials remain. Across the Irish Sea, William was soon dignified, even deified, by Anglican Protestants, anxious to bestow legitimacy on their regime and to foster an heroic legend. Ten years on from the battle, the city fathers of Dublin commissioned a sculpture of their hero from Grinling Gibbons. Unveiled on College Green on 1 July 1701, the Boyne's eleventh anniversary, the equestrian statue portrayed William in classical mode, dressed in Roman tunic with a wreath of laurels on his head and riding a prancing horse. Cakes, claret and gun salutes entertained the crowds but the Corporation's compliment to the King went unreturned: William did not attend the ceremony, nor apparently did he acknowledge this singular honour.

The statue became the focus of Dublin's official celebration to mark the anniversary of William's birthday, and soon took on a pattern which went largely unchanged throughout the eighteenth century. The choice of 4 November as opposed to the anniversaries of Boyne (1 July) or Aughrim (12 July), was significant in itself. The Anglican Protestants were attempting to stress the constitutional and political values of the Glorious Revolution, and put less emphasis on military conquest. Civic and local authorities ceased to take part in celebrations of the Boyne and Aughrim, which were increasingly associated with lower-class Protestants, and were seen as a nuisance as bonfires raged out of control and fireworks frightened the horses.

The official contribution to each 4 November's celebrations usually took the same form. The Lord Lieutenant or Lords Justices held a levée at the Castle, and then led a procession of city dignitaries, nobility and gentry, escorted by troops, to the statue in College Green. They would then head for St Stephen's Green, before returning to the Castle. Those taking part often wore cockades of orange and blue, thus combining the colours associated with William and St Patrick. The official celebration concluded with a banquet at the Castle for the Administration's leading officials.

From the earliest years, however, Williamite celebrations and commemorations were denied universal reverence. During the politically disputatious years of Anne's reign, Trinity College was suspected as a hotbed of Toryism. A student was expelled for drinking to the memory of Sorrel, the horse which threw William, causing him the injuries which led to his death in March 1702. The Provost, Peter Brown, who was also Bishop of Cork, in his tract, *Of drinking in remembrance of the dead*, attacked the practice of toasting the dead King's memory. The fervent Williamites gave their riposte. Their toast 'To the glorious, pious and immortal memory of William III, Prince of Orange, who saved us all from popery, brass money and wooden shoes', was extended to incorporate a new phrase: 'And a fart to the Bishop of Cork'.

Dublin's equestrian statue of William was an inviting target for students at Trinity, as it stood with its back to their main gate. On Tuesday 27 June 1710, readers of the *Dublin Intelligence* learnt that 'On Sunday night, some Disaffected Villain or Villains had the Impudence to Steal away the Truncheon out of the Hand of the Statue of King William on College-Green.' The authorities were appalled. As well as removing the King's truncheon, his face had been smeared with mud. So seriously did the Privy Council take the insult to William's memory that they offered a reward of £100 to anyone with information leading to the arrest of the offenders. This was a very large sum at a time when a skilled craftsman might earn three shillings a day. The Lord Mayor promptly increased the reward by a further £50.

In mid-August, three Trinity College students, Harvey, Vinegin and Crafton, were charged with the attack. The latter two confessed, but Harvey escaped. The icon was again intact, to the evident relief of Dublin's ruling Protestant establishment. As the *Dublin Intelligence* reported,

> Thursday [the 17th] being the Day of the Franchises of this City, the Truncheon was Replaced to the said Statue in the presence of the Lord-Mayor, at the Head of the 24 Corporations, who all marched by the Statue in good Order, being well Mounted on Horseback, and all in general, made very gallant Appearance.

The occasion prompted a late-night throng of sedan chairs in College Green, as 'a great many Gentlemen' assembled, 'and on their Knees Drank many Noble and Loyal Healths, among them the Queen's, the Glorious and Immortal Memory of King William, the Duke of Marlborough, &c.'

At their trial in November, the statue's assailants were sentenced to six months' imprisonment and fined £100 each. Yet the severity of the sentence acted as little deterrent. A further attack was made in 1714, but the culprits were never found. Although this prompted the posting of guards and the building of a watch-house, the statue was subjected to frequent indignities, sometimes a scarecrow figure of straw being seated behind William.

A few weeks after the unveiling of William's statue in Dublin, a play opened in London at the old Lincoln's Inn Fields theatre, which became another focus for Williamite celebrations during most of the eighteenth century. *Tamerlane*, by Nicholas Rowe, was a political allegory, in which the hero Tamerlane represents William and the villain of the piece, Bajazet, Louis XIV. As a 'paean of praise' to William, *Tamerlane* appealed to English Whigs and was also one of the most popular productions staged at Dublin's Smock Alley theatre, which

revived after the Williamite war. During Anne's reign, however, as Whigs
and Tories jostled for power, the play provoked controversy. In 1711, Sir
Constantine Phipps, the Tory Lord Chancellor of Ireland, was attacked for
ordering the prosecution of a Whig who read out a prologue in favour of 'no
peace without Spain' at the performance on William's birthday.[40] The Whig
domination of politics from the consolidation of the Protestant, Hanoverian
succession, guaranteed the play's popularity for sixty years, until the late
1770s. Astute theatre managers staged the play on 4 or 5 November and were
guaranteed a full house.

William had become an establishment hero. He was toasted at dinner
parties, and Williamite toasting glasses, complete with engravings of their hero
and a range of suitable inscriptions, became a speciality. The mammoth goblet
which belonged to Charles Cobbe, an eighteenth-century Protestant Archbishop of Dublin, can be seen in the Ulster Museum. Complete with William
on a prancing horse, sword aloft and rows of cavalry and infantry in the background, it bears the inscription 'The glorious and immortal memory of King
William and his Queen Mary and perpetual disappointment to the Pope, the
Pretender, and all the enemies of Protestant religion'. A glass on display in the
National Museum of Ireland, which bears the inscription 'The glorious
memory of King William, 1 July 1690', has a large bubble in the stem
representing a tear to express sorrow for his departure from Ireland.

William became a popular subject for paintings in private houses and public
buildings. In 1733, the walls of the chamber of the House of Lords of the new
Houses of Parliament in College Green were decorated with specially commissioned tapestries, the *Battle of the Boyne* and the *Defence of Londonderry*.
Initially, their manufacturer, Robert Baillie of Dublin, was contracted to produce six, but only the two were woven. The designer is thought to have been
Johann van der Hagen, a landscape, marine and scene painter, and the chief
weaver Jan Van Beaver. Many of the weavers came from Flanders, their origin
and their subject-matter prompting W. B. Yeats to assert:

> When Huguenot artists designed the tapestries for the Irish House of Lords,
> they celebrated the defeat of their old enemy Louis XIV, and the establishment
> of a Protestant Ascendancy which was to impose upon Catholic Ireland, an
> oppression copied in all details from that imposed upon the French Protestants.

The tapestries can still be viewed in the original room, which is part of the
Bank of Ireland building.

In 1736, an obelisk was erected on the banks of the Boyne, as a result of 'the
grateful contributions of several Protestants of Great Britain and Ireland'. The
inscription on it read:

> Sacred to the glorious memory of King William III, who on 1 July 1690 crossed
> the Boyne near this place to attack James II at the head of a Popish army

advantageously placed on the south side of it, and did on that day, by a successful battle secure to us and our posterity, our liberty, laws and religion.

The Boyne's golden jubilee on 1 July 1740 was celebrated, according to the
Dublin newspapers, with the greatest rejoicing ever known. As part of the
festivities, ten veterans of the battle were reunited, the youngest of them being
seventy-seven years old. *Reilly's Dublin Newsletter* reported that the 'Boyne
Club' in the Earl of Meath's liberties attended church and then marched
through the town with orange cockades in their hats, preceded by drums and
trumpets.

As the zenith of Anglican Protestant power passed, the cult of King Billy
was exposed to new pressures. In response, its hero would assume a fresh guise.

II

Compare William's horse in Jan Wyck's famous painting of the Battle of the
Boyne and the tapestry installed in the Irish House of Lords in 1735, with his
mount in another well-known representation of the battle by the English court
painter, Benjamin West, in 1778. In Wyck's painting and the tapestry, the
King rides a chestnut horse, but in West's work the royal steed has been
transformed into the white charger more familiar to us today from the streets
of Northern Ireland.[41] The transformation was no accident. The white horse
was the Hanoverian emblem. William symbolized the Protestant succession.
By bringing the two together, William and the Hanoverians were represented
as indivisible.

But why should William on his white charger be considered a suitable subject by West in the late 1770s? It was not, after all, a jubilee, diamond, or any
special Williamite anniversary. By far the most plausible explanation is to be
found in the politics of the period. The American colonies were in revolt and
France entered the war in support of the American rebels. The British Empire
was under threat. Rebels in America, and critics of the Government in England and Ireland, were claiming to be the true heirs to the principles of the
Glorious Revolution. George III and his ministers were accused of arbitrary
government and oppression, the very allegations which the Williamites had
levelled against James II.

Viewed in the context of revolutionary upheaval, West's painting appears as
a restatement by the Hanoverian establishment in England of their position as
the true heirs to William and the Glorious Revolution. It remained the foundation of their claim to rule, and they could not afford to abandon it to their
liberal and radical critics. Moreover, West's association of the Hanoverians
with the military success at the Boyne would not come amiss with the English,
when their army were fighting to subdue a rebellious people, as William had
subdued the Irish almost ninety years earlier.

But the view from Ireland gave a different perspective. As the Anglo-Irish became more critical of arbitrary, despotic rule from London, the radical strand in the Williamite legend became more pertinent. There were clear parallels with the American colonies. The American rebels themselves had been strongly influenced by Irish thinking. William Molyneux's tract, *The case of Ireland's being bound by acts of parliament in England stated*, which appeared in 1698, had highlighted the iniquitous position of people having laws imposed upon them by a parliament in which they had no representation. The Scots-Irish Presbyterians, who were emigrating to America in large numbers, had also infused the colonies with dissenter radicalism.

By the late 1770s, the political tide was flowing strongly back across the Atlantic. The shock-waves from the American War of Independence soon hit Ireland. The Irish economy was plunged into deep recession as trade slumped and England imposed tougher war-time restrictions on Irish exports. In 1778, France declared war on England, and an old Anglo-Irish spectre reappeared – the combined threat of domestic unrest and a foreign invasion. Moreover, the Anglo-Irish felt terribly exposed. English red-coats had poured from Irish barracks and garrisons to fight in the American campaign, but the Administration in Dublin Castle refused to allocate the funds required to raise a militia.

Ireland's Protestants mobilized. In Belfast, in spring 1778, a paramilitary corps was set up to organize and train its members in self-defence against invasion. In the spirit of the times, the Volunteers fashioned themselves on liberal and radical ideals. Their aims were non-sectarian. They were independent of the Government and organized themselves on democratic lines, their officers elected by the membership. Such was the impact of the Volunteers that the idea of militias quickly spread across the country, though there were local variations. By 1779, with the threat of French imminent invasion, their numbers increased dramatically, from 15,000 in the spring to 40,000 by December. Grudging official recognition was given in the summer when the Administration gave them light arms. At the same time, Ireland's political crisis, brought on by the economic recession, was worsening. Dublin Castle had lost control of the Irish Parliament. MPs and many people outside Parliament joined in demanding the removal of the trade restrictions imposed from London.

In this atmosphere of political turbulence there occurred, on 4 November 1779, the most remarkable celebration of all the annual gatherings held at William's statue. The Volunteers corps in the Dublin area, some 900 strong, assembled at St Stephen's Green at eleven o'clock. Among those present were Liberty Volunteers, the companies of Lawyers, Goldsmiths and Merchants, the Uppercross Fusiliers, and companies from the Barony of Castleknock and the Barony of Coolock. Some wore mainly blue uniforms, others mainly red. They marched in files to College Green, gathering round the statue, which was decorated in orange and blue ribbons and its pedestral festooned with placards: 'The Volunteers of Ireland', 'Relief to Ireland', 'Short Money Bills –

A Free Trade – Or——', and 'The Glorious Revolution'. The official celebration was held at three o'clock that afternoon, when a troop of horse preceded the Lord Lieutenant, riding to College Green in 'a superb carriage'. In the evening, 'A general illumination took place, attended by every mark of real rejoicing. The different corps of our Volunteers, consisting of near a thousand persons, dined with their commanders and officers.' A ball at Dublin Castle, a play at the Theatre Royal, the ringing of bells and bonfires rounded off the day's festivities.

As the campaign for political reform was stepped up, William's revived role as liberal hero was maintained. The scenes as the Volunteers gathered at their annual celebrations around William's statue are captured in Wheatley's famous painting. At the November 1782 gathering, one of the placards placed on the statue demanded 'an unequivocal bill of rights'. The Volunteers' non-sectarian appeal attracted some Catholic financial and moral support, although the movement remained almost entirely Protestant.

By the 1780s, it seemed that the old sectarian tensions might finally be banished. The process of repealing the penal laws was under way, and some landowners and local authorities were willing to provide financial support for Catholic schools and churches. At Derry, on 7 December 1788, Catholics, as well as Protestants, joined in the commemorations on the hundredth anniversary of the apprentice boys' shutting the city gates to keep out Antrim's troops. But any notion that the old divisions might wither away was an illusion. Instead, the old questions and attitudes had merely been frozen over. From the 1770s, the pressures for a thaw were steadily growing. The political heat of the 1790s would fashion a new sectarianism, which would make a lasting impression on Irish society.

III

The French Revolution and the subsequent war between Britain and France had a profound effect on Ireland. Their impact was greater than any other European event since 1689–91. In the turmoil of the last decade of the eighteenth century, King William emerged as a reactionary, sectarian hero.

Ireland was already experiencing considerable change by the time of the French Revolution. The process of repealing the penal laws had begun, splitting Protestant opinion between liberals and conservatives. A newly assertive Catholic middle class was making its voice heard in the campaign for further reform. The economy was expanding and a more market-oriented approach was having an unsettling impact in some rural areas. The country had experienced agrarian disturbances since the 1760s. But the Oakboys, the Hearts of Steel, the Whiteboys and the Rightboys were all essentially conservative protests and did not challenge the existing order. From the 1780s, however, a sectarian feud, involving sporadic attacks and clashes, developed in County Armagh, and came to be dominated by two secret societies, the

Catholic Defenders and the Protestant Peep-of-day boys. Although initially rooted in the particular economic and social circumstances of Armagh, sectarian violence spread across southern Ulster. From the mid-1790s Ireland's sectarian and political conflicts became interlocked.

In 1791, the French Revolution impinged directly on Irish politics, prompting a revival of the Volunteers. But this reflected a division within the Protestant community about Ireland's future. The radical wing, based mainly in Belfast and to some extent in Dublin, identified with the events in France. William and the 'Glorious Revolution' looked tame by comparison. On 14 July, they celebrated Bastille Day. Later in the year, the French Revolution inspired the formation of a new radical political organization in Belfast and Dublin, the Society of United Irishmen. The case for a radical alliance of Catholics and Protestants was persuasively argued by a young Dublin Protestant lawyer, Wolfe Tone.

By 1792, the Volunteer Earl of Charlemont found that few others were any longer prepared to parade at William's statue. Some Volunteers took to wearing green instead of the traditional orange cockades, and stated a preference for celebrating 14 July rather than William's birthday. Elsewhere, however, the newly revived Volunteers reflected the more conservative views of many in the Protestant community, acting as a Protestant, or loyalist, private police force. Although this was largely a result of Dublin Castle's failure to deal with a rash of agrarian and sectarian disturbances during 1792–3, the Government were none the less perturbed at the growth of a potential challenge to their authority. This prompted the possibility of raising a militia in Ireland, an option which appeared increasingly necessary with the mounting threat of war against France, and the consequent need to ensure the security of Ireland.

In turn, the question arose of whether the militia should be entirely Protestant. The Lord Lieutenant, Lord Westmorland, who had introduced only minor reforms to the penal laws despite London's demands that more should be done, believed that a Protestant militia would reassure the Protestant community. But the Catholic Committee, the main pressure group campaigning for emancipation, seized their opportunity, and appealed over the Lord Lieutenant's head. Their deputation to London was granted an audience with George III. Faced with imminent war against Revolutionary France, William Pitt's Government were anxious to prevent any alliance between discontented Catholics and radical Protestants. Westmorland was urged to push through the crucial concessions being demanded by Catholics – the right to vote and the right to carry arms. As the British Home Secretary, Henry Dundas, wrote to Westmorland, the Government's aim 'was to connect all lovers of order and good government in a union of resisters to all the abettors of anarchy and misrule'.

In April 1793, two months after the outbreak of war with France, the royal assent was granted to the Catholic Relief Bill and the Militia Bill. Their passage marked a turning-point. The century-long Anglican Protestant domination was seriously undermined. The rationale behind reform showed that as far as London was concerned Ireland's Protestants were merely another form of Irishmen.

It seemed to many Catholics, however, that compulsory recruitment to the militia, through a random ballot of the names of all cess-payers, was designed to deny them their newly won rights. The violence of the subsequent anti-militia riots and the ferocity of the army's response revealed that the old social order was breaking down. Its erosion, the British Government's rejection of any further Catholic concessions and the repression of protest when Ireland was once again under threat of invasion, combined to create a highly volatile society by the mid-1790s.

In September 1795, sectarian feuding spread to northern Armagh. The Defenders attacked the Winter's Inn, at the Diamond, Loughgall, but were defeated by a large party of Protestant weaver–farmers. In imitation of the Defenders, the Protestants established their own secret society, the Orange Order, with local 'Orange' lodges. William had long since entered the folk-memory of Ulster Protestants. Like the lower-class Protestants of Dublin, northern Protestants had continued to celebrate the Boyne and Aughrim, long after the official celebrations had been limited to William's birthday.

The Protestant local gentry started to give open support to the Orangemen. Following attacks against Catholic smallholders during the winter of 1795–6, rumours of Protestant outrages and Government complicity spread across the country. The reaction among the Defenders was to become more uncompromisingly anti-Protestant and anti-state. The authorities were initially perturbed at the emergence of the Orange Order, since it represented a further challenge to central authority. But Orangemen were active in the local militias and yeomanry, on whom the authorities relied to help to counter the revolutionary plans of the United Irishmen. The alliance between the Defenders and the United Irishmen prompted some Protestants to leave the latter organization. The Government's concern to break the link between the northern Presbyterian radicals and Catholics gave them an interest in the continuation of sectarian division. Excesses by the militia and yeomanry, to which the authorities increasingly turned a blind eye, spread fear of massacre throughout the Catholic community. In turn, the Catholics increasingly looked for protection to the Defenders, the United Irishmen and the French, who were attempting invasion from 1796. The division between conservatives and radicals became more closely aligned with the sectarian divide.

During the early summer of 1798, the country was rocked by a series of insurrections. Poor leadership, bad luck, lack of support from the French and the effects of the Government's repression prevented their developing into a full-blown revolution. The largest uprising, in County Wexford, was crushed at Vinegar Hill, when about 20,000 rebels were defeated. Later in the summer, General Humbert led a small French invasion force ashore at Killala, County Mayo, but despite the enthusiasm of local volunteers it was no match for the Government forces and was defeated at Ballinamuck, County Longford. A larger invasion force in October was unable to effect a successful landing. Among those captured was Wolfe Tone, wearing a French uniform.

The Boyne's anniversary had already become the cause for patriotic celebrations by the Anglo-Irish during the war against France. In November 1798, following the defeat of the insurrections and the French invasion, the Anglo-Irish marked William's birthday 'with a spirit of preparation beyond what has been usual on the celebration of this anniversary'. Orange cockades and gun salutes were again the order of the day. The decoration of William's statue symbolized a victory for the Anglo-Irish status quo, as the following day's press report made clear:

A cincture [garland] formed of orange and green ribbons surrounded the head of the Monarch, whose shoulders were ornamented with a rich orange sash terminated with shining tassles, orange reins to the horse, and orange and blue ribbons at the saddle skirts and in every appropriate situation, were liberally arranged, the whole exhibiting a studious attention to detail.

Official condemnation of the rebels was also represented: 'Under one of the animal's feet . . . was placed a piece of green silk tied with pale yellow, indicative of trampling underfoot those colours, as being the adopted emblems of revolutionary union during the late rebellion.' William's statue was celebrated by the Orange societies in Dublin which had been formed in 1797, but it became a target for their opponents. In 1798, the King's sword was wrenched off and an attempt made to file off his head.

The first members of the Orange Order were lower-class Protestants, who portrayed their hero as aggressively sectarian. As Lecky later observed, 'the most worthless Protestant, if he had nothing else to boast of, at least found it pleasing to think that he was a member of a dominant race.' Today's Orange Day marches derive from the late 1790s, with subsequent Victorian embellishments. From the earliest days they featured processions with drums and banners depicting 'King Billy' on his white charger, the Hanoverian symbol, and the singing of 'Orange' songs including 'The Spirit of William', sung to the tune of 'Lilliburlero' and regarded as the original song of the Orange institution.

The New Style, Gregorian, calendar was soon adopted for the anniversary of the Boyne. During the eighteenth century, eleven days were added to Old Style dates to adjust them to the New Style calendar. The Boyne's anniversary date of 1 July therefore became 12 July, and has remained so ever since. But the Boyne had occurred in the seventeenth century, when the difference between the two calendars was in fact ten days. The correct date of the anniversary is therefore 11 July and not the 12th.

The original Orange oath enjoined its adherents 'to support the King and his heirs as long as he or they support the Protestant Ascendancy'. The Orangemen's loyalty is thus conditional. Underpinning Ulster's 'loyalist' tradition is the notion of the 'covenant', derived from Scottish presbyterianism. The 'covenanters' owed unconditional loyalty only to God, not to any 'earthly prince'. The conditionality of Ulster loyalism has remained a consistent strand in the Orange tradition, and has baffled successive generations of British politicians and officials as they try to come to terms with self-professed 'loyalists' whose loyalty attaches to a Protestant monarchy, not to the modern symbol of authority in the British state, the Crown-in-Parliament.

IV

The British reaction to the Irish insurrection was to rewrite the constitution. In 1800, the Act of Union abolished the Irish Parliament and created the United Kingdom of Great Britain and Ireland. The first Irish MPs arrived at Westminster in early 1801, but London was slow in honouring its promise to remove the remaining penal laws.[42] The issue of Catholic emancipation was to remain unresolved for the first three decades of the nineteenth century. Orangemen led the opposition to Daniel O'Connell's campaign and, in the process, the cult of King Billy became exclusively partisan.

The tradition of the state procession to College Green on William's birthday, established in 1690, was broken in 1806. Earlier that year, after Pitt's death, the new 'ministry of all the talents' in London included several liberal Whigs who favoured Catholic emancipation. The Orangemen's 12 July celebrations in College Green were criticized by liberal Protestants. On 4 November, as the *Freeman's Journal* reported, 'The Anniversary of William III's Birth Day was not observed with the usual demonstrations of regard. A few yeomen, a few fifes and drums, a few orange ribbons, and a few shots were all the symptoms we heard of extraordinary exultation.' As the paper added, the new Lord Lieutenant, the Duke of Bedford, 'did not parade the streets, as was usual with former Viceroys', although the Lord Mayor gave a grand public dinner. From this time on, Williamite celebrations were seen as partisan, not state, occasions, even when the incumbents of Dublin Castle were opposed to Catholic emancipation. Liberal Protestants increasingly turned to St Patrick for their national day.

As the struggle over Catholic emancipation continued, Orange Lodges spread throughout Britain. Orangemen occupied powerful positions in central and local government, their influence in the English army increased, and they even won support from members of the royal family. But their readiness to defy the Government and the sectarian invective of their supporters ultimately limited their influence and narrowed their appeal. In Ireland, their annual celebrations provoked growing confrontations with Catholics. On 12 July

1813, the liberal *Freeman's Journal* reported:

> The entire of the morning was spent in most outrageous freaks of Orange
> revelry; shoutings, firings, etc. etc. The evening was passed in a different des-
> cription of disorder – the people, seeking retribution by similar clamour, and by
> assailing the devoted statue with all description of filth.

The civic authorities eventually intervened. In 1822, the Lord Lieutenant,
the Marquis Wellesley, elder brother of the Duke of Wellington and a supporter of Catholic emancipation, imposed a ban on Orange decoration of
the statue on William's birthday. The Orangemen demonstrated their anger
the following month during a performance of Goldsmith's *She Stoops to Conquer* at the Theatre Royal. At the close of the Fifth Act, 'When Old Hardcastle
and Tony Lumpkin appeared with their tankards of ale, the Orangemen called
on them to drink the Glorious, Pious and Immortal Memory.' The curtain
came down and the band played 'God Save the King', 'when a quart glass
bottle was thrown from the gallery' and fell on the stage. The band completed
the national anthem, then played 'Patrick's Day', 'the time of which the
Marquess Wellesley also marked. Many bars of this national air had not been
performed when another missile, a large wedge of timber, which formed the
heavy part of a watchman's rattle, was aimed at the Lord Lieutenant's box.' At
the following year's Boyne anniversary, troops lined College Green to prevent
any decoration of the statue. July 1823 marked the end of Williamite celebrations in Dublin.

By the time that Catholic emancipation finally came in 1829, the division
between Orange and Green was being accentuated by Ireland's uneven economic development. Eastern Ulster was industrializing, while the rest of Ireland
remained a predominantly agrarian society with commercial activity based
around its ports. As a result, an increasingly important element within the
northern Protestant community was coming to identify ever more closely with
Britain, economically and politically, and was set even further apart from rural
and commercial Catholic Ireland. The terrible ravages of the famine in the
1840s widened the gulf.

The stresses and strains of social change in Belfast, generated by
industrialization, were the seed-bed of sectarian violence. The town's population was swollen by huge immigration from the countryside, creating a substantial Catholic minority. In 1784, only 8 per cent of the Belfast population
were Catholic, but by 1835 this had increased to nearly one-third. In the mid-
1830s, the sectarian, anti-Catholic sermonizing of Dr Henry Cooke made a
considerable impact. On 12 July 1835, serious rioting broke out in Belfast at
the end of the day's Orange celebrations. It was to set a pattern for the rest of
the nineteenth century, reflecting the function which the marches had come to
perform in Ulster's mish-mash of Catholic and Protestant communities:
'Where you could walk you were dominant, and the other things followed.'

Although the Orange Order was virtually eliminated in Britain and most of Ireland as a result of a determined political campaign against it during the late 1830s, Orangeism continued to grow in the north. Increasingly, it bore the hallmarks of Cooke's teaching. In 1843, O'Connell brought his campaign for the repeal of the Union to Belfast, but his espousal of a Catholic, popular nationalism alarmed Ulster's Protestants. Union with Britain preserved their position as part of a larger Protestant majority throughout the United Kingdom. This one issue overrode all the differences of interest and outlook which characterized Ulster's Protestants, uniting the bosses and workers of eastern Ulster, the landowning gentry and tenants of the west, the farmers and weavers of Armagh, the Calvinist settlers of the Antrim coast. They feared that Home Rule would condemn them to their worst nightmare – sectarian Catholic, majority rule. From the 1860s and 1870s, as the Fenians threatened and the Nationalist-led land war challenged Protestant power, the Orange movement expanded throughout Ulster. A new siege was beginning.

'All Ulster is Ours!' proclaimed the Nationalists after the victory of their candidate, T. M. Healy, in the 1883 Monaghan by-election. Their public meetings in the province were seen as an invasion, and Protestant counter-demonstrations were organized. As the northern Protestant minority mobilized to resist the spectre of Catholic majority rule, they deployed the imagery and revived folk-memories of the Williamite period. In October 1883, Protestants in Fermanagh were urged to mobilize against a meeting in Garrison, which would be addressed by the Nationalist MPs, Thomas Sexton and William O'Brien. A loyalist colour-poster proclaimed:

1688–90 LOYALISTS OF FERMANAGH, Messrs. SEXTON & O'BRIEN, Following in the footsteps of Healy and Sullivan, intend to INVADE your county on Thursday next . . . ASSEMBLE IN YOUR THOUSANDS and show these Teachers of Murder, Assassination and Outrage, that NO DISTANCE will Prevent you Personally Protesting against such a Policy . . . MEN OF DONEGAL. Remember BUNDROUSE 5th July 1689. MEN OF FERMANAGH. Remember BELLEEK, 6th May 1689.

At the November 1885 general election, the Irish Nationalists won eighty-six seats, giving them the balance of power at Westminster. Their leader, Parnell, had initially supported the Tories, who had won most seats, but the Liberal leader, Gladstone, indicated his readiness to introduce Home Rule for Ireland. With Nationalist support, he formed a minority government in February 1886. Ulster Protestants faced their most serious challenge since the late seventeenth century. The imagery of that period would provide a community of disparate and disputatious groups with an essential, unifying focus.

V

During the British Cabinet meeting of 26 March 1886, Joseph Chamberlain, President of the Local Government Board, announced that he could no longer remain in the Government, gathered his papers, and walked from the room. Gladstone, the Liberal Prime Minister, had just confirmed to ministers his intention to press ahead with Home Rule for Ireland. Lord Randolph Churchill, the Tory 'Young Turk', had already played the 'Orange card', visiting Ulster and inciting Protestants to resist Home Rule in rabble-rousing speeches, declaring 'Ulster will fight and Ulster will be right!' Although the late nineteenth and early twentieth centuries saw two other contentious Irish issues – disestablishment of the Church of Ireland and land reform – largely settled, Home Rule dominated British and Irish politics for a generation. This one issue caused one of the most bitter partisan conflicts ever witnessed in the United Kingdom. Chamberlain's Liberal Unionists fought with the Conservatives against Home Rule, eventually merging to form a single party.

When Gladstone's Home Rule Bill was defeated in June 1886, serious rioting broke out in Belfast. The wrecking and looting of Catholic shops and public houses was only stopped by the arrival of 5000 additional police. The anniversary of the Boyne, the following month, 'was celebrated with processions and customary distinctions upon a larger scale than usual, and with more enthusiasm'. Serious violence followed. Within two days, the Chief Constable and a British soldier were shot. Rioting continued on and off throughout the summer, resulting in 32 deaths, 377 police injured, 442 arrests and 31 public houses wrecked. The Orange Order was criticized for its intolerance and incitement in the Commission of Inquiry report into the rioting.

At the bi-centenary celebrations of the Boyne in 1890, the Unionist MP, Colonel Waring, warned that 'If Mr. Gladstone was returned to power they might find another Tyrconnell in Dublin Castle, and might have to combat another conspiracy for the extinction of Protestants in our native land.' The imagery of the late seventeenth century endured into the new era of modern democracy because it represented more than simply a myth of past, heroic achievements. It provided the focus around which the diverse groups in the Ulster Protestant community could rally, and offered the means for political unity in a society where religious dissent and schism were the norm. The struggles of 1688–91 became the warp and weft of Unionist rhetoric.

But more than rhetoric and unfocused demonstrations would be required if Home Rule were to be resisted. The last two decades of the nineteenth century saw the growth of an organized Unionist movement and the development of a more coherent case against Home Rule. The Ulster Unionist Council was founded in the early 1880s to elect MPs to Westminster. By the early 1900s, the leadership of the Unionist movement was largely drawn from the landed gentry, but the policies came to reflect the harder-line, non-negotiable opposition to Home Rule identified with Ulster's urban businessmen.

The Conservative Prime Minister, Lord Salisbury, encouraged the Ulster Unionists. Speaking at the annual meeting of the Primrose League in the Covent Garden Theatre in 1892, he argued that Parliament had the right to govern the people of Ulster, but it had no right to sell them into slavery. He recalled how the people of Ulster had met the challenge of James II. If a similar abuse of power on the part of Parliament or a King should ever again occur, he did not believe that 'the people of Ulster have lost their sturdy love of freedom nor their detestation of arbitrary power'.

On 17 June 1892, Ulster Protestant opposition to Home Rule was harnessed in a great Unionist Convention, held in a specially constructed wooden pavilion at Belfast's Botanic Gardens. 'A more momentous occasion prior to a political occasion has never been experienced in the history of Belfast,' proclaimed the *Belfast Telegraph* 'and nothing of equal importance has transpired since the historic siege of Derry.' Over 12,000 delegates attended, and a crowd of 120,000 massed outside. The exterior of the building was decorated with flags, shields and emblems, while inside tapestries portaying famous moments in Protestant history were hung from the walls and ceilings. 'We are children of the revolution of 1688,' Thomas Sinclair, a former Gladstonian Liberal MP, told the meeting, 'and, cost what it may, we will have nothing to do with a Dublin Parliament.' The following year, the second attempt by a Liberal government to introduce Home Rule was defeated in the House of Lords. No further effort was made until the Liberals were again dependent on Irish Nationalist support in the Commons, after the two indecisive general elections of 1910.

The third Home Rule crisis brought the United Kingdom to the brink of civil war. The Ulster Unionists, led by the Dublin Protestant lawyer, Sir Edward Carson, were given remarkable support by the official Opposition party at Westminster. The then Leader of the Conservative and Unionist Party, Andrew Bonar Law, himself a lowland Scot with Ulster connections, gave his unequivocal backing to a threatened insurrection against the elected Government of the day. Accompanied by seventy British MPs, Bonar Law addressed a mass rally of Unionists near Belfast in April 1912, and chose to deploy the imagery of the 1680s:

> Once again you hold the pass, the pass for the Empire. You are a besieged city. The timid have left you; your Lundys have betrayed you; but you have closed your gates. The Government have erected by their Parliament Act a boom against you to shut you off from the help of the British people. You will burst that boom. That help will come . . .

By 1912, Carson was recruiting and drilling his own private army, the Ulster Volunteers. Dominated by the Orange Order, it was pledged to resist Home Rule by force. But Carson needed to channel and discipline Unionist resistance. The solution was to persuade his followers to enter into a binding covenant to resist Home Rule. Later that year, on 28 September, which the Unionists designated 'Ulster Day', a 'Solemn League and Covenant' was signed by 237,368 men. A Declaration expressing similar sentiments was signed by 234,046 Ulster women, giving a grand total of 471,414 signatories. Some had signed in their own blood. The following July, 150,000 Orangemen and loyalists rallied at Craigavon, and in the autumn of 1913 the Provisional Government of Ulster was formed.

Immediately beforehand, in their determination to resist Home Rule, some Ulster Protestants had seen the Kaiser's Germany as a potential ally. The guns supplied to the Volunteers, for use against the British army, were supplied from Germany, and in 1911 James Craig observed that the Kaiser would be preferable to Redmond. The Kaiser had given a large equestrian statue of William III as a gift to the British people only a few years earlier, and some Ulstermen saw the German monarch as a latter-day William, as a letter in the *Irish Churchman* of 14 November 1913 made clear: 'should our king sign the Home Rule Bill the Protestants of Ireland will welcome this Continental deliverer as their forefathers, under similar circumstances did once before.'

In the event, Carson's Ulster Volunteers fought against the Kaiser, as did thousands of other Irishmen, many of them supporters of Redmond's Nationalists. The Volunteers, however, were allowed to serve as a separate regiment, the 36th (Ulster) Division. They were an army within an army, bound by their own oath and committed to the survival of Protestant Ulster as much as to the survival of Britain. In his moving account of the Ulster Division, Philip Orr quotes a popular Ulster poem of the period, which shows that Unionists saw loyalty to Britain in terms of a covenant:

> What of the men of Ulster?
> Hark to the armèd tread,
> As they turn their backs on the Province,
> And face to the front instead;
>
> The sword half drawn on her own behalf
> In Ulster's Red Right Hand
> Will leap from the scabbard and flash like fire
> For the common Motherland.
>
> And wherever the fight is hottest,
> And the sorest task is set,
> ULSTER WILL STRIKE FOR ENGLAND –
> AND ENGLAND WILL NOT FORGET.

The Ulster Division was steeped in the Orange tradition. At its training camp at Clandeboye, many of the tents were decorated with Union Jacks and Orange emblems, at night the troops sang Orange songs, and each battalion acquired its own regimental marches, including 'King William's March' and 'Billy's March'. Although the authorities shipped the men across the Irish Sea before the anniversary of the Boyne in 1915, the troops none the less celebrated 12 July in the incongruous setting of their new camp at Seaford, on the Sussex coast. A soldier on a white horse representing King William led a group of his comrades marching round the parade ground. Bemused local inhabitants witnessed a procession, complete with band and banners.

It was the fate of the Ulster Division to be drafted in Picardy, near the River Somme, where in the summer of 1916 the British were planning a major offensive. The Ulstermen were ordered to attack on Saturday 1 July. Some saw it as a good omen, since the Battle of the Boyne had been fought on the first day of July. For many others it was the last thing on their mind, but, in the few remaining moments before they went over the top, some placed wild flowers in their battledress, including orange lilies, the symbolic flower of the Boyne celebrations. Others donned their Orange sashes. Last-minute Orange Lodge meetings were held as German shells exploded around them.

Cries of 'No surrender, boys!' were heard as the first Ulstermen reached the enemy's frontline. But they were cruelly exposed to unrelenting gunfire from the German positions on higher ground. They displayed immense bravery, pushing the Germans back, taking hundreds of prisoners and winning four VCs, but the battle became a slaughter. Among the carnage, 'Some of the men were whistling Orange songs and now and again you'd get a few words from "Dolly's Brae" or "The Sash".' As few as one in ten soldiers from the battalions who led the assault survived. In just two days, the Ulster Division suffered more than 5000 casualties, of which at least 2000 died. In addition, many Ulstermen were killed in other regiments in which they served.

On 12 July 1916, the celebration of the Boyne was abandoned. Instead of the traditional Orange parades, a five-minute silence was observed at noon all across Ulster. As the rain poured down on Belfast,

> On the stroke of 12 all traffic came to a standstill, men raised their hats, ladies bowed their heads, the blinds in business and private houses were drawn, and flags were flown at half-mast. The bells at the Assembly Hall tolled, and after the interval of five minutes chimed the hymn 'Abide with me'.

The impact on a tightly knit community was devastating. The message from memorial services across the province was the same: 'Ulster Protestants took their stand where their fathers stood ... [in] costly self-sacrifice to our Empire.' Many nationalist Irishmen died in the trenches, but the Somme became the unionist blood-sacrifice.

EPILOGUE

I

Like the rest of Europe, Ireland was transformed by the First World War. The Easter before the Somme, Sinn Fein's uprising had triggered the events which led to Irish independence. But the price was partition. The British believed that the 'Irish problem' had finally been solved, and proceeded on the whole to ignore what was happening in the part of Ireland which remained under their control, until they were rudely awakened by the explosion of the troubles in the late 1960s.

The tricolour of the new Irish state proclaimed the coming together of Green and Orange in a united Ireland. But there were few Protestants south of the border, and a state was developed which embodied Catholic nationalism as opposed to a more pluralist republicanism.[43] In the six counties which comprised Northern Ireland, almost two-thirds of the population were Protestant. Orangemen virtually monopolized the institutions of government. But their own sense of being a minority within the island of Ireland persisted, and conditioned their response to the sizeable minority of Catholics north of the border. The siege mentality persisted.

Predictably, the cult of King Billy fared very differently north and south of the border. Its impact on the majority of Irish people had earlier been vividly described by the nineteenth-century English historian, Lord Macaulay:

> To them every festival instituted by the State was a day of mourning, and every public trophy set up by the State was a memorial of shame. We have never known, and can but faintly conceive, the feelings of a nation doomed to see constantly in all its public places the monuments of its subjugation. Such monuments everywhere met the eye of the Irish Roman Catholics. In front of the Senate House of their country, they saw the statue of their conqueror. If they entered, they saw the walls tapestried with the defeats of their fathers.

In the Free State, which later became the Republic of Ireland, two of the most notable Williamite monuments soon met their end. In 1923, a group of soldiers from the Irish army garrison at Drogheda, angered at Protestant attacks on the Catholic areas in Northern Ireland, drove along the Boyne Valley and destroyed with a landmine the obelisk commemorating William's victory. In 1929, the IRA attempted to blow up the equestrian statue of William in College Green, Dublin. It was never repaired. Instead, the City authorities decided that the statue was a traffic hazard, and it was removed to a builder's yard. The IRA completed their task by entering the yard and sawing off William's head. The statue of the poet, Thomas Davis, now stands in College Green.

The Huguenot tapestries still hang on the walls in what is now the Bank of Ireland building on College Green, but the equestrian statue outside now lives on only in the everyday life of Joyce's Dublin. Johnny, the old mill-horse, pressed into action 'to drive out with the quality to a military review in the park', did splendidly until he 'came in sight of King Billy's statue: and whether he fell in love with the horse King Billy sits on or whether he thought he was back again in the mill, anyhow he began to walk round the statue'.[44] And as the viceregal procession sweeps from Phoenix Park after luncheon, passing the city landmarks, 'Where the foreleg of King Billy's horse pawed the air Mrs Breen plucked her hastening husband back from under the hoofs of the outriders.'[45]

The impact of 1689–91 could not be erased as easily as its monuments. But to search for the present-day effects of the events of three centuries ago, as though they can be as readily identifiable as a statue or a tapestry, is too reductionist. History's shapes are more complex, its threads more tangled, its sculptors and weavers not consciously creating the patterns sought by later generations.

The folk-memory survives. South of the border, Aughrim and Limerick often evoke a stronger response than the Boyne. The first of July 1690 proved the turning point of the Williamite war, but Aughrim remains the last defeat of the old Irish Catholic army on Irish soil. Sarsfield secured the Irish army's survival at Limerick, but it was for ever lost to its own people as the Wild Geese flew down the Shannon and the Lee, never to return from the battlefields of Europe. The white cockade, emblem of the Jacobites, lived on in Irish song, but as the decades passed there were new demands to be made, new ideas to believe in, new emblems of inspiration. The shock of the 1790s snapped the old political threads.

Yet the new was informed by the old. Loss, betrayal, dispossession left their mark. Ireland had lost its Catholic aristocracy, the political and military leaders of their day. The sense of loss was compounded by betrayal after Limerick and the dispossession which followed. The 'Glorious Revolution' and its aftermath appeared Janus-faced. Bloodless in Britain, but bloody in Ireland. Heralding parliamentary government, but enlisting British and Irish soldiers and taxpayers in European war, and removing access to public service for Irish Catholics and Presbyterians; entrenching the recognition of basic rights in the constitution, but imposing a 'communal humiliation' on a majority in Ireland.

An Irish perspective is provided in the gaelic poem, 'The Tears of Hibernia for the Battle of Aughrim', written around 1700. The 'ill-got' gains of the Anglican Protestants are shown to have been made at great cost, not only to the Irish, but also to themselves:

> Mourn lost Hibernia ever mourn
> thy freedom lost, thy laurels torn,
> thy warriors sunk on Aughrim's plains,
> And Britain loading thee with chains.
>
> Her stern oppression grinds the land,
> and bows thee with its iron hand.
> Thy nobles a degenerate race,
> corrupt, rapacious, sordid, base,
> anxious their ill-got wealth to save,
> and slaves themselves to rule the slave;
> barter their rights, betray thy cause,
> and abject bow to British Laws.

Modern historians have properly debunked the old stereotypes, showing the diversity, in some limited cases even the prosperity, of the Catholic Irish after the Williamite settlement. But the political and cultural legacies, the impact of that settlement on assumptions and attitudes, cannot be gainsaid. Historical events which are the centre-piece of the loyalist tradition – the 1688 Revolution, the Boyne and securing the Protestant succession – symbolize the old sufferings and wrongs.

II

North of the border, the imagery of three centuries ago proved a powerful instrument of political unity for the Protestant majority. The new state created in 1921 was dignified with its own Parliament and accorded the honour of being opened by King George V, the first royal attendance at a State Opening in Ireland since James II over 230 years earlier. Orangemen monopolized the state institutions, James Craig, later Lord Craigavon, the first Prime Minister of Northern Ireland, later describing Stormont as a 'Protestant Parliament and a Protestant State'.

The imagery of the Boyne, King Billy and the siege are embedded in Ulster Protestant folklore. These images had been refashioned in the upheaval of the 1790s, revivified in the struggle against Home Rule, and sanctified in the blood-sacrifice at the Somme. After partition, they flourished as a potent expression of Protestant solidarity, a badge of identity in the face of a perceived threat. '"No Pope here", "Not an inch", "God save the King", and "Remember 1690" were signs we saw every day,' recalled Robert Harbinson of his 1930s childhood in the Belfast Protestant stronghold of Sandy Row. It was, and still is, a culture rich in the ballads and music of the Orange tradition, and where the events of 1689–91 were taught as part of their heritage. Earliest memories invariably still feature 'brightly coloured Orange banners, a figure in restoration dress near a river, and seeing the bands go by'.[46]

Orange Day marches inescapably combine folk festival and sectarian triumphalism. As Sam Hanna Bell recalled, Protestants in the Orange Order could joke with their counterparts in the Catholic Ancient Order of Hibernians, who march on 15 August, about borrowing drums from each other:

> Divil the one o' the Hibs walking on the fifteenth knowed it was King Billy was on the drum ye borrowed from the Orange Lodge. We slapped a coat o' green whitewash on his rid jacket and they all thought 'twas Patrick Sarsfield ridin' to blow up the siege train at Ballyneety!

At another level, however, Orange marches have served to reinforce sectarian division in Northern Ireland. To recall Macaulay on the annual celebrations of the raising of the siege of Derry, 'The faults which are ordinarily found in dominant castes and dominant sects have not seldom shown themselves without disguise at her festivities.' Growing up in Derry, John Hume, the leader of the Social and Democratic and Labour Party, recalls that for most of the year he and his fellow Catholics would get on perfectly well with Protestants, but as the summer marching season approached, 'they distanced themselves from us, the tensions emerged and the siege mentality was there again.'[47] The troubles which began in the late 1960s had their origins in economic and political problems, but the riots which led to British troops being sent on to the streets of Northern Ireland in August 1969 started with the violence which flared following the Derry Apprentice Boys' march.

A society long neglected came under the spotlight. Fifty years earlier, the young Louis MacNeice, born in Carrickfergus, had been shocked to find that although his English governess 'was a Protestant, she knew almost nothing about King William'. Little had changed. From the late 1960s, images of the Orange marches on television screens and in the press were greeted across the Irish Sea with incredulity and incomprehension. They still are. As A.T.Q. Stewart, the Ulster historian, has observed:

> The BBC is quite wrong when it says with ill-concealed astonishment every 12 July that so many thousand Orangemen celebrated the victory of Protestant over Catholic in 1690. It is not about that at all. It is about the continued survival of Protestants against the unitary Catholic State.[48]

The incredulity can be mutual. 'Doesn't everyone have a twelfth?' was the shocked response from a young boy, reared in the Protestant community, when he discovered that Orange Day was not universal.[49]

'How many were out? Who did you see?' are stock questions at the end of Orange Day.[50] The marches are exercises of annual reassurance, an expression of solidarity in a community which feels under threat and insecure. Protestants fear becoming a minority. Their sense of insecurity is heightened by the danger of division in a community where the dissenter tradition is strong, and which is continually breaking and shattering on religious lines. Religious schism reinforces the need for monolithic politics. A tradition characterized by dissent has been paralyzed by the fear of public disunity. The wall-poster's call, 'Remember 1690', is not about the past, but urges the need for solidarity in the present and future, a need reinforced by the terrorist threat.

Yet 1690 and the Boyne can also serve as a metaphor for the unionist approach, as one of their number acknowledges:

> The Boyne symbolizes all our political battles. Every battle has to be fought with us on one bank of a river, and an enemy on the bank opposite. The leader on his white charger has to declare openly beforehand the price he is willing to pay if he is to retain the trust of all those behind him.[51]

There is thus 'no flexibility in thought, a lack of preparedness to consider tactics'.[52] On the limiting nature of the loyalist view of history, Tom Paulin, the Ulster poet, has written: 'There is so little history / we must remember who we are.'[53] The unionist view, at least since the 1880s, is a remarkably simple one. In this sense, 'a community that superficially might appear to be burdened by historical awareness can accurately be said to possess "so little history".'[54]

At the heart of the loyalist tradition is a radical readiness to resist authority. This was reflected from the very first, in the original Orange oath. Loyalty still lies solely to the monarch, on condition that he or she remains Protestant. The overriding concern for the Protestant succession, and the consequent protection of Protestant civil and religious rights, has meant that loyalists have never accepted that their loyalty lies to the modern British state as such. A direct result is their providing the one example in the history of the United Kingdom of a workers' strike bringing down a government, when the Ulster Workers' Council succeeded in ending Northern Ireland's power-sharing Executive in the spring of 1974.

Successive British politicians have been perplexed by what seems an incomprehensible paradox: disloyalty by self-proclaimed 'loyalists'. In July 1975, Enoch Powell, the former Conservative MP, who was elected Ulster Unionist MP for South Down, declared that:

> To be loyal is, for the Unionist, to accept the will of Parliament as expressed in the law of the land, which is made by the Crown in Parliament. What, however, no person who calls himself a Unionist can do without self-contradiction, is to place limits or conditions upon his obedience to the Crown in Parliament.[55]

The riposte from other Unionists was blunt and immediate. Harry West, Powell's own party leader at the time, recalled that if Unionists had always been loyal to the British Parliament, there would have been no Northern Ireland, explaining that 'While we proclaim loyalty to the British Crown, we do not necessarily follow the dictates of any British political party in power at Westminster.' The Rev. Ian Paisley, leader of the Democratic Unionist Party,

commented that Unionists 'hold no allegiance whatsoever to the Wilsons and
Heaths of this world. If the Crown in Parliament decided to put Ulster into a
united Ireland, according to Mr Powell we would have to obey if we were loyal.
This is utter nonsense.'[56]

Loyalists are thus set apart not only from the majority with whom they share
the island of Ireland, but also, by their view of politics, from those with whom
they share citizenship of the United Kingdom. The point is illustrated in their
determined opposition to the Anglo-Irish Agreement, signed in November
1985 at Hillsborough, County Down, by Dr Garret FitzGerald, the then
Taoiseach, and Margaret Thatcher, the British Prime Minister, and ratified by
both the Dáil and Westminster. In John Hume's view, the Agreement brought
a marked improvement in the handling of parades, and Orange parades in
particular. Hume says that he has 'no objection whatsoever to the Orange
tradition being celebrated in Ireland. It's part of our tradition. But it should be
done in a manner that is neither triumphalist nor provocative. It should be
done in a genuinely celebratory manner.'[57] Hume's comments reflect a greater
readiness to recognize the validity of both Irish traditions, nationalist and
loyalist, which has developed in Ireland, and which has been given notable
expression in Dr FitzGerald's Richard Dimbleby Lecture and the Forum for a
New Ireland, initiated in 1983. Notwithstanding their opposition to the Anglo-
Irish Agreement, younger Unionist politicians have recently indicated their
readiness to try to find ways in which the nationalist and loyalist traditions can
co-exist. It is, however, far too early to conjecture whether any flesh can be put
on the bones.

III

More than sixty years ago, Winston Churchill surveyed the upheaval wrought
by the First War, and reached a gloomy conclusion as he turned to Ireland:

> The whole map of Europe has been changed. The mode and thought of man.
> The whole outlook on affairs, the groupings of parties, all have encountered
> violent and tremendous changes in the deluge of the world, but as the deluge
> subsides and the waters fall we see the dreary steeples of Fermanagh and
> Tyrone emerging once again. The integrity of their quarrel is one of the few
> institutions that have been unaltered in the cataclysm which has swept the
> world.[58]

Too often, the events of recent decades have appeared to vindicate Churchill's view. Yet, inexorably, deeper changes are affecting the island. Its uneven
economic development, between industrial eastern Ulster and agricultural and
commercial Ireland, which for so long accentuated the division between loyalists and nationalists, has faded considerably since the 1970s. New industries
and services have developed north and south of the border, while the old
industries of the Belfast area have dwindled. Of course, economic change does

not, in itself, recast people's political identities. But at least the potency of one of the factors which polarized Ireland's two traditions is reduced.

As this book has shown, Europe has exerted a decisive impact on Ireland's history. Arguably, it is about to do so again. Europe's importance in recent years is perhaps greater than is often appreciated, as British and Irish membership of the European Community since 1973 has helped to foster closer ties between London and Dublin. For the future, the Single European Act and the lifting of frontiers in 1992 seem likely to signal a further transformation.

The consequences are already being debated. What will be the impact on relations between the Republic, Northern Ireland and Great Britain? If national boundaries in the European Community become less important, what of the prospects for greater autonomy to the regions? John Hume's advocacy of a strong, European regional policy finds an echo among some Unionists, because they feel betrayed by London over the Anglo-Irish Agreement and are alert to the example of Scotland where politicians increasingly look to Europe to further their country's prospects. Following the June 1989 European elections, there was an intriguing development at the Strasbourg Parliament, where the newly elected Ulster Unionist MEP became an allied member of the European People's Party (Christian Democrats), sitting alongside Ireland's Fine Gael MEPs. Time will tell whether the move is a straw in the wind, or nothing more than a tactical convenience in a distant talking-shop.

In the 1690s, and again in the 1790s, events in Europe left an indelible imprint on Ireland. But crucially their impact was channelled and shaped in the ferment of Ireland's differing identities and traditions: in the 1690s, these were Gaelic catholic, 'old English' catholic, 'new English' protestant and the Scots–Irish presbyterian; and in the 1790s, Anglo-Irish protestant, catholic and presbyterian radicals, and catholic and presbyterian conservatives. So too in the 1990s will Europe's impact be adapted and refashioned in the debate between Ireland's present-day identities and traditions, nationalist and unionist, republican and loyalist, and the various strands within them.

NOTES

1 In 1641, an estimated 4000 Protestants were killed, and a further 8000 died from privation. Contemporary and subsequent accounts gave exaggerated estimates, ranging between 20,000 and 100,000 murdered. See T. W. Moody, F. X. Martin and F. J. Byrne, 1978, pp. 290–2.

2 Penn sailed for America early in September 1682. During subsequent visits to Britain, he advised James, and was a supporter of the King's proposals for religious toleration.

3 Surveys of 1619 and 1622 indicate the presence of 6000 adult British males on the Ulster plantation estates. By the time of the 1659 census, 32 per cent of the total population were of English or Scottish extraction.

4 The start of a new reign was traditionally accompanied by the election of a new Parliament, a convention only broken at the end of Queen Victoria's long reign when there was no election on the accession of King Edward VII to the throne.

5 Monmouth claimed that Charles II had secretly married his mother, Lucy Walters, and that he was therefore the lawful heir to the throne.

6 On 15 February 1972, *The Times* published a letter from the poet Robert Graves, suggesting that 'the use of Lilliburlero be at once suspended by the Overseas News, and that the melody "Top of the Cork Road" be substituted for it'. Graves wrote as a member of an Irish Protestant family 'which has always lived on the best possible terms with the Catholics'.

7 'Lilliburlero' was originally chosen by the editor of the BBC's Chinese Service, and first used as a transmission signature in January 1943. It was taken on by the English transmissions in November of that year, and was chosen because it was a good tune. (Information provided by BBC World Service.)

8 line 3: 'debittie': Tyrconnel was appointed only Lord Deputy, not Lord Lieutenant.

line 6: 'Lero lero' etc.: although there are various suggestions about the meaning of the refrain, the phrases are probably meaningless.

9 The terms Tory and Whig were coined during the Exclusion Crisis of 1678–81 to describe the rival groupings. They were designed to portray opponents as extremists: the Whiggamores were Scots covenanting rebels; the Tories, Irish Catholic outlaws. The chief *raison d'être* of the Whigs was 'preserving the Protestant Succession as the guarantee of the nation's liberties, religion, properties and independence, a principle that was first formulated in the policy of Exclusion and then embodied in what were termed Revolution principles'. The Tories 'saw themselves as the defenders of domestic peace and order against the spirit of faction and rebellion, allegedly active in demagogic whig politics and a continuing threat to the Anglican church'. J. R. Jones, 1978, p. 42.

10 Prorogation of Parliament means that the monarch has stood a particular Parliament down, usually for a specified period. It is thus not the occasion for fresh elections.

11 Despite the reference to 'many murders', there appears to have been only one such murder.

12 Derry's loss of its Protestant garrison and its proposed replacement by the Catholic Antrim's troops were the background to the apprentice boys' shutting the city gates.

13 James cancelled his request in a postscript to the letter.

14 James and Henry Fitzjames were both sons of James II by Arabella Churchill, sister of John Churchill, later Earl of Marlborough.

15 The French ships were flying English colours at James's request. The last visit by an English king had been Richard II's between October 1394 and May 1395.

16 Although the evidence suggests that one of the Plunkett family was the author of one of the most important Jacobite accounts of 1688–91, it is less certain that it was written by Nicholas Plunkett, as has been suggested (for further discussion see P. Kelly, '"A Light to the blind": the voice of the dispossessed élite in the generation after the defeat at Limerick', 1985, Irish Historical Studies, xxiv, no. 96, pp. 431–57). Plunkett's account was edited by J. T. Gilbert and published in 1892.

17 William's statement came in the form of an Answer, read by the Speaker, to an Address of both Houses, declaring that they 'would stand by him, &c., with their Lives and Fortunes'.

18 The Irish Parliament thus gathered on the north bank of the Liffey, and not at Chichester House, on College Green, which was their customary meeting place.

19 It would never be repeated in Dublin, and would not be repeated on the island of Ireland for more than 230 years.

20 Tyrconnel wrote to Mary of Modena from Dublin Castle on 16 June (OS), and then later from the Jacobite camp at Ardee. He plumps for delay in the later letter, not in the earlier one as has been suggested.

21 J. G. Simms, 1969, cites the anecdote from the *Dublin Penny Journal* of 1832–3.

22 Sterne was born in 1713 in Clonmel, Ireland; the first two books of *Tristram Shandy* were published in 1759.

23 De Tourville remained off the Devon coast until 4 August 1690.

24 Stevens suggests that there was little activity, but he was based at Limerick throughout the winter months and therefore saw none of the action elsewhere.

25 Sir Charles Porter, the Lord Chancellor of Ireland, had been sworn in as a Lord Justice on 24 December 1690. Coningsby and Sydney continued to serve as Lords Justices.

26 Stevens's eye-witness account ends abruptly on 12 July 1691, which has led to conjecture that his copy fell from his knapsack. After the Irish war, Stevens returned to exile on the Continent, where he became a scholar of literature, translating works from Spanish. He died in October 1726.

27 The exact day was still be to decided.

28 A Select Committee was set up on 1 January 1694 and a bill introduced on 3 February 1694.

29 R. H. Murray, 1911, cites these same figures, but gives them the wrong way round.

30 William's successor, Anne, was Protestant, like her elder sister, the late Queen Mary. But in 1700 Anne's only surviving child, the Duke of Gloucester, had died. On Anne's death the crown would pass to a Catholic, unless the conditions of the succession were revised.

31 The 'sacramental test' required that any person holding any position, civil or military, must not only take the usual declaration against substantiation, but must also, within three months of entering upon office, produce a certificate of having received the testament of the Lord's supper 'according to the usage of the church of Ireland . . . in some public church, upon the Lord's day commonly called Sunday, immediately after divine service and sermon'. J. C. Beckett, 1948, pp. 46–7. The 'sacramental test' was not repealed until 1780.

32 The term 'Protestant Ascendancy' was first used in the 1780s by conservative Anglicans, who sought to justify Anglican Protestant political and religious domination of Ireland as essential to the survival of Protestantism on the island.

33 Daniel Corkery's *The Hidden Ireland* was published in 1924, and, as R. F. Foster has commented, 'encouraged his countrymen to seek their cultural heritage in an exclusively Gaelic past' (1988, p. 167n).

34 Liam de Paor, 1985, 'The Rebel Mind: Republican and Loyalist', in *The Irish Mind* (ed. Richard Kearney).

35 In 1701, Louis XIV recognized James Stuart, the son of James II, as James III of England.

36 Princess Clementina was the granddaughter of John Sobieski, King of Poland, who raised the siege of Vienna in 1683.

37 Ormonde, son of Charles II's Lord Lieutenant of Ireland, had been a Williamite, but later became a Jacobite.

38 This is taken from Psalm 18, verse 2.

39 The Duke of Berwick had been killed by a cannon-ball at Philippsburg on 12 July 1734, during the War of the Polish Succession, but the Regiment kept his name; Roth's Regiment later became known as Walsh's; Lally's Regiment was founded in 1744.

40 The cry of 'no peace without Spain' reflected Whig fears that the Tory Administration would sell out Britain's allies in order to make peace with France and withdraw from the War of the Spanish Succession.

41 Jan Wyck's portrayal of the Boyne features a prominent figure on a white horse, but this is not William. The King can be seen on his chestnut horse. Wyck's painting can be viewed at the National Gallery of Ireland, and another version at the National Army Museum, London; West's painting is owned by the Duke of Westminster.

42 The galleries of the old Chamber of the House of Commons at Westminster were extended to accommodate the arrival of 100 Irish MPs. Today, Northern Ireland elects seventeen MPs.

43 The distinction between these two strands in the nationalist tradition was drawn by Dr Garret FitzGerald, in 'Irish Identities', the Richard Dimbleby Lecture, 1982, BBC London.

44 James Joyce, 1977, *Dubliners*, London, Grafton, pp. 237–8.

45 James Joyce, 1986, *Ulysses*, Harmondsworth, Penguin, p. 208.

46 Interview with author.

47 Interview with author.

48 Quoted in the *Guardian*, 5 October 1988.

49 Interviews with author.

50 Ibid.

51 Ibid.

52 Ibid.

53 *Liberty Tree*, 1983, quoted by T. Brown, 1985, Derry, Field Day.

54   T. Brown, 1985, p. 5.
55   *The Times*, 7 July 1975.
56   Ibid, 8 July 1975.
57   *The Irish Times*, 26 August 1989.
58   W. S. Churchill, 1929, *The World Crisis: the Aftermath*, London, p. 319.

SELECT
BIBLIOGRAPHY

Abbreviations: HMC, Historical Manuscripts Commission; MS(S), Manuscript(s); RIA, Royal Irish Academy; TCD, Trinity College, Dublin.

EYE-WITNESS, CONTEMPORARY AND DOCUMENTARY SOURCES
[The following cover the period 1689–91 and are quoted in the text.]

Analecta Hibernica, i, 1930, and iv, 1932, Letters of the Earl of Tyrconnel; x, 1941, George Clarke's Irish war correspondence, 1690–1; xxi, 1959, Franco-Irish correspondence.

T. Bellingham, 1908, *Diary*, ed. A. Hewitson, London, George Toulmin.

Berwick, James, Duke of, 1779, *Memoirs*, 2 vols, London.

G. Bonnivert, 1933–6, 'Some Extracts Relating to Ireland from the Journal of Gideon Bonnivert', in *County Louth Archaeological Journal*, viii, pp. 18–21.

G. Burnet (Bishop), 1823, *History of His Own Time*, 6 vols, Oxford University Press.

Calendars of State Papers, Domestic series, London, various years.

J. S. Clarke, 1816, *The Life of James II*, 2 vols, London.

J. Dalrymple, 1773, *Memoirs of Great Britain and Ireland*, London.

K. Danaher and J. G. Simms, 1962, *The Danish Force in Ireland, 1690–1*, Dublin, Irish Manuscripts Commission.

R. Davies, 1857, *The Journal of the Very Rev. Rowland Davies, Dean of Ross*, ed. R. Caulfield, Camden Society.

'Diary of the Siege of Athlone, 1691, by an Engineer of the Army', *Irish Sword*, iii, pp. 88–92.

Documents on the Reduction of Ireland, 1689–91, RIA.

General J. Douglas, 1862, Letter to the Duke of Queensbury, Dublin, 7 July 1690, in *Memorials and Letters Illustrative of the Life and Times of John Graham of Claverhouse, Viscount Dundee*, iii, ed. M. Napier, Edinburgh.

Dublin Intelligence.

J. Evelyn, 1955, *Diary*, 6 vols, ed. E. S. de Beer, Oxford, Clarendon Press.

J. de la Fouleresse, 1877, Danish Ambassador, Letters to Christian V on the Battle of the Boyne 1690 and the Siege of Limerick 1691, in L. Barbé, *Notes and Queries*, 5th series, viii, pp. 21–3, 121–3.

J. T. Gilbert (ed.), 1892, *A Jacobite Narrative of the War in Ireland, 1688–91*, Dublin.

R. Hayes (ed.), 1949–53, 'Reflections of an Irish Brigade Officer', in *Irish Sword*, i, pp. 68–74.

HMC Dartmouth MSS, 1887.
HMC Ginkel correspondence, de Ros MSS, 1874.
HMC Ormonde MSS, new series, viii, 1920.
HMC Finch MSS, ii, 1922, and iii, 1957.
HMC Leyborne-Popham MSS (George Clarke's autobiography), 1899.
HMC Stuart MSS, vi, 1916.
W. King, 1691, *The state of the Protestants under the late King James's government*, London.
London Gazette.
J. Mackenzie, 1690, *A narrative of the siege of Londonderry*, London.
J. Macpherson, 1775, *Original papers*, 2 vols, London.
S. Mulloy (ed.), 1983, *Franco-Irish Correspondence: December 1688 – February 1692*, Stationery Office for the Irish Manuscripts Commission, Dublin.
C. O'Kelly, 1850, *Macariae excidium, or the destruction of Cyprus*, ed. J. C. O'Callaghan, Dublin.
R. Parker, 1747, *Memoirs of the Military Transactions . . . from 1683 to 1718*, London.
Parliamentary History of England, 1809, v, ed. William Cobbett, London.
Portland, Earl of, 1690, *Narrative of the fight at the Boyne*, RIA.
The Present State of Europe, or Historical and Political Mercury.
RIA Proceedings, ix, Lord Meath's account of the Battle of the Boyne, July 1690, Dublin.
J. Richardson, 1938, 'Plan and Narrative of the Battle of the Boyne', in *5th Royal Dragoon Guards Journal*, vii, No. 4, May, pp. 146–8.
S. W. Singer (ed.), 1828, *Clarendon and Rochester correspondence*, 2 vols, London.
J. Stevens, 1912, *Journal, 1689–1691*, ed. R. H. Murray, Oxford, Clarendon Press.
G. Story, 1691, *A true and impartial history . . . etc.*, London, and 1693, *A Continuation of the impartial history of the wars in Ireland*, London.
G. Walker, 1689, *A true account of the siege of Londonderry*, London.

LATER WORKS
Many references relevant to the issues discussed in this book are to be found in the following periodicals and books: *An Cosantoir, Éire–Ireland, The Historical Journal, History, History Today, Irish Economic and Social History, Irish Historical Studies, The Irish Sword, Past and Present*; the Gill and Macmillan *History of Ireland* and *New History of Ireland*, and the Helicon *History of Ireland*.

P. Arthur and K. Jeffery, 1988, *Northern Ireland Since 1968*, Oxford, Basil Blackwell.
R. Bagwell, 1909–16, *Ireland Under the Stuarts and During the Interregnum*, 3 vols, London, Longman Green.
S. E. Baker, 1973, 'Orange and Green: Belfast 1832–1912', in H. J. Dyos and M. Wolff (eds), *The Victorian City. Images and Realities*, London.
T. Bartlett and D. W. Hayton (eds), 1979, *Penal Era and Golden Age: Essays in Irish History 1690–1800*, Belfast, Ulster Historical Foundation.
S. Baxter, 1966, *William III*, London, Longman.
J. C. Beckett, 1948, *Protestant Dissent in Ireland 1687–1780*, London, Faber & Faber.
R. Beddard, 1988, *A Kingdom Without a King*, Oxford, Phaidon Press.
S. H. Bell, 1956, *Erin's Orange Lily*, London, Denis Dobson.
P. Berresford Ellis, 1976, *The Boyne Water*, London, Hamish Hamilton.
P. Bew and H. Patterson, 1985, *The British State and the Ulster Crisis*, Verso.

D. Boulger, 1911, *The Battle of the Boyne*, London, Martin Secker.

H. Boylan, 1988, *A Valley of Kings: The Boyne*, Dublin, O'Brien Press.

P. Brooke, 1988, *Ulster Presbyterianism*, Dublin, Gill & Macmillan.

T. Brown, 1985, *The Whole Protestant Community: The Making of a Historical Myth*, Derry, Field Day.

P. Buckland, 1973, *Ulster Unionism and the Origins of Northern Ireland 1886–1922*, Dublin, Gill & Macmillan.

I. Budge and C. O'Leary, 1973, *Belfast: Approach to Crisis*, London, Macmillan.

N. Canny, 1988, *Kingdom and Colony: Ireland in the Atlantic World 1560–1800*, Baltimore, Maryland, John Hopkins University Press.

J. Carswell, 1969, *The Descent on England*, London, Barrie & Rockliff.

R. Cathcart, 1988, 'Ireland and King Billy: Usage and Abusage', *History Today*, xxxviii, July, pp. 41–5.

J. Childs, 1980, *The Army, James II and the Glorious Revolution*, Manchester, Manchester University Press.

J. Childs, 1987, *The British Army of William III 1689–1702*, Manchester, Manchester University Press.

J. Clark, 1986, *Revolution and Rebellion*, Cambridge, Cambridge University Press.

J. Clark, 1989, 'English History's Forgotten Context: Scotland, Ireland, Wales', *Historical Journal*, xxxii, pp. 211–28.

S. Clark and J. S. Donnelly Jr (eds), 1983, *Irish Peasants*, Manchester, Manchester University Press.

S. J. Connolly, 1982, *Priests and People in Pre-Famine Ireland 1781–1845*, Dublin, Gill & Macmillan.

C. Coogan Ward and R. E. Ward, 1979, 'The Ordeal of O'Conor of Belanagare', in *Éire – Ireland*, Summer 1979.

P. J. Corish (ed.), 1985, *Radicals, Rebels and Establishments*, Belfast, Appletree Press.

A. Cosgrove and D. McCartney (eds), 1979, *Studies in Irish History*, Dublin, University College.

R. Crawford, 1988, *Loyal to King Billy: A Portrait of the Ulster Protestant*, Dublin, Gill & Macmillan.

L. M. Cullen, 1972, *An Economic History of Ireland Since 1660*, London.

M. W. Dewar, D. Bryce and S. E. Long, 1988, *William of Orange*, Belfast, Orange Order.

D. Dickson, 1987, *New Foundations: Ireland 1660–1800*, Dublin, Helicon.

C. Duffy, 1964, *The Wild Goose and the Eagle: A Life of Marshal von Browne, 1707–57*, London, Chatto & Windus.

J. Ehrman, 1953, *The Navy in the War of William III 1689–97: Its State and Direction*, Cambridge, Cambridge University Press.

M. Elliott, 1982, *Partners in Revolution*, New Haven, Yale University Press.

M. Elliott, 1985, *Watchmen in Sion: The Protestant Idea of Liberty*, Derry, Field Day.

M. Farrell, 1980, *Northern Ireland, the Orange State*, London, Pluto Press.

K. Ferguson, 1980, 'The Army in Ireland from the Restoration to the Act of Union', PhD thesis, Trinity College.

R. F. Foster, 1988, *Modern Ireland 1660–1972*, London, Allen Lane.

J. A. Froude, 1887, *The English in Ireland in the Eighteenth Century*, 3 vols, London.

P. Gibbon, 1975, *The Origins of Ulster Unionism*, Manchester, Manchester University Press.

J. T. Gilbert, 1854–9, *A History of the City of Dublin*, 3 vols, Dublin, McGlashan & Gill.

K. D. Haley, 1985, *Politics in the Reign of Charles II*, Historical Association Studies, Oxford, Basil Blackwell.

R. Harbinson, 1960, *No Surrender: An Ulster Childhood*, London, Faber & Faber.

J. F. Harbison, 1974, *The Ulster Unionist Party 1882–1973*, Belfast, Blackstaff Press.

R. Hatton (ed.), 1976, *Louis XIV and Europe*, London, Macmillan.

G. A. Hayes-McCoy, 1989, *Irish Battles*, Belfast, Appletree Press.

D. Hayton (ed.), 1976, *Ireland After the Glorious Revolution 1692–1715*, Belfast, Public Record Office of Northern Ireland.

M. R. Hennessy, 1973, *The Wild Geese*, London, Sidgwick & Jackson.

J. R. Hill, 1984, 'National Festivals, the State and "Protestant Ascendancy" in Ireland, 1790–1829', *Irish Historical Studies*, xxiv, No. 93, May 1984, pp. 30–51.

P. Hopkins, 1986, *Glencoe and the End of the Highland War*, Edinburgh, John Donald.

H. Horwitz, 1977, *Parliament, Policy and Politics in the Reign of William III*, Manchester, Manchester University Press.

F. G. James, 1973, *Ireland in the Empire 1688–1770*, Cambridge, Mass., Harvard University Press.

C. Jones (ed.), 1987, *Britain in the First Age of Party 1680–1750*, London, Hambledon Press.

D. W. Jones, 1988, *War and Economy in the Age of William III and Marlborough*, Oxford, Basil Blackwell.

J. R. Jones, 1972, *The Revolution of 1688 in England*, London, Weidenfeld & Nicolson.

J. R. Jones, 1978, *Country and Court, England 1658–1714*, London, Edward Arnold.

R. Kearney (ed.), 1985, *The Irish Mind*, Wolfhound Press.

R. Kee, 1972, *The Green Flag*, London, Weidenfeld & Nicolson.

P. Kennedy, 1976, *The Rise and Fall of British Naval Mastery*, London, Allen Lane.

J. P. Kenyon, 1958, *Robert Spencer, Earl of Sunderland*, London, Longman.

W.E.H. Lecky, 1892, *History of Ireland in the Eighteenth Century*, 5 vols, London, Longmans, Green & Co.

P. A. Lucas, 1982, 'Irish Armies in the Seventeenth Century', PhD, Manchester University.

F. S. L. Lyons, 1979, *Culture and Anarchy in Ireland 1890–1939*, Oxford, Clarendon Press.

Lord Macaulay, 1848–61, *The History of England*, 3 vols, London.

P. Macrory, 1980, *The Siege of Derry*, London, Hodder & Stoughton.

M. MacCurtain, 1972, *Tudor and Stuart Ireland*, Dublin, Gill & Macmillan.

O. MacDonagh, 1983, *States of Mind: A Study of Anglo-Irish Conflict 1780–1980*, London, George Allen & Unwin.

R. B. McDowell, 1979, *Ireland in the Age of Imperialism and Revolution 1760–1801*, Oxford, Clarendon Press.

D. McKay and H. M. Scott, 1983, *The Rise of the Great Powers 1648–1815*, Harlow, Longman.

M. G. McLaughlin, 1980, *The Wild Geese*, London, Osprey.

F. McLynn, 1981, '"Good Behavior": Irish Catholics and the Jacobite Rising of 1745', *Éire–Ireland*, xvi, pp. 43–58.

E. MacLysaght, 1979, *Irish Life in the 17th Century*, Dublin, Irish Academic Press.

F. L. MacNeice, 1965, *The Strings are False*, London, Faber & Faber.

A. P. W. Malcolmson, *John Foster, The Politics of the Anglo-Irish Ascendancy*, 1978 Oxford, Oxford University Press.

P. Melvin, 1977–9, 'Irish Soldiers and Plotters in Williamite England', *Irish Sword*, xiii, pp. 256–86.

D. W. Miller, 1978, *Queen's Rebels*, Dublin, Gill & Macmillan.

J. Miller, 1977, 'The Earl of Tyrconnel and James II's Irish Policy', *Historical Journal*, xx, No. 4, pp. 803–23.

J. Miller, 1978, *James II: A Study in Kingship*, Hove, Wayland.

T. W. Moody, F. X. Martin and F. J. Byrne (eds), 1978, *Early Modern Ireland 1534– 1691*, Oxford, Clarendon Press.

T. W. Moody and W. E. Vaughan (eds), 1986, *Eighteenth-Century Ireland 1691–1800*, London, Clarendon Press.

J. A. Murphy, 1959, *Justin MacCarthy, Lord Mountcashel*, Cork.

R. Murphy, 1968, *The Battle of Aughrim*, London, Faber & Faber.

R. H. Murray, 1911, *Revolutionary Ireland and Its Settlement*, London.

C. C. O'Brien, 1972, *States of Ireland*, London, Hutchinson.

G. O'Brien (ed.), 1989, *Parliament, Politics and People: Essays in Eighteenth-Century Irish History*, Dublin, Irish Academic Press.

J. C. O'Callaghan, 1870, *History of the Irish Brigades in the Service of France*, Glasgow, Cameron & Ferguson.

P. O'Farrell, 1971, *Ireland's English Question*, London, Batsford.

P. O'Flanagan, P. Ferguson and K. Whelan (eds), 1987, *Rural Ireland 1600–1900*, Cork, Cork University Press.

P. Orr, 1988, *The Road to the Somme*, Belfast, Blackstaff Press.

S. O'Tuama (ed.), 1981, *An Duanaire – 1600–1900: Poems of the Dispossessed*, Dublin, The Dolmen Press.

M. Perceval-Maxwell, 1973, *The Scottish Migration to Ulster in the Reign of James I*, London.

Sir Charles Petrie, 1973, *The Great Tyrconnell*, Cork, The Mercier Press.

C.H.E. Philpin (ed.), 1987, *Nationalism and Popular Protest in Ireland*, Cambridge, Cambridge University Press.

E. B. Powley, 1972, *The Naval Side of King William's War*, London, John Baker.

J. P. Prendergast, 1887, *Ireland from the Restoration to the Revolution*, London, Longman.

L. von Ranke, 1875, *A History of England, principally in the seventeenth century*, 6 vols, Oxford.

D. Rea (ed.), 1982, *Political Co-operation in Divided Societies*, Dublin, Gill & Macmillan.

F. J. Riegler, 1983, *Anglo-Catholics, the Army of Ireland, and the Jacobite War*, 2 vols, PhD thesis, Temple University, USA.

P. S. Robinson, 1984, *The Plantation of Ulster*, Dublin, Gill & Macmillan.

L. G. Schwoerer, 1977, 'Propaganda in the Revolution of 1688–89', *American Historical Review*, lxxxii, pp. 843–74.

H. Senior, 1966, *Orangeism in Ireland and Britain 1795–1836*, London, Routledge & Kegan Paul.

P. W. Sergeant, 1913, *Little Jennings and Fighting Dick Talbot: A Life of the Duke and Duchess of Tyrconnel*, London, Hutchinson.

J. G. Simms, 1969, *Jacobite Ireland 1685–1691*, London, Routledge & Kegan Paul.

J. G. Simms, 1974, 'Remembering 1690', *Studies: An Irish Quarterly Review*, lxiii, pp. 231–42.

J. G. Simms, 1986, *War and Politics in Ireland 1649–1730*, ed. D. W. Hayton and G. O'Brien, London, Hambledon Press.

J. G. Simms, 1956, *The Williamite Confiscation in Ireland 1690–1703*, London, Faber & Faber.

W. A. Speck, 1988, *Reluctant Revolutionaries*, Oxford, Oxford University Press.

A. T. Q. Stewart, 1967, *The Ulster Crisis*, London, Faber & Faber.

A. T. Q. Stewart, 1977, *The Narrow Ground: Aspects of Ulster 1609–1969*, London, Faber & Faber.

L. Swords (ed.), 1978, *The Irish–French Connection 1578–1978*, Paris.

J. H. Todhunter, 1895, *The Life of Patrick Sarsfield*, London.

W. Troost, 1983, 'William III and the Treaty of Limerick (1691–1697): A Study of His Irish Policy', PhD thesis, Leiden University.

M. Walsh, 1987, 'The Wild Goose Tradition', *Irish Sword*, xvii, Summer, no. 66.

J. R. Western, 1972, *Monarchy and Revolution: The English State in the 1680s*, London, Blandford Press.

W. R. Wilde, 1849, *The Beauties of the Boyne and Its Tributary, the Blackwater*, Dublin, James McGlashan.

T. Wilson, 1988, *The Ulster Problem*, Oxford, Basil Blackwell.

F. Wright, 1988, *Northern Ireland: A Comparative Analysis*, Dublin, Gill & Macmillan.

INDEX